Philopatry, Inbreeding, and
the Evolution of Sex

Philopatry, Inbreeding, and the Evolution of Sex

WILLIAM M. SHIELDS

State University of New York Press

ALBANY

Published by
State University of New York Press, Albany

© 1982 State University of New York

Printed in the United States of America

For information, address State University of New York Press, State University Plaza, Albany, N.Y. 12246

Library of Congress Cataloging in Publication Data

Shields, William M., 1947–
    Philopatry, inbreeding, and the evolution of sex.

    Bibliography: p. 199
    Includes index.
    1. Sex (Biology) 2. Inbreeding. 3. Evolution.
I. Title.
QH481.S55   574.1′66   82-729
IBSN 0-87395-617-6
ISBN 0-87395-618-4 (pbk.)

Contents

Preface   vii

1 Philopatry, Inbreeding, and Sex: An Overview   1

2 Why Philopatry: Dispersal and Inbreeding   6

3 The Relativity of Relatedness and Inbreeding   29

4 The Disadvantages of Inbreeding   50

5 An Advantage for Inbreeding: Coadaptation and
   Outbreeding Depression   66

6 Inbreeding and Sex: Paradox Lost?   103

7 The Who and How of Inbreeding: Predictions and
   Evidence   139

8 Low Fecundity Species: Population Structure,
   Inbreeding and Evolution   173

   References   199

   Author Index   235

   Subject Index   241

Preface

Teleonomic analysis has been defined as the systematic study of adaptive function (e.g., Pittendrigh, 1958; Williams, 1966; Mayr, 1974). Questions of function are often posed as why questions, with the understanding that why refers to the ultimate selective causes controlling a character's frequency in nature. My initial question was, why philopatry, or why do so many organisms disperse relatively short distances before settling to breed? In order to answer this question I was forced to address other questions, including: why inbreed, why outbreed, and why reproduce sexually? This teleonomic odyssey led me into more arenas than I had envisioned would be necessary in posing the initial problem. I have drawn on theory and data from the fields of behavior, ecology, and genetics in an attempt to provide a comprehensive evolutionary framework for exploring these questions.

In developing the arguments reported here, I have explored, in detail, many definitions, concepts, or theories, that experts in particular disciplines may find trivial or common knowledge. I apologize to the experts and suggest that they can skip appropriate portions of the work without loss. I present all the details, so that the internal logic of the synthesis that is the final argument is more open to the critical analysis of *all* readers regardless of their particular expertise.

Readers of earlier versions of the manuscript have all commented, usually critically, on the absence of novel mathematical analysis bearing on the verbal arguments. I chose not to attempt such analyses for two reasons, (1) I agree with Williams (1975, p. 7) that, ''For answering questions on function in biology, comparative evidence is more reliable than mathematical reasoning.''

Thus, I have directed the bulk of my effort to gathering and presenting comparisons, and (2) I am not competent in the necessary mathematics. Undoubtedly, mathematical analysis would be of great help in exploring the arguments, but I can only hope that my presentation will act as a stimulus to those with the requisite interests and expertise.

The ideas presented here are a collective effort. My personal endeavor has been shaped by the written and spoken words of colleagues too numerous to mention individually. Yet, I would feel remiss if I failed to publicly acknowledge those whose extraordinary patience and perseverance were most directly responsible for the final product. It is to them that most of the clarity in what follows owes its existence. I hope that it is obvious that any turbidity is my own, and my gratitude implies no responsibility for the errors that undoubtedly follow.

My primary intellectual debt is to the work of George C. Williams, which introduced me to teleonomy, and clarified my thoughts on many other topics as well. I owe an open mind on the question of inbreeding to science fiction writer Theodore Sturgeon, though I hope our vocations are not confused.

I initiated this project while a student at Livingston College, Rutgers University. I thank the many faculty members and students who listened to my initial ramblings with tolerance. I am especially grateful to Julia Chase, Timothy Perper, and Bertram G. Murray, Jr. for encouraging me to actively pursue unorthodox ideas. I am also grateful to all my colleagues at Ohio State University for generously tutoring me in many necessary disciplines. Those who gave inordinately in continuous and challenging discussion included K. Beal, K. Bildstein, C. B. Brownsmith, C. Cook, J. Downhower, A. Gaunt, R. Mitchell, S. Peters, W. Peters, G. Pierce, L. Putnam, and B. Schaal.

I have discussed my ideas, at length, with T. Wood, E. Waltz, C. Doner, L. Wolf, and W. T. Starmer. I am particularly grateful to P. Greenwood and P. Harvey who unselfishly shared their thoughts and data on inbreeding, dispersal, and the social structure of science.

I am grateful to C. W. Birky, P. A. Colinvaux, J. R. Crook, M. A. Cunningham, J. Felsenstein, P. J. Greenwood, T. C. Grubb, Jr., A. Hopkins, J. Mitton, B. G. Murray, Jr., G. Williams and a number of anonymous reviewers who have waded through the en-

tire manuscript making telling and critical comments that have saved
me considerable embarrassment.

I acknowledge the following for their kind permission to make
extensive use of previously published and copyrighted materials:
R. Selander and Academic Press, New York (Figs. 7 and 27); J.
Johnston and University of Chicago Press (Fig. 2); G. Rheinewald
and Ardea (Fig. 2); J. Crow and Harper and Row (Fig. 9); K. Mather
and Chapman and Hall (Fig. 10); S. Wright and University of
Chicago Press (Fig. 13); M. Price and N. Waser and MacMillen
Press (Fig. 19); J. Maynard Smith and Cambridge University Press
(Fig. 20); R. Highton and Plenum Press (Fig. 25); G. L. Stebbins and
Columbia University Press (Table 11); Cold Spring Harbor
Biological Laboratory (Table 12); and Oxford University Press,
Figs. 3, 10, 15, and 24 as well as extensive textual material. All of
the figures were drawn or redrawn by D. Dennis or K. Vournakis. I
am especially grateful to Ruth Piatoff who patiently typed and
retyped the manuscript.

Finally, I am indebted to the very special people whose intellectual and emotional support not only influenced this work profoundly, but also made life more bearable, stimulating, and joyous.
I thank C. Barbara Brownsmith, Janice R. Crook, Michael A. Cunningham, Thomas C. Grubb, Jr., Bertram G. Murray, Jr., and most
especially Lea Shields. The entire enterprise certainly would have
been impossible without them.

CHAPTER 1

Philopatry, Inbreeding, and Sex: An Overview

Dispersal is defined as the movement of an individual from its site of origin to a more or less distant area or succession of areas. Successful dispersal is expected to result in breeding in the new area (Howard, 1960). At some stage of every organism's life, propagules are produced with a capacity to move. Powered by external forces (passive dispersal), or their own locomotive powers (active dispersal), they do move from their origin to new locales. When propagules are marked, and the distribution of dispersal distances they move is surveyed, one of three species-characteristic patterns usually emerges. When one stage of the life cycle (usually adult) shows site tenacity (i.e., a relatively fixed attachment to a specific piece of real estate), dispersal is usually, (1) philopatric, with propagules remaining at or very near their origin, or (2) vagrant, with propagules traveling greater distances before settling (Ch.2). (3) Nomadism is characterized by individuals that do not attach to specific sites, wandering more or less widely throughout their lives (e.g., many ungulates, Leuthold, 1977).

This analysis originally focused on the question, why philopatry? As it unfolded, it expanded to include the questions, why inbreed and why sex? My choice of philopatry, inbreeding, and sex for a teleonomic analysis was not based on *a priori* considerations of a relationship among them. Rather the possibility of such a relationship emerged during the course of the analysis. I believe that a brief presentation of the historical sequence of the argument's development will highlight important logical and empirical connections both within and between the groups of hypotheses that together form the final argument. Such a procedure should increase the potential for critical analysis and help guard against the possibility of circular reasoning by illustrating all the factors which entered into the development of each hypothesis. This may prevent the use of these factors as corroborating evidence for the hypotheses they helped generate.

Why philopatry?

Why do so many organisms remain at, or near, their birthplace throughout their lives? When many organisms disperse, why are their movements so localized, regardless of the organism's mobility, migratory status, ecology, or trophic relations? After considering many of the traditional explanations of philopatry, I conclude that its one inevitable consequence is to increase the relatedness of potential mates. Rather than viewing the increased inbreeding that results from philopatry as a price paid for some other unspecified advantage, I view inbreeding as the primary but not sole function of philopatry (Ch. 2).

Why inbreed?

If philopatry is adaptive because it promotes inbreeding, then inbreeding must be adaptive as well. For now, I define inbreeding as a system in which mates are regularly more similar genetically than a pair chosen at random from a reference population or species (Falconer, 1960; Crow and Kimura, 1970). A more extensive discussion of inbreeding's meanings is found in chapter 3. The new question is, then, Is the mating of genetically similar individuals sufficiently advantageous to outweigh the often discussed disadvantages of inbreeding (Ch. 4)? Inbreeding's disadvantages result from its tendency to decrease heterozygosity thereby speeding the chance (nonadaptive) fixation of alleles and decreasing the genetic variability of individuals and populations (for extensive discussions, see Wright, 1921; 1932; 1940; 1977; Haldane, 1936; 1937; Fisher, 1949; Lerner, 1954; Darlington, 1958; Falconer, 1960; Carson, 1967; Crow and Kimura, 1970; Mather, 1973; Jacquard, 1975). Inbreeding's advantages may result from a tendency to preserve complexes of interacting alleles at different loci that have been coadapted by a common selective history (Ch. 5).

Why sex?

Embedded in the question why should mates be similar, is the question, why mate at all? Williams's (1975) monograph on the evolution of sex was a necessary stimulus for me to perceive this connection. I was able to take ideas concerning advantages of inbreeding, and integrate them with Williams's ideas about the costs of sex, synthesizing what I hope is a simpler and clearer set of hypotheses dealing with both inbreeding and sex.

Philopatry, inbreeding, and sex: an overview

Leaving most of the details for the main body of this work (Chs. 5 and 6), I will turn to the final argument which proposes that individual (inclusive) fitness is enhanced in low fecundity ($< 10^4$ zygotes/female/lifetime) organisms by transmitting parental genomes as faithfully as possible. Sexual reproduction by genetically similar individuals maximizes the conservation of genetic information during transmission across generations. Stated in another way, inbreeding sex is capable of greater precision (though never perfection) in transmitting successful parental genomes, and thus phenotypes, than either outbreeding sex or asexuality, under a wide variety of conditions.

Sexual reproduction by genetically dissimilar individuals (outbreeding) has two major theoretical disadvantages for the individuals involved, meiotic loss and recombinational load (for recent reviews, see Williams, 1975; Thompson, 1976; Maynard Smith, 1978). Meiotic loss is a product of "sharing" offspring. For a female, outbreeding yields a 50% share of the genome for each zygote produced. This represents a two-fold loss, when compared to the 100% share available to a female reproducing the same number of zygotes asexually (e.g., parthenogenetically). Recombinational load results from the intrinsic organization of nucleic acid genomes, which depend heavily on gene-gene (interlocus) interactions to produce phenotypes. In an outbreeding system, once an integrated, "coadapted" combination of alleles, at many interacting loci, is produced by an incidence of parental recombination and gamete fusion, it is not transmissible to subsequent generations, being broken apart by subsequent recombination events (Wright, 1932). Outbreeding yields a lower fitness potential than the theoretically exact duplication available through asexuality (Maynard Smith, 1971 a and b; Williams, 1975). This disadvantage of outbreeding stems from the impossibility of faithfully reproducing successful parental genomes. The greater the genetic difference between mates, the greater the recombinational load, as more and more alleles with different selective histories are thrust together into a single novel genome.

3

Although asexuality does prevent meiotic loss and does permit exact transmission of parental genomes, preventing recombinational load, it, too, is unable to transmit precise duplicates of *successful* parental genomes. Muller (1964) observed that asexuality is accompanied by an inevitable "ratchet" effect. Once a mutation occurs in an asexual organism, the continued presence of that mutation (barring back-mutation) is assured in all its descendants. Given expected mutation rates of 10^{-9}–10^{-4} events/locus/generation (Wright, 1977), and the overwhelming probability that most mutations will be detrimental (Fisher, 1930), then if an entire genome is considered, asexuality cannot conserve a successful genome for longer than a single generation (Ch. 6).

Because of the inevitability of mutation, asexuality is limited to copying a master blueprint that contains newly arisen errors. Outbreeding cannot even copy the blueprint faithfully, as it constantly mixes halves of two different blueprints to produce a new one. In contrast, inbreeding simultaneously solves the problems of outbreeding and asexuality, while conserving most of the advantages of both. With inbreeding the magnitude of meiotic loss is inversely proportional to the relatedness of mates. There can be no loss in a selfing organism and the potential loss will decrease as the level of inbreeding approaches selfing. The more related are mates, the less damaging is recombinational load. Chromosomes with a common ancestral history are less likely to contain totally novel alleles and produce outbreeding depression. Finally, inbreeding obviates the ratchet by permitting more precise replication of a successful ancestral genome in the face of mutation. If inbreeding is intense enough, parental genomes will be similar at all loci except those at which mutation has occurred within a single generation. During gametogenesis, recombination can combine such mutations, drawing from each homologous chromosome, into a single "waste" gamete. At the same time the process will have produced a gamete free of these new mutations, an almost exact duplication of the ancestral gamete. The process is repeated in close relatives, one of which mates with the first individual. Fertilization will then produce a significant number of diploid ancestral genomes, unbiased by recent mutation. This editing effect of sex and thus inbreeding will only work efficiently if the number of novel mutations per chromosome is low. Editing also entails some waste (i.e., a segregational load, Wallace, 1970), but all this means to the organism is an upward adjustment of fecundity to balance expected losses.

4

In summary, I propose the following general argument, now presented in logical rather than historical sequence. I assume that transmission of exact duplicates of a successful ancestral genome is advantageous for the individuals concerned. For a variety of conditions, the only pattern of reproduction which can approach the favored fidelity is inbreeding sexuality. If inbreeding is adaptive, mechanisms promoting its occurrence should be found in nature. The most common pattern of dispersal observed in nature is philopatry which, as one of its consequences, promotes inbreeding. It is likely that philopatry evolved because it increases inbreeding intensity, and that inbreeding is a primary function of philopatry.

Stated this way it is obvious that had I developed the idea that inbreeding is adaptive, independently of my ideas about philopatry, then the occurrence and consequences of philopatry could have been used as supporting evidence for the inbreeding hypothesis. Since the idea that philopatry functions to promote inbreeding preceded the inbreeding hypothesis, this would not be a legitimate postdictive test. Valid postdiction requires that the empirical evidence available in the literature being used to test novel hypotheses must not have been used in developing the hypotheses (Hempel, 1966). Hopefully, this caution, and the historical background, will help illustrate the power of the mostly comparative postdictive tests I have developed during this analysis (Chs. 7 and 8).

CHAPTER 2

Why Philopatry:
Dispersal and Inbreeding

If an organism's environment is inherently unstable or it offers
many empty but ephemeral sites for occupancy, then the production of propagules that disperse will obviously benefit both propagules and their parents (Cohen, 1967; Levins, 1968). Recently,
Hamilton and May (1977) reached a less obvious but apparently
valid conclusion that temporally stable and saturated environments also require some minimal level of dispersal as an
evolutionarily stable strategy (Maynard Smith and Price, 1973). By
agreeing with their reasoning and assuming that, in most situations dispersal will be adaptive, we can investigate the functions of
the dispersal patterns observed in nature. Given that propagules
disperse, why do they move the distances they do? Whatever an
organism's phylogeny, ecology, mobility, migratory status, or
mode of dispersal (active or passive), one of three dispersal
strategies is usually realized, either philopatry, vagrancy, or
nomadism. Leaving the latter two for later discussion (Ch. 7), I will
concentrate here on the occurence, distribution, and consequences
of philopatry.

Dispersal Analysis

Dispersal distances are normally reported as population averages
of the absolute distances individual propagules move. This er-
roneously implies that dispersal is a continuous phenomenon, ignoring the contributions of normal individual spacing to dispersal.
Consider an animal which possesses breeding home ranges or ter-

ritories 100 m in diameter (assuming circular ranges, Fig. 1). A young animal born near the center of range (A), whose same sex parent survives, cannot disperse less than 50 m unless it displaces the parent. If there is an empty range (B), adjacent to (A), and a juvenile chooses to settle there, it will have dispersed between 50 and 150 m. If all (B) territories are occupied, it cannot disperse less than 150 m, and at the nearest must settle between 150–250 m from its origin (Fig. 1). Dispersal is really a discrete process, occurring in quantal leaps, with the quanta determined by a species characteristic use of space. Whether spacing results from individual aggression (e.g., territorial species), chemical interactions (e.g., plant allelopathy), or simply avoidance of established conspecifics, dispersal distances are expected to reflect the number of filled home ranges passed by a propagule before it settles successfully.

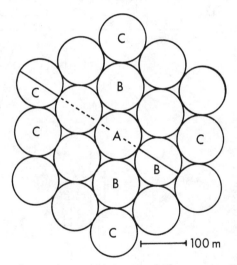

Fig. 1. Division of an environment into normal "home ranges" illustrating the necessity for a discrete measure of dispersal. An individual born in territory A must disperse a distance that is a quantal function of normal home range size in order to settle in an empty territory one (B) or two (C) home ranges away from its birthsite.

Whether dispersal is reported in absolute distances, or as some function of interindividual spacing, the resulting frequency distributions are usually skewed and leptokurtic (Fig. 2; for review, see Endler, 1977; Baker, 1978). Thus, the majority of propagules

7

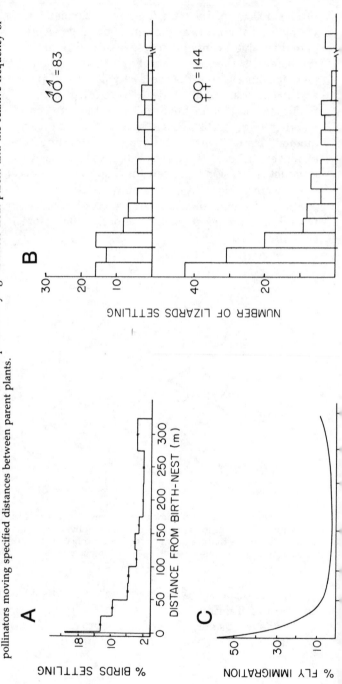

Fig. 2. A composite of philopatric dispersal distribution illustrating the normal skew and the typical leptokurtosis for a variety of otherwise disparate organisms. **A.** The avian migrant house martin, *Delichon urbica* (after Rheinewald, 1975). **B.** The fence post lizard, *Sceloporus olivaceus* (data from Blair, 1960). **C.** The cactus fruit fly, *Drosophila nigrospiracula* (after Johnston and Heed, 1976). **D.** The field mouse, *Peromyscus maniculatus* (data from Dice and Howard, 1951). **E.** The outcrossing plant, *Lupinus texensis* (redrawn from Schaal, 1980). **A-D.** Either the number or percentage of total juvenile individuals settling to breed for the first time at varying distances from their birth sites. **E.** The number of seeds dispersed varying distances from parent and the relative frequency of pollinators moving specified distances between parent plants.

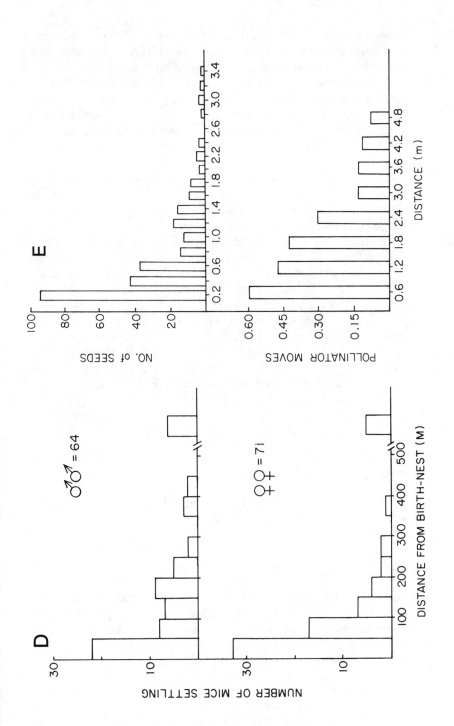

move very short distances. Fewer than expected (based on a normal distribution) move intermediate, and still fewer, but more than expected, move the greatest distances. If such a dispersal distribution is averaged, as is normally done (e.g., Sherman, 1977), a few disproportionately long movements can inflate the population mean enough to provide overestimates of what the "average" propagule is doing. A better measure of central tendency for such nonnormal distributions might be median (or modal) dispersal distance.

An ideal statistic for reporting dispersal, then, should reflect the nonnormal nature of dispersal distributions, and the interindividual spacing (e.g., sessile plants or invertebrates) or home range sizes (mobile organisms) characterizing a species. One such measure is effective dispersal (E), which I (Shields, 1979; 1982a) have defined as a group's median dispersal divided by the average diameter of the area occupied exclusively by sedentary individuals (e.g., home range diameters). In effect, E indicates roughly how many quanta are traveled before a majority of propagules settle. More loosely, it is an indication of how many home ranges away from its birthplace an "average" propagule disperses. Effective dispersal, then, should be useful in estimating effective population size (N_e), itself important in determining the genetic and evolutionary consequences of dispersal (e.g., Ch. 8; Dobzhansky and Wright, 1943; Wright, 1978; and for an independent analysis of the importance of spacing in determining effective dispersal, see Greenwood et al., 1979a).

What Is Philopatry?

Philopatry was originally used to describe an absence of dispersal, that is when propagules capable of movement remained at their birthplace (e.g., Mayr, 1963). Defined more broadly as relatively localized dispersal, philopatric propagules remain at their origin, or as near it as local ecological conditions (e.g., nest site availability or local density) permit. Operationally, and arbitrarily, a philopatric dispersal distribution is one with a median effective dispersal less than 10 spacing units in magnitude (Fig. 3). Vagrancy, then, is any dispersal of greater magnitude, with the implication that the average vagrant propagule will travel much further than the average philopatric individual (Fig. 3).

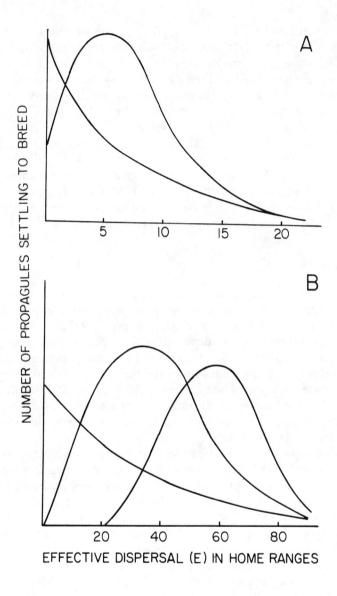

Fig. 3. Hypothetical distributions of propagule dispersal distances reflecting the actual patterns observed in many organisms in nature. A. Philopatric dispersal with median effective dispersal (E = median dispersal/average home range size) less than 10 units. B. Vagrant dispersal with E > 10 home range units.

Philopatric species typically display age and sex dependent differences in dispersal. In most species, adults are either sessile, or if mobile, show site tenacity, remaining at, or returning to, areas where they have bred successfully. Movements between breeding seasons (breeding dispersal) are usually small relative to the movements of younger propagules from birthplace to first breeding locale (natal dispersal); see Fig. 4A and for reviews, see Mayr, 1963; Endler, 1977; Baker, 1978; Greenwood et al., 1979a). To be classified a philopatric species, both sexes should disperse philopatrically. Nonetheless, in most species there is a small but consistent sexual bias in dispersal, with members of one sex (e.g., males in most mammals, females in most birds) moving consistently further than the other (Fig. 4B; for review, see Greenwood, 1980).

Who Is Philopatric?

Based on these definitions, philopatry is a widespread phenomenon. In the context of passive dispersers, in insect-pollinated plants, pollen is normally dispersed philopatrically. In many of these species, seed dispersal is also philopatric, resulting in what Grant (1971) calls "vicinism." Seed and pollen philopatry are common in many annual and perennial plants living in a variety of habitats (for reviews, see Bateman, 1950; Grant, 1971; Levin and Kerster, 1974; Harper, 1977). Philopatry is also found, though less frequently, in passively dispersing animals (e.g., some marine invertebrates, Thorson, 1950).

Philopatry appears to be the usual strategy in actively dispersing animals. As Mayr (1963, p. 568) noted, ". . . such a preference for staying on the home ground is widespread among animals. It has been documented for mice, lizards, turtles, snakes, fish, snails, butterflies, and, in fact, for nearly all species in which movements of marked individuals were carefully recorded." Adult site tenacity combined with juvenile philopatry has been documented in invertebrates (e.g., *Drosophila* spp., Dobzhansky and Wright, 1943; Wallace, 1968a; Begon, 1976; Johnston and Heed, 1976), in fish (Gerking, 1959; Harden-Jones, 1968), in reptiles (Blair, 1960; Tinkle, 1967), in birds (for reviews, see Miller, 1947; Johnston, 1961; Berndt and Sternberg, 1968) and in many mammals (e.g., Dice and Howard, 1951; Erlinge, 1977). Adult site tenacity has been demonstrated directly in many semiaquatic animals (in urodeles, e.g., Twitty, 1961; Forester, 1977), in anurans (e.g., Bogert, 1947;

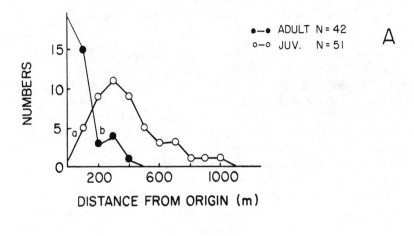

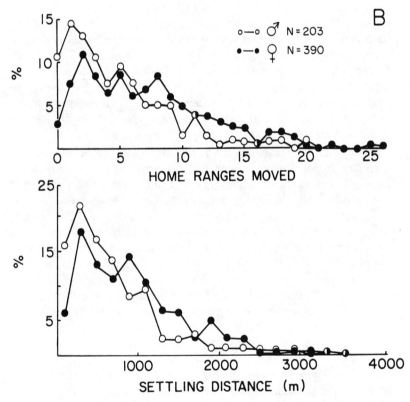

Fig. 4. Typical age and sex differences within philopatric species with: A. adults showing greater site tenacity than philopatric juveniles (tree sparrow, *Passer montanus*, after Balat, 1976), and B. one sex showing a tendency to disperse slightly further, on average, than the other. (In the Great tit, *Parus major*, illustrated here, as in most birds, females disperse further. In most mammals and other vertebrates, e.g., Fig. 2, males disperse further, data from Greenwood, et al., 1979a).

Jameson, 1957; Heusser, 1969; Daugherty, pers. comm.), in turtles (e.g., Cagle, 1944; Carr and Giovanelli, 1957; Carr and Carr, 1972; Loncke and Obbard, 1977) and in seals (e.g., Kenyon, 1960; Coulson, 1971). The difficulties of following the aquatic stages of such species makes conclusive demonstration of complete philopatry very difficult. Yet what indirect evidence exists is consistent with a view that these species are truly philopatric (e.g., Twitty, 1961; Daugherty, pers. comm.).

Effective dispersal (E) can be used to compare dispersal strategies between otherwise very different species. Since most dispersal studies fail to report home range size and fail to present entire distributions of dispersal distances, our sample is necessarily limited. Within these constraints, and using data available in the literature, I have calculated E for a variety of vertebrates (Table 1). These statistics are subject to several sources of error. When forced, I used reported averages, rather than preferable median dispersal distances. For some species it was necessary to use home range and dispersal estimates from different studies. In addition, many of the studies did not control for potential age and sex differences in home range size, dispersal magnitude, or both.

Owing to such factors, and the disparate methods used to calculate dispersal distances and home range sizes, one would not expect that the statistics generated would reflect exact dispersal magnitudes. Nevertheless, the consistency of the emerging pattern, both within and among these otherwise disparate species, suggests that the observed trend is likely to be real. There is a positive and statistically significant correlation ($r = 0.84$; $p < .05$) between home range size and absolute dispersal distance. This relation tends to mask similarities in effective dispersal between sexes within species and among different species, if only absolute dispersal is examined. For example, the apparently large differences observed in absolute dispersal (range; 13–1400 m) disappear on reanalysis, unmasking a consistent trend of localized dispersal of the same effective magnitude (range; 0.4–9.3 diameters; Table 1). Based on absolute dispersal, Berndt and Sternberg (1968) concluded that the pied flycatcher (*M. hypoleuca*) is less philopatric than the blue tit (*P. caeruleus*) or the nuthatch (*S. europaea*). If we examine effective dispersal, the opposite conclusion is more consistent with the data (Table 1). Rather than the huge sexual difference in dispersal strategies reported for Belding's ground squirrel (Sherman, 1977), effective dispersal suggests a

Table 1. Effective dispersal (median absolute dispersal/mean home range diameter) for selected vertebrate species.

Species[c]	Absolute[a]			Effective[b]		
	M	F	Avg.	M	F	Avg.
Amphibians						
Plethodon glutinosus	17.5	14.3	–	4.3	3.5	–
Reptiles						
Chelonia mydas	–	1400.0	–	–	7.0	–
Uta stansburiana	17.7	12.8	–	0.8	1.0	–
Sceloporus olivaceus	40.8	31.3	–	1.4	1.7	–
Birds						
Diomedea immutabilis	19.0	24.0	–	4.0	5.1	–
Muscicapa hypoleuca	–	1000.0	–	–	2.5	–
Parus major(1)	475.0	775.0	–	3.0	5.0	–
Parus major(2)	558.0	879.0	–	4.4	6.9	–
Parus caeruleus	–	–	700.0	–	–	9.3
Sitta europaea	–	–	900.0	–	–	5.9
Sylvia atricapilla	–	–	240.0	–	–	3.5
Passer montanus	–	–	300.0	–	–	3.0
Zonotrichia leucophrys	375.0	450.0	–	2.6	3.1	–
Melospiza melodia(1)	–	–	265.0	–	–	3.7
Melospiza melodia(2)	–	–	225.0	–	–	1.6
Mammals						
Peromyscus maniculatus	103.0	57.0	–	1.6	1.0	–
Tamias striatus	45.1	24.9	–	2.0	1.2	–
Spermophilus beldingi	449.7	47.0	–	2.6	1.3	–
S. richardsonii	–	–	50.0	–	–	0.4

[a]Median (or when median not available mean) dispersal distance in meters.

[b]Effective dispersal, absolute dispersal/average home range diameter, assuming circular home ranges.

[c]Data from, P. glutinosus, Wells and Wells, 1976; C. mydas, Carr and Carr, 1972; U. stansburiana, Tinkle, 1967; S. olivaceus, Blair, 1960; D. immutabilis, Fisher, 1976; M. hypoleuca; Berndt and Sternberg, 1968; P. major(1), Bulmer, 1973; P. major(2), Greenwood et al., 1979a; Perrins, 1956; P. caeruleus and S. europaea, Berndt and Sternberg, 1968; S. atricapilla, Bairlein, 1978; P. montanus, Balat, 1976; Z. leucophrys, Baker and Mewaldt, 1978; M. melodia(1), Nice, 1964a; (2), Halliburton and Mewaldt, 1976; P. maniculatus, Dice and Howard, 1951; T. striatus, Elliot, 1978; S. beldingi, Sherman, 1977; S. richardsonii, Michener and Michener, 1977.

slight, though real, difference (Table 1), with both sexes being philopatric.

The clearest generalization emerging from this analysis is that whatever a philopatric species' mobility or migratory status, whatever its ecological needs, trophic status, or ranging behavior, the magnitude of effective dispersal is remarkably constant and extremely localized. This conclusion is bolstered by the replicated studies in two bird species. In the song sparrow (M. melodia), two studies (Nice, 1964; Halliburton and Mewaldt, 1976) separated by 40 years and 3400 km, yielded similar estimates of effective dispersal. Likewise, two studies of the same population of the great tit (*P. major*) covering 18 years of work produced similar quantitative results (Bulmer, 1973; Greenwood et al., 1979a; Table 1).

Without exception, in these well-studied species, dispersal and normal spacing distances are similar in magnitude. Effective dispersal is as skewed as absolute dispersal, often accentuating the appearance of philopatry if the two are compared (Fig. 5). While there are exceptions (see Ch. 7), the impression remains that philopatry is the rule in actively dispersing species, especially vertebrates. This conclusion is supported by an abundance of less rigorous and less complete data gleaned from studies of a variety of organisms (a partial list could include snails, Selander and Hudson, 1976; mosquitoes, Saul et al., 1978; grasshoppers, White,

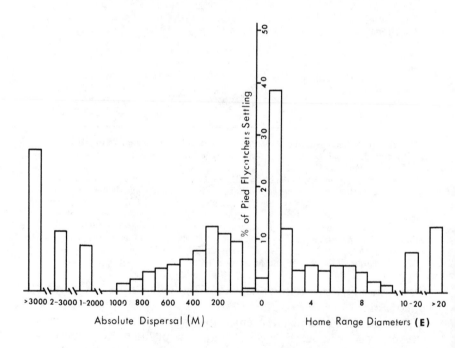

Fig. 5. Comparison between absolute dispersal distance and effective dispersal (using 400 m home range diameter) in the pied flycatcher (females only; data from Berndt and Sternberg, 1968; also see Fig. 4B).

1957; crickets, Morvan and Campan, 1976; butterflies, Ehrlich et al., 1975; Cook et al., 1976; fish, Harden-Jones, 1968; Hasler et al., 1978; antelope, Buechner and Roth, 1974; Leuthold, 1977; rodents, Blair, 1953; Smith, 1974; wolves, Mech, 1970; nonhuman primates, Altmann and Altmann, 1970; Tenaza and Tilson, 1977; and perhaps even humans, Wallace, 1968b; and for general reviews, see Endler, 1977; Baker, 1978).

Why Philopatry?

The ubiquitous and at times striking character we are calling philopatry (it also appears in the literature as *ortstreue*) has received considerable attention. Previous investigations of the problem have, however, often addressed pieces of the problem. Much has been written regarding the proximate control of dispersal in a variety of organisms, but with little discussion of dispersal's ultimate consequences (for reviews, see Johnson, 1966; Hilden, 1965; Bekoff, 1977). More numerous are the important studies exploring the consequences of philopatry without explicitly addressing the question of function (e.g., Miller, 1947; Ehrlich and Raven, 1969; Levin and Kerster, 1974; Endler, 1977; Wright, 1977). Still remaining is a substantial body of work which does attempt to deal with the function of philopatry.

Different interpretations of the skewed and often leptokurtic distributions of dispersal distances observed in nature (Fig. 6), divide opinion into two camps. One group appears to concentrate on the distribution's consequences for the population (species), another on its adaptive implications for individual propagules and their parents. The biotic adaptation school appears to believe that the distribution results from a polymorphism in propagule types (e.g., Howard, 1960; Johnston, 1961; Wynne-Edwards, 1962; Berndt and Sternberg, 1968; Van Valen, 1971; Halliburton and Mewaldt, 1976). They distinguish between innate dispersers, responsible for longer movements, and environmental dispersers, responsible for the bulk of local movements (Fig. 6). Innate dispersers are believed to travel some minimal distance, passing suitable empty sites, before settling in response to an intrinsic psychological motivational state. If given the opportunity, environmental dispersers are expected to remain at, or return to, their birthplace. Their limited dispersal movements are considered responses to local environmental pressures. These include territorial aggression by

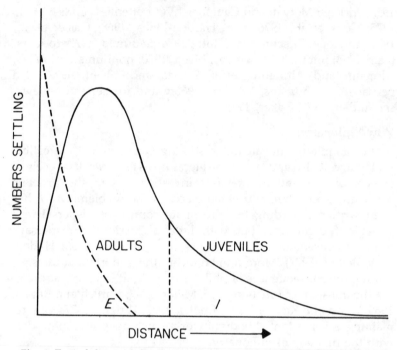

Fig. 6. Typical dispersal distribution illustrating adult site tenacity and juvenile philopatry. Polymorphic propagule types could lead to the juvenile pattern through a balance of short-distance environmental dispersers (E) and long-distance innate (I) dispersers.

dominant residents, local overcrowding, or a shortage of nest sites or other necessary resources. If ecological conditions force movement, environmental dispersers are expected to settle at the suitable empty site nearest their birthplace.

To accentuate the difference between the two types of propagules and the movements that result from their action, some (e.g., Johnston, 1961; Berndt and Sternberg, 1968; Gauthreaux, 1978) have proposed calling the externally controlled movements of environmental dispersers ''spacing,'' referring only to innate movements as dispersal. I believe that this is an unnecessary narrowing of the meaning of dispersal, based on a still hypothetical relationship, and will continue to refer to any movements between birth and breeding sites as dispersal.

With the exception of Van Valen (1971), adherents to this polymorphic hypothesis appear to view the balance between the two propagule types in a single population as a biotic adaptation benefiting the population or species. Either tacitly (Johnston, 1961; Howard, 1960; Halliburton and Mewaldt, 1976), or explicitly (Wynne-Edwards, 1962; Van Valen, 1971), all view the polymorphism as a compromise between individual selection reducing, and group selection promoting, dispersal (see also, Mayr, 1963). The group advantage is thought to result from the consequences of increased gene flow (Howard, 1960; Lidicker, 1962; Mayr, 1963; Wilson, 1980), pioneering new or empty habitats or niches, and extensions of species' range (Johnston, 1961; Mayr, 1963; Udvardy, 1969), and countering the effects of local population extinction (Van Valen, 1971; Gadgil, 1971).

Adherents to the individual selection hypothesis (e.g., in places Lidicker, 1962 and especially Murray, 1967) assume that only environmental dispersers exist. They feel that the leptokurtosis (and even the bimodality seen in some species, e.g., Fig. 5) can be explained as strict environmental dispersal. Through simulation, Murray (1967) was able to show that a population of environmental propagules would produce such distributions, given a few reasonable assumptions (Table 2), despite a real preference for settling as near their birthplace as possible. In his model, the tail of the distribution results from dominance interactions, with dominant residents forcing subordinate dispersers to wander widely before settlement becomes possible. Murray suggested further that the highly visible population consequences of dispersal were merely unselected side effects of the behavior (also, see Gauthreaux, 1978).

Both monomorphic and polymorphic hypotheses, and their proponents, assume that individual selection will tend to minimize dispersal magnitudes. Their reasoning is often coincident and has produced a variety of tentative functions for philopatry. But, these are often proposed on a case-by-case basis with little thought of generality. The resulting pantheon of functions, offered widely and repeatedly, has assumed the guise of a truism and is often accepted uncritically.

Nonadaptive models

The simplest of these explanations are complementary. In sedentary species, individuals are thought to be philopatric because they are incapable of long-distance movements. They are either not mobile enough (e.g., snails) or are passive and must rely on outside agencies that necessarily limit dispersal (e.g., seeds and

Table 2. Simulated distribution of dispersal in two populations. Juveniles disperse distances in arbitrary units and settle empty sites. Dominance, and thus successful settlement, depend on prior residence (Murray, 1967).

Population	Dispersal Distances						
	0–5	6–10	11–20	21–30	31–40	41–50	left area
A[a]	0	10	5	0	0	0	8
B[b]	0	13	6	1	0	1	41

[a]23% survival of young; 50% adult survivorship.
[b]62% survival of young; 50% adult survivorship.

pollen). Both arguments are blinded by proximate factors, overlooking the fact that mobility and mode of dispersal are subject to selection and therefore *could* have evolved differently. A conclusion of adaptation, rather than chance, is strongly supported by those species using identical modes of dispersal, and having similar mobility, that are vagrant dispersers. The individuals in a philopatric species which move considerably farther than the average propagule also imply that their greater dispersal could become the mean if this were adaptive.

In contrast, the philopatry of highly mobile and migratory animals cannot be due to an inability to disperse widely. A common alternative explanation for these species is that "homing" serves to bring the sexes together, after their separation during the nonbreeding season (e.g., Orr, 1970; Hasler et al., 1978). This explanation is commonly used when the distribution of breeding sites is limited compared with the distribution of individuals during the nonbreeding season (e.g., island populations of turtles, pinnipeds, or sea birds, Orr, 1970; Carr and Carr, 1972). If a species' range includes more than one nesting colony, getting the sexes together does not require *birthsite* philopatry. Individuals that return to a general breeding area and then choose breeding sites at random from *all* those available, would still get the sexes together. Instead, they usually return to their birth colonies and settle within meters of their birthplace (e.g., Austin, 1949; Kenyon, 1960; Carr and Carr, 1972; Fisher, 1976). Neither "they can't do anything else" nor "to bring the sexes together" unequivocally answers the question, Why philopatry?

Somatic models

A second set of explanations purports to explain philopatry, or at least adult site tenacity, as a result of the somatic benefits gained by individual propagules. They suggest that nondispersing organisms are likely to benefit because, (1) movement *per se* increases the risk of predation, energetic stress, or both, and (2) individuals familiar with an area are more efficient at using resources, or predator refuges, or at finding nest sites, or at defending resources against conspecific intruders (e.g., Burt, 1940; Blair, 1953; Lack, 1954; 1958; Hinde, 1956; Lidicker, 1962; Cohen, 1967; Gadgil, 1971; Van Valen, 1971; Greenwood and Harvey, 1976; Leggett, 1977; Hamilton and May, 1977; Bengtsson, 1978; Baker, 1978).

While such considerations will apply for many organisms and, therefore, are implicated in the selective maintenance of philopatry, they are less satisfactory in other instances. For example, while the predation costs of (1) may apply, there are few, if any, energetic costs associated with increased *passive* dispersal. Similarly (2) can only apply to actively dispersing animals. More tellingly, (1) will not apply to many migratory species. Members of a bird species that migrate south for the winter, would spend less time on their northerly movements, and therefore less time at risk, if they chose to settle in suitable habitat prior to reacing their birthplace. Should somatic gain be the key benefit, such species would not disperse philopatrically (Fig. 6). Though (2) is probably important in the maintenance of some adult site tenacity, it is less satisfying as an explanation of juvenile philopatry. Juveniles that disperse, even philopatrically, are likely to enter unfamiliar areas (but, see Baker, 1978). Why do such juveniles move 4 or 5 home ranges and not 10, 100, or more, since they have left familiar ground anyway? For mobile birds, the difference would be a few minutes flight. Finally, neither (1) nor (2) applies with much force to philopatry in colonial breeders. Most gulls are likely to be familiar with their entire breeding colony, and the risks of moving a few hundred meters, and thereby dispersing vagrantly, are certainly minimal.

While the somatic models fail as a universal explanation of philopatry, the factors they implicate are likely to be major contributors to a positive selective value for philopatry in many instances. Although, there is no logical imperative that every manifestation of philopatry be explained by a single hypothesis,

21

such a hypothesis, with a domain including *every* example of philopatry, would be worth exploring. At the very least, it might offer additional advantages that could be added to the putative somatic advantages.

Ecogenetic models

A final pair of hypotheses has been proposed to explain philopatry. They are more general and richer in implications than the somatic models. The problem, if any, is that they are so obviously true that their acceptance has been achieved without a thorough analysis of their logical structure or implications.

Ghiselin (1974) eloquently advances a "phenotypic" hypothesis, "Seals can hardly be expected to know, through abstract reasoning, when to seek a better place for giving birth. Rather they ought to go where they were born, where everyone else goes, or both. That mother succeeded in a given place is clear and sufficient evidence that daughter may." He appears to argue that if one's parents were successful in a given area, a reasonable assumption since one *is* alive and ready to reproduce, then one is also likely to be successful in the same area (for similar views, see Murray, 1967; Harden-Jones, 1968; Alcock, 1975; Forester, 1976; Hasler et al., 1978). Of course the problem is that evidence that is clear and sufficient to the investigator may be neither to the seal. The hypothesis should explain why seals that wander more widely would actually be less successful than those that follow Ghiselin's dictum. This would explain how philopatry is maintained. As stated, the "explanation" neither explains nor predicts the required disadvantages of wider dispersal. It is not really an argument, but rather an example of circular reasoning. Why return home? Because mother was successful. Why was mother successful? Because she returned home. Perhaps the power of this argument stems from an underlying, and perhaps unconscious, reliance on the ecogenetic hypothesis presented in greater detail by other investigators. Clearly the "phenotypic" hypothesis relies on an assumption of some minimal genetic resemblence between parents and progeny, a keystone of the ecogenetic hypothesis.

The ecogenetic hypothesis, *sensu strictu*, suggests that philopatry both permits and maintains local adaptations, thereby benefiting individuals, or in some cases, populations (e.g., Mayr, 1942; 1947; 1963; Dobzhansky, 1951; 1970; Blair, 1953; Fisher, 1930; Ford, 1964;

22

Wilson, 1975; Immelmann, 1975; Hasler et al., 1978). Fisher (1930; pp. 140–42) has even provided an intuitive model of how individual selection could favor philopatry. In discussing "heterogeneous" environments, he suggested that two different areas could act as selectively different regions such that,

> . . . the instincts governing the movements of migration or the means adopted for dispersal or fixation, will influence the frequency with which the descendants of an organism, originating in one region, find themselves surrounded by the environment prevailing in another. The constant elimination in each extreme region of the genes which diffuse to it from the other, must involve incidentally the elimination of those types of individuals which are most apt to diffuse. If it is admitted that an aquatic organism adapted to a low level of salinity will acquire, under Natural Selection, instincts of migration, or means of dispersal, which minimize its chances of being carried out to sea, it will be seen that selection of the same nature must act gradually and progressively to minimize the diffusion of germ plasm between regions requiring different specialized aptitudes.

His argument relies on two assumptions: (1) that the ecological environment is spatially heterogeneous, and more specifically, that the scaling of that heterogeneity is small enough that individuals moving more than 10–12 home ranges (i.e., 1.0–24 km; from Table 1) will often encounter selectively different conditions, and (2) that these different regions favor genetically different and "incompatible" selective peaks (Wright, 1956).

Without ever stating it explicitly, the argument implies a major genetical consequence of philopatry. If all the members of a local population breed at their birthplace, or as near as ecological conditions allow, then the average relatedness of mates will increase. This increase is only with respect to alternative dispersal patterns. Just as philopatry increases inbreeding, vagrancy will tend to minimize it. It is the increased level of inbreeding, resulting from philopatry, that maintains locally adapted genomes. Inbreeding protects a local gene complex by preventing its dilution by "unrelated" alleles from different areas with different selective properties. Philopatry minimizes migrational genetic load (Crow and Kimura, 1970, p. 298).

There is a great deal of empirical evidence from a variety of organisms, including both active and passive dispersers and migrants and nonmigrants, which is consistent with the ecogenetic hypothesis. Its wide applicability and support are partially the reason that it has been accepted without detailed analysis. It is obvious that wide dispersal will be maladaptive in plant species living in soils on gradients of heavy metal contaminants. Free interbreeding between genetically resistant individuals and those beyond the influence of the contamination, often results in progeny poorly adapted to either condition (for review, see Antonovics et al., 1971). Similarly, there are two populations of sockeye salmon (*Oncorhynchus nerka*), one breeding on the inlet, the other on the outlet side of a lake (Brannon, 1967). After development in their birth streams, juveniles move to the lake, where they develop further before their seaward migration. This juvenile lakeward migration is controlled behaviorally. At the proper stage of development, when migration would normally occur, members of the downstream population display a positive rheotaxis, swimming upstream in an experimental situation. Members of the upstream population show a reversed taxis, swimming downstream with the current. Under natural conditions this behavioral difference would be adaptive, bringing the fry to the lake. Experimental crosses of adults from the two populations simulated the results of straying in comparison to the actually observed birth stream philopatry. Broods resulting from interpopulational crosses showed segregation for the taxis. Some individuals swam upstream, some down, some both in alternation. Such a "crossbred" family would be likely to lose at least half its numbers, based on the disruption of this single character (Brannon, 1967). Under these conditions, or others sufficiently like them, philopatry will be adaptive.

In presenting this ecogenetical hypothesis, I have assumed that the less detailed presentations of many of its adherents (e.g., Mayr, 1963; Dobzhansky, 1970), reflect the same opinion evident in Fisher's detailed explanation quoted above. The hypothesis is consistent with a large body of data and is amenable to explanation by individual selection as Fisher (1930) proposed. The next question is, What is the domain of the hypothesis? We have seen that it is more general than the somatic models, but how inclusive is it?

The hypothesis predicts that if an environment is heterogeneous, with ecological conditions changing on a specified spatial scale, and if these changing conditions select for different and incompatible genomes, then (1) selection will reward phenotypes displaying limited dispersal which prevents the movement of propagules into selectively novel environments, and (2) that the ultimate function of (1) is its genetic consequence of increased inbreeding. Inbreeding produces offspring adapted to their native environment that are not burdened by alleles from another region.

In his monograph on the effects of spatial scaling of selective environments, Levins (1968) reaches similar conclusions. He predicts that species perceiving their environments as coarse-grained (consisting of large spatially separate patches with different selective properties) should remain in their natal patches and adapt to local conditions through inbreeding. Symmetrically, he predicts that species perceiving their environments as fine-grained (consisting of less discrete patches) should outbreed, as they adapt to a wider range of circumstance. His analysis extends and echos Ford's (1964) conclusion that low levels of dispersal will permit independent adaptation to local environmental differences, while wider dispersal with its consequent gene flow will only permit adaptation to average conditions over a wider range of environments.

If these models are true, then, (1) dispersal distances should reflect the spatial scale of environmental grain for a particular species, and (2) philopatry, if it is defined as a tendency to remain at, or near, one's birthplace, implies extremely small patches differing from nearby patches in some selectively important ecological condition. For these predictions to hold, for example, we would expect the environment of the great tit to show significant ecological differences ever 2 or 3 km, since their median dispersal is less than 1 km (Table 1).

While such small-scale differences are apparent in metal-stressed plants and sockeye salmon, and may be plausible for the great tit and especially many plant species (e.g., Price and Waser, 1979), they are less than obvious for many other philopatric species. The major exceptions are the many philopatric species living in apparently homogeneous (fine-grained) environments. An ideal example of an exceptional species is the Laysan Albatross (*Diomedea immutabilis*) studied by Fisher and his colleagues for 13 years (Fisher, 1966; 1971a; 1971b; 1975; 1976; Fisher and Fisher, 1969; Van Ryzin and Fisher, 1976).

The Laysan Albatross is a large (2–3 kg), long-lived (about 25 years), extremely mobile, and migratory seabird. During the nonbreeding season, individuals are pelagic, ranging widely over the entire North Pacific. They breed in loose colonies in sandy, sparsely vegetated areas on 11 atolls in the leeward Hawaiian archipelago, with the largest colonies on Laysan and Midway islands (Palmer, 1962). They begin breeding at 8 or 9 years and almost invariably settle on the island of their birth (only 2 of hundreds of breeders banded as nestlings were *known* to have changed islands though searches for vagrants were made). Their philopatry extends further than choosing the island of birth. In a specific study of site tenacity, Fisher (1976) reported that juvenile males breeding for the first time nested an average of 19 m, females 24 m, from their birthsites. Adult albatrosses were even more sedentary with < 1% of 1288 repeat nesters changing nest sites at all, and those that did moving very short distances and only after the loss of a mate.

Since they can home precisely, there must be some difference among nest sites that is perceptible to these birds. Yet, is it likely that sparsely vegetated beach sand in the interior of a single mid-Pacific island is selectively heterogeneous on a scale of decameters? The Laysan, after all, is a large, mobile, homeostatic vertebrate. It is forced to endure much greater variation in ecological conditions during its life than is offered on a single breeding island. It is exactly the sort of creature that Levins (1968) suggests will perceive its environment as fine-grained. Its only use of the breeding island is as an egg and chick depository, and it creates their microenvironment with its own body. There are no natural predators on the islands, and all food is gathered far offshore (usually 200–600 km). At the very least, any environmental heterogeneity on a breeding island is exceedingly subtle. When this putative lack of heterogeneity is compared to the intensity of philopatry the species displays, the contrast tends to belie a hypothesis relying on ecological heterogeneity.

While the albatrosses may be a problem, a single exception cannot overturn an otherwise useful hypothesis. But this exception is one of many. The same coincidence of philopatry and fine-grained environment occurs for many other colonial island nesters (e.g., Austin, 1949; Richdale, 1957; Warham, 1964; Coulson, 1971; Stirling, 1975; Carr and Carr, 1972). In terrestrial species, the apparent lack of dispersal between isolated populations of house mice in *single* barns belies the hypothesis (Selander and Yang, 1969; Selander, 1970). This hypothesis is endangered further by philopatric populations of snails (Selander and Hudson, 1976) and butterflies (Ehrlich et al., 1975) living in relatively homogeneous fields. Finally, the hypothesis is an unlikely explanation for the reproductively isolated populations of brown trout observed in a *single* lake (Ryman et al., 1979).

Levins (1968) suggested that fine-grained species should out-breed widely. In fact, it is a generally held view (though there is much ambiguity about the implications of this view because of ter-minological problems, see Ch. 3) that most "higher" animals are, and should be, outbreeders (Dobzhansky, 1951; 1970; Falconer, 1960; Mayr, 1963; Crow and Kimura, 1970; Wilson, 1975). It ap-pears that most of these species are philopatric. Since one of the consequences of philopatry is increased inbreeding (see Ch. 5), either outbreeding is less desirable than is supposed, or some level of inbreeding might be advantageous. Given the occurrence of philopatry, in both coarse and fine-grained species, we can extend the hypothesis by noting that any advantage of inbreeding should be unrelated to the spatial scale of ecological heterogeneity. Perhaps inbreeding, *per se* is valuable, increasing fitness potential in some, as yet, unspecified way.

Which is intrinsically more adaptive in a given situation, in-breeding or outbreeding? The Laysan Albatross offers a pre-liminary and inconclusive test between alternatives. If out-breeding were advantageous, a species should attain a state of at least random mating (Crow and Kimura, 1970). I can think of no species that could as easily and with minimal somatic costs attain species-wide panmixia than this seabird. They are extremely mobile, are known to island-hop as prebreeding juveniles, presumably becoming acquainted with the entire breeding range of the species. There appears to be little that could act as selectively important ecological heterogeneity on their breeding grounds. All that would be necessary for them to attain panmixia would be for first-time breeders to choose an initial nest site at random from among any and all suitable sites available to the entire species. At the very least, they could choose sites at random on their natal island. They do not. They are intensely philopatric, with the resulting reduction in panmixia and increase in inbreeding intensity. One potential inference is that this inbreeding is adaptive.

Philopatry may evolve because it increases the level of in-breeding, which is itself in some way adaptive. This would answer the original question, Why philopatry? The answer, because it pro-motes inbreeding, would also be philopatry's function and ultimate cause. But this answer is ultimately unsatisfying. It is an answer by exclusion, ruling out alternatives until one possibility is left. Such exclusionary analyses, while helpful, do not rule out the possibility of simple, correct, yet overlooked, answers. In addition, the hypothesis fails to explain the existence of nonphilopatric dispersal. Many marine invertebrates and at least a few plant species are neither philopatric nor inbreeding and the hypotheses discussed here make no suggestions as to why. If inbreeding is to be our ultimate answer to the question, Why philopatry?, we must first answer the question, Why inbreed?

CHAPTER 3

The Relativity of
Relatedness and Inbreeding

Exploring the selective value of inbreeding requires an understanding of what inbreeding is. As Jacquard (1975) notes, it is "one word, several meanings," though even he underestimated its many connotations. Ambiguity may enhance poetry, but at best it generates misunderstanding in teleonomy. Thankfully, there are some constants. Inbreeding does refer to the fusion of gametes drawn from related individuals, while related refers to individuals that share common ancestors. One source of ambiguity is the relativity of relatedness, which permits wide latitude in defining the limits of inbreeding. A second is a tendency by some to define inbreeding, not as a pattern of mating, but as one of the pattern's theoretically possible consequences, i.e., as the production of homozygotes.

Concepts of Relatedness: Definitions of Inbreeding

Prior to the rediscovery of Mendel, indeed prior to the development of any formal science, humans had probably developed concepts of relatedness (kinship). Simple observation may have indicated that full siblings appeared more similar to each other and to their parents then to members of other families. Similarly, cousins, while less similar than sibs, were more similar to each other than to other tribesmen. This primitive hierarchical concept of relatedness was, and is, remarkably similar, though rarely identical, to its modern genetic counterpart (Alexander, 1977). It encompassed the realization that kinship reflects an underlying continuum of similarity ranging from "identical" twins to the nonrelatedness reflected by an Eskimo's restricted use of the word "human" for Eskimos and relegation of Indians or whites to "nonhuman" status. The correlation between phenotypic similarity and common ancestry did not escape our primitive geneticists' attention. It would be baseless speculation to guess whether kin classifications first emerged from consideration of phenotypic similarity or patterns of shared ancestry. The importance of the latter, however, is indicated by the maintenance of oral and written records of who begat whom (e.g., the Old Testament).

Regardless of precedence, even today patterns of coancestry do permit pedigree evaluations of relatedness that are independent of genetic effects (e.g., Wright, 1968; 1969). This pedigree concept of relatedness assumes that the more ancestors two individuals share, the more related they are. Thus, full sibs have all their ancestors in common. Cousins share half their ancestors beyond the parental generation via common grandparents, and unrelated individuals have no ancestors in common (Fig. 7). The correspond-

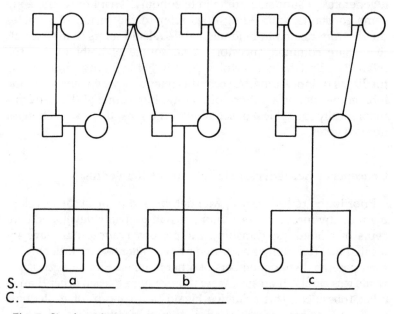

Fig. 7. Simple pedigrees to indicate relatedness. Squares and circles indicate males and females, respectively. The S line groups individuals into three different full sibships (a, b, and c). The C line groups the sibships (a and b) as they are cousins. (See text for further explanation.)

ing definition of inbreeding refers to the mating of individuals with common ancestors. It also reflects a continuum, with inbreeding intensity determined by the proportion of ancestors (100–0%) actually shared by mates. If mates have no ancestors in common, they are "outbreeding" (a × c or b × c). Cousin (a × b) or full-sibling (a × a, b × b, or c × c) matings are examples of increasingly intense inbreeding owing to increasing degrees of coancestry (Fig. 7).

Pedigree analysis also illustrates a second property of continuous inbreeding (each generation inbreeding to produce subsequent generations). A diploid organism produced sexually is the product of two gametes, usually one male and one female. The parents contributing those gametes were also the product of two ancestors each, and so on. Any individual then, will have 2^t ancestors, t generations ago, and a total of $(2^{t+1} - 2)$ ancestral gametes through that generation. In an idealized (perfect) outbreeding system each of those gametes will have been contributed by a unique individual ancestor. No single individual will be found in any pedigree more than once. Through the fourth generation an outbred individual will have 16 (2^4) unique great-great-grandparents (i.e., fourth-degree ancestors) and a total of 30 ($2^5 - 2$) unique ancestors (Fig. 8). Inbreeding invariably reduces the number of unique ancestors by narrowing the pedigree (Pearl, 1914; East and Jones, 1919). For example, by making two grandparents cousins (Fig. 8, dashed line), the reference individual will have only 12 fourth-degree ancestors and a total of 24 (vs. 30) unique ancestors. With continuous full-sib mating, an individual has only 2t unique ancestors through generation t, while selfing reduces to the minimum of 1 per generation, and a total of t (Fig. 8, Table 3).

In order for perfect outbreeding to occur, all of the ancestors of two mates must be mutually exclusive and unique individuals. Ten generations ago, each individual would necessarily have had 1,024 different ancestors. If a population today consists of 10,000 members, then an ancestral population would have had to consist of 1.024×10^7 individuals, half male and half female, and all equally successful at reproducing to insure outbreeding. Obviously, perfect outbreeding does not exist other than as an abstraction against which to measure actual levels of inbreeding. In any finite population, then, some degree of common ancestry and inbreeding is a necessity (East and Jones, 1919; Darlington, 1958; Falconer, 1960; Crow and Kimura, 1970).

Since all organisms are, of necessity, inbreeding we might expect

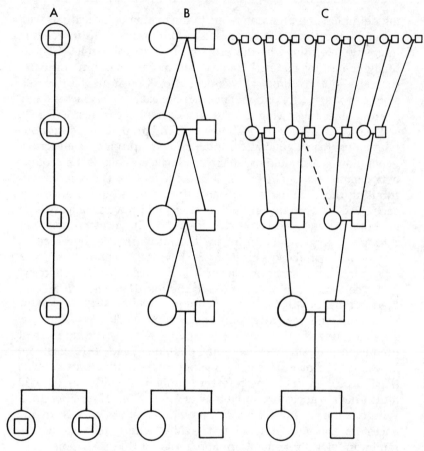

Fig. 8. Pedigrees indicating the relation between inbreeding intensity and patterns of shared ancestry. A. illustrates continuous selfing, B. continuous full-sib mating, and C. "perfect" outbreeding. The dashed line indicates the reduction in unique ancestry resulting from inbreeding, in this case the mating of full cousins.

to hear less about outbreeding. Actually, any text on genetics, population biology, natural history, or evolution is sure to mention both inbreeding and outbreeding, and their properties and potential consequences (e.g., Mayr, 1942; 1963; Stebbins, 1950; 1971; Dobzhansky, 1951; 1970; Lack, 1954; Lerner, 1954; Falconer, 1960; Wright, 1969; 1977; Crow and Kimura, 1970; Grant, 1971; 1975; Wilson, 1975; Dobzhansky et al., 1977). This putative inconsistency results from the relativity of relatedness, which leads to wide variation in the levels of shared ancestry used to define inbreeding. In-

Table 3. Pedigree characteristics for various levels of inbreeding.

Breeding Pattern	Possible	% Ancestors in Common	# of Unique Ancestors
Selfing	Yes	100%	t^a
Incest[b]	Yes	100%	$2t$
Mixed	Yes	$0 < x < 100\%$	$(2^{t+1}-2) < x < 2t$
Perfect Outbreeding	No	0%	$(2^{t+1}-2)$

[a] t = the number of generations prior to the mates in question.
[b] Incest includes continuous parent-offspring, or full-sibling matings.

breeding intensity is determined by the relatedness of mates, and relatedness is a quantitative, rather than qualitative, property, despite the frequent use of the appelation unrelated. Inbreeding intensity can range from a maximum with continuous self-fertilization, to a theoretical minimum with perfect outbreeding (Table 3). Although the latter can only be approximated for short periods of time, the remainder of the continuum is often arbitrarily (and at times implicitly) divided into "inbreeding" and "outbreeding" levels. These cryptic divisions are then used in subsequent discussion.

One common division of the inbreeding continuum, used mostly by botanists (but, see Ford, 1964, p. 177) limits inbreeding to refer exclusively to self-fertilization. By contrast, any form of biparental reproduction is classified as outbreeding (e.g., Faegri and van der Pijl, 1971; and review in Jain, 1976). Dobzhansky (1970, p. 19) once stated, "among higher organisms, especially animals, including man, sexual reproduction and outbreeding are prevalent." I suspect he was not referring to perfect outbreeding; perhaps he was simply referring to biparental reproduction. The question remains, was he implying something more than this? To lessen this sort of ambiguity and insure consistent treatment across kingdoms, I will use selfing and outcrossing to distinguish between uni- and biparental reproduction. I will employ inbreeding and outbreeding to describe patterns of relatedness observed between mates in sexual species.

Unfortunately this distinction does not clear up the ambiguity surrounding inbreeding. Though they are rarely made explicit, there appear to be other arbitrary divisions which equate incest (defined here as parent-offspring or full-sibling matings) and inbreeding in outcrossing species. By default, lesser intensities of inbreeding are considered outbreeding (Table 3). The nebulous nature of these arbitrary divisions makes it difficult to characterize the levels of inbreeding observed in the mixed-mating situations characteristic of nature.

Since perfect outbreeding is impossible, one method of resolving some of the ambiguity has been to arbitrarily define some reference group as outbreeding. Random mating (panmixis), with each individual in a group having an equal probability of mating with any other group member of the opposite sex, is often defined as outbreeding (e.g., Falconer, 1960; Dobzhansky, 1970; Crow and Kimura, 1970; Mather, 1973). By this definition inbreeding occurs if "mates are more closely related than they would be if they had been chosen at random from the *population*," and " . . . the extent of inbreeding is related to the *amount* of ancestry that is shared by the parents of the inbred individuals" (Crow and Kimura, p. 61, emphasis added). The reference group can vary from an entire species down to a localized Mendelian population (deme). Dobzhansky (1950) defined the latter as "a reproductive community of individuals which share a common gene pool." Mayr (1963, p. 136) defines deme even more explicitly as "a group of individuals so situated that any two of them have equal probability of mating with each other and producing offspring. The local population is by definition and ideally a panmictic unit."

If we define inbreeding as nonrandom mating, and then use the deme as reference group, we define away the very possibility of inbreeding regardless of observed patterns of coancestry. Consider a population founded by a single hermaphroditic individual that produces 10 offspring. All survive, mate among themselves at random and produce 10 offspring each. Of the hundred, 10 survive, mate at random, and so on. Despite the high levels of coancestry that would be revealed by pedigree analysis, the consistent parental panmixia would imply *no* inbreeding *within* the population. This occurs because mating within the population is independent of patterns of coancestry. Thus, the population meets Mayr's definition of an ideal, panmictic, and by implication outbreeding, deme. If this same population were then compared to the rest of its species, it would be equally obvious that its members are the product of intense inbreeding, since they have more ancestors in com-

34

mon, than would any two drawn from different conspecific demes. In the end, inbreeding is relative, requiring a reference group before comparisons of inbreeding intensity can be made (Wright, 1965; Jacquard, 1975).

In any functional analysis, our interest focuses on the consequences of a trait. Because the consequences of increasing coancestry are identical, whether the coancestry is a proximate result of finite population size or nonrandom mating, any functional analysis should refer to both sorts of inbreeding. In this context, inbreeding can be conceived as having two contributing components. Nonrandom inbreeding occurs with positive assortative mating based on patterns of relatedness within demes. Random inbreeding occurs when deme size is limited, and inbreeding intensity will be inversely proportional to effective population size (N_e, see Ch. 8; and Kimura and Crow, 1963). Global inbreeding, then, can be defined as random mating over many generations in small $N_e < 1000$) demes. Inbreeding can be further subdivided into mild $100 < N_e < 1000$), intense ($2 < N_e < 100$), or extreme inbreeding, the last being associated with incest ($N_e = 2$), or obligate selfing ($N_e = 1$; for review, see Crow and Kimura, 1970). In contrast, global outbreeding can be defined as continous random mating in large ($N_e > 10,000$) demes. While specific matings in an outbred deme are likely to entail inbreeding (e.g., occasional full-sib matings are expected), this nonrandom inbreeding will be swamped by mutation and gene flow at this or greater population sizes (for review, see Wright, 1977). While inbreeding will occur in large, but finite demes, its expected intensity is weak enough that its consequences may be considered negligible.

Consequences of Inbreeding

The theoretical consequences of inbreeding are well known (Malecot, 1948; Falconer, 1960; and especially Wright, 1969; 1977). All of the genetic consequences of inbreeding stem from the increased genetic similarity of mates that share ancestors. Sexual reproduction requires mechanical transmission of parental chromosomes and their constituent DNA to offspring. Individuals with many common ancestors are expected to share more chromosomes and allelic DNA sequences which are identical, than are individuals with less coancestry. Inbreeding is expected to increase the probability (in diploids) of bringing identical chromosomes and alleles together into single progeny.

Pioneered by Pearl (1914), and especially Wright (1921; 1922), a number of mathematical treatments have been developed to indicate the genotypic consequences of inbreeding. Wright's inbreeding coefficient (f) was originally defined as the correlation between the homologous genes of uniting gametes due to common ancestry. It can be calculated through a path analysis (a series of partial regression coefficients, Wright, 1968), which traces the contribution of all ancestors shared by an individual's parents, by summing the contribution of each unique path such that,

$$f = [(1/2^{t_f + t_m + 1} (1 + f_a)] \qquad \qquad 1$$

where f and f_a are the inbreeding coefficients of the individual in question and its parents' common ancestor on each unique path, and t_f and t_m are the number of generations from "father" and "mother" back to the common ancestor for each path. The correlation between the parents' gametes, their coefficient of relatedness (r_{mf}), is, in the absence of inbreeding, twice their offspring's inbreeding coefficient (2f). If there is some background level of inbreeding, then the coefficient of relatedness is calculated by,

$$r_{mf} = \frac{2f}{\sqrt{(1 + f_m)(1 + f_f)}} \qquad \qquad 2$$

Wright (1943; 1951; 1965) later extended his methods to permit computation of "inbreeding" effects in hierarchically subdivided populations. He defined F_{IT} as the correlation between uniting gametes, relative to the gametes of the entire population. F_{IS} is the average correlation over all subpopulations between uniting gametes relative to those of their own subdivision (the nonrandom component). F_{ST} is the correlation between gametes drawn at random in a subdivision, relative to those of the entire population (random component). He showed that these F-statistics were related by,

$$F_{IT} = F_{ST} + (1 - F_{ST}) F_{IS} \qquad \qquad 3$$

which can be translated into a panmictic index, P (where $P = 1 - F$) such that,

$$P_{IT} = P_{IS}P_{ST} \qquad\qquad 4$$

If these relationships are considered at an allelic level, they can be considered a measure of the likelihood that homologous loci will carry alleles that are identical owing to their descent through common ancestors from a single ancestral allele.

Malecot (1948) explicitly derived a probabilistic model which is computationally equivalent to Wright's, but specifically refers to allelic states. He defined a coefficient of consanguinity, f_i, as the probability that the two alleles drawn from a single, randomly selected locus in an individual, are identical by descent. If the individual's parents are m and f, then f_i will equal the coefficient of kinship ($\varphi_{mf} = r_{mf}/2$) of its parents. The coefficient of kinship is defined as the probability that an allele taken at random from m will be identical with an allele drawn at random from the same locus in f. Computation of f_i and φ_{mf} use methods identical to Wright's (eq. 1), when pedigrees are available. In Malecot's system, the mean coefficient of consanguinity of a population is $\propto$ ($\simeq F_{ST}$). It is the probability that the two alleles carried at a single locus in a randomly chosen individual are identical by descent. Finally, β is the average coefficient of kinship, or the probability that two alleles from the same locus, drawn at random from two individuals in a population are identical by descent (Malecot, 1948; Jacquard, 1975).

The probabilistic model can also account for subdivision and finite population size by using the expected increase in $\propto$, in a population of size N, so that after t generations,

$$\propto_t = 1 - e^{-t/2N} \qquad\qquad 5$$

which can be used to generate a partitioning relationship analogous to eq. 3,

$$f_t = f_0 + (1 - f_0)\propto_t \qquad\qquad 6$$

where f_0 is calculated through parental genealogies ($\simeq F_{IS}$), $\propto_t$ is calculated by eq. 5 ($\simeq F_{ST}$), and f_t is the total consanguinity ($\simeq F_{IT}$) of the individual or class of individuals in question (Jacquard, 1975).

The major difference between the correlation and probabilistic models is in interpretation. The F-statistics measure the correlation between gametes relative to some standard gametic array. They do not imply deterministic changes in genotype frequency. In contrast, the probabilistic models imply that the genotypic consequences expected of inbreeding are necessarily occurring (Wright, 1965).

Despite these theoretical differences, in practice both the F-statistics and their probabilistic counterparts are used to predict the genotypic structure of inbreeding groups. All imply that inbreeding increases the level of homozygosity in individuals. The initial discussions of inbreeding effects (e.g., Wright, 1921; 1922; Haldane, 1936; Fisher, 1949; Lerner, 1954; Falconer, 1960) noted that all treatments assumed that mutation, migration, and selection were absent. There are recent treatments which also state, ''inbreeding leads to homozygosis . . . other things being *equal''* (Mather, 1973, p. 30, emphasis mine; see also Carson, 1967; Lande, 1977; Franklin, 1977). Just as often, modern workers ignore these key assumptions (possibly because they are so well known they are considered trivial) and categorically state, ''The genetic significance of inbreeding is the consequential increase in homozygosity'' (Mettler and Gregg, 1969, p. 53), ''Thus inbreeding increases the amount of homozygosity'' (Crow and Kimura, 1970, p. 61), or ''. . . it also decreases heterozygosity in the population . . . '' (Wilson, 1975, p. 73). Indeed, in Crow and Kimura's classic textbook, the entire 53-page chapter entitled ''Inbreeding'' makes little suggestion that homozygosis is anything but an inevitable result of inbreeding. (They do discuss selection and inbreeding in their sections on selection.) As Grant (1963) warned, ''Our thinking tends to be channeled by the terminology we employ.'' The channelization has proceeded far and deep enough that in much modern discussion a new definiton of inbreeding has emerged which replaces a particular pattern of mating with its ''inevitable'' genetic consequence.

For example, Wallace (1968b, p. 112) states explicitly, ''By inbreeding is meant the bringing together at fertilization of two alleles that are identical by descent from some specified earlier generation.'' Wallace is not alone in making this transformation (e.g., Allen, 1965); he is just more explicit than most. While definitions are often considered above reproach, especially if used with internal consistency, I believe that this definition is misleading. Empirical studies of the genetic structure of natural populations currently use the frequency distributions of electrophoretic "genotypes" to determine mating systems and levels of inbreeding (Ch. 8). All compare observed frequencies with those expected from a panmictic (Hardy-Weinberg) model (e.g., Wright, 1965; Cockerham, 1969; 1973; Rothman et al., 1974; Jacquard, 1975). If observed and expected are not significantly different, panmixia is assumed. Only if there is a deficiency of heterozygotes is there a conclusion that inbreeding may be occurring. Equating inbreeding and homozygosis in this manner redefines inbreeding into *one* of its theoretically *possible* results. Since inbreeding can occur without the predicted changes in adult genotype frequencies (Ch. 4), this cannot be an inclusive or the exclusive definition of inbreeding. Recognizing this difficulty, Wright (1965) suggested that if F-statistics are used to refer to homozygosity, they should be called "fixation indices" rather than the more usual term "inbreeding coefficients." Following his suggestion would preserve the distinction between the mating pattern of inbreeding and its theoretically possible consequence of homozygosis. For now, I would suggest that any such equivalency should not be cast in concrete or be allowed to structure research and expectations about inbreeding and its importance in nature. Jacquard (1975) goes even further, suggesting that the multiple concepts and usages of inbreeding cause sufficient confusion that the word ought to be abandoned entirely. I prefer a return to the pedigree definition, which is useful, and perhaps necessary for functional analysis. A reduction in ambiguity is accomplished by restricting the definition to mating patterns that limit the number of ancestors, regardless of the resultant genetic consequences.

Genotypic Consequences of Inbreeding

Given the pedigree definition of inbreeding, its genetic consequences are still conditioned by the occurrence of mutation, migration, and selection. Although each can independently reinforce or oppose the action of the others, in terms of theory each is usually treated individually (e.g., Crow and Kimura, 1970). With respect to the action of selection, there are two basic assumptions, (1) a neutral model which assumes that alternative alleles and genotypes posses equal fitness potential (no selection), or (2) a selective model which assumes that alternative alleles and genotypes are not selectively equivalent.

Neutral model

Under the neutral model the primary genotypic (single locus) consequence of inbreeding is an increase in homozygosity. This corresponds to the traditional models of the consequences of inbreeding (Wright, 1921; 1922; 1977; Haldane, 1936; Malecot, 1948; Fisher, 1949; Li, 1955; Falconer, 1960; Carson, 1967; Jacquard, 1975). Secondary consequences include (1) random fixation (drift) of alleles in divergent subpopulations (inbred lines), and (2) an overall reduction in the genetic variability carried in each such line and its individual members as they tend towards fixation at all loci.

All of these consequences may be viewed as a result of sampling error in finite populations, of consanguineous mating, or some combination of both. The intensity of inbreeding determines the speed and extent of allelic dispersion and ultimately of fixation. Continuous and intense inbreeding (e.g., selfing) is expected to quickly (< 10 generations) lead to many homozygous and genetically identical individuals distributed into different subpopulations (Haldane, 1936). This complete homozygosis is the eventual result expected of any continuous inbreeding. Only the rate of fixation (heterozygote loss) varies, increasing with inbreeding intensity whether measured by consanguinity of mates (Fig. 9), or by finite population size (Fig. 10). As far as genotypic consequences are concerned, continuous selfing is equivalent to random mating in a population of one (Crow and Kimura, 1970, p. 62).

Under the neutral model inbreeding is not expected to affect allele frequencies in the megapopulations. The frequency of sublines fixed for alternate alleles is expected to equal the initial frequencies of those alleles in the original population, so that inbreeding does not result in a loss of genetic information, rather it simply changes its distribution.

Most of the theoretical treatments of the effects of mutation and migration on inbreeding are embedded in the neutral model (for comprehensive reviews, see Crow and Kimura, 1970; Kimura and Ohta, 1971). Continuous mutation can limit the degree of fixation (F) expected in a finite deme, such that approximately,

$$F = \frac{1}{4N_e u + 1} \qquad 7$$

where N_e is effective population size, and u is the rate of mutation to novel alleles per locus per generation. If either u or N_e is large

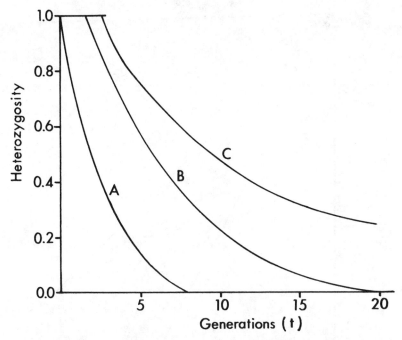

Fig. 9. Different rates of loss of heterozygosity as a function of inbreeding intensity assuming no selection, mutation and migration. A. Selfing; B. Full-sib mating; C. Double first-cousin mating, all relative to an unspecified base population (from Crow and Kimura, 1970).

enough, F can be negligible. On the other hand, if effective population size is so small that $N_e \simeq \frac{1}{u}$ then $F \simeq 0.20$, and considerable inbreeding effects are expected. A conservatively high estimate of the u's likely to occur in nature (e.g., 10^{-4} per locus per generation), suggests that N_e must be greater than 10,000 to significantly limit fixation. This will be true only if such mutations are neutral or favored in current environments. It is this relationship that earlier led me to define inbreeding as occurring in demes of $N_e < 1000$, while demes of $N_e > 10,000$ were classed as outbreeding (Shields, 1979; 1982a; 1982b).

Gene flow (or as others call it, migration) among demes is analagous to mutation, in that it is also capable of limiting fixation. The actual consequences of gene flow depend on the spatial and genetic structure of the species in question. Wright's (1940; 1951) early island and isolation by distance models, and the more recent and realistic stepping stone models (Kimura and Weiss, 1964;

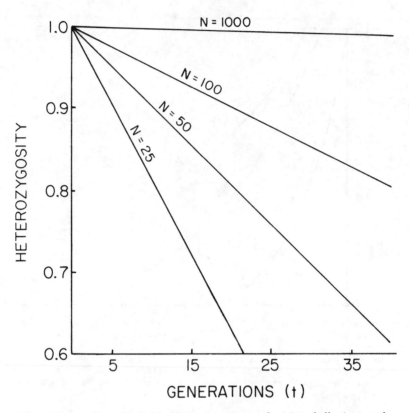

Fig. 10. Rates of loss of individual heterozygosity as a function of effective population size (N_e). The heterozygote decay is relative to the level of an unspecified base population at generation zero, in the absence of disturbing selection, mutation or migration (curves are based on Jacquard's (1975) version of my equation 5).

Weiss and Kimura, 1965), all indicate that if migrants carry novel alleles into otherwise inbred demes, they will reconstitute the heterozygosity lost to inbreeding effects. Others (e.g., Maruyama, 1970; Nei and Feldman, 1972) also indicate that only minimal rates of neutral migration (e.g., one migrant carrying a significantly different genetic complement) are sufficient to limit fixation and prevent local genetic differentiation in all but the smallest ($N_e < 25$) of populations (for a comprehensive review, see Kimura and Ohta, 1971).

Selective models

The development of models of the joint effects of inbreeding and selection lags behind those assuming neutrality. One reason for this is that there is no single, inevitable result if inbreeding and selection occur together. Equilibrium genotype frequencies are jointly determined by the form and intensity of selection conditioned by inbreeding intensity. Since there are many forms of selection (Haldane, 1932), there are also many selective models of inbreeding. I will investigate three such conditions: dominance, underdominance, and overdominance. Unless stated otherwise, I assume migration and mutation are absent.

Dominance

I assume that dominance refers to the case where one allele (A) results in an advantageous "wild-type" phenotype (P_1), whether it occurs in double dose or in association with a recessive alternative (a). Assuming complete dominance, two phenotypes are possible, P_1 (AA, Aa) and P_2 (aa). Inbreeding, then, will increase the zygotic frequencies of homozygous genotypes, relative to the frequencies characterizing the adult parent generation. Selection will increase the frequency of the AA genotype at a rate determined by the selective difference between the two phenotypes ($P_1 > P_2$), and the frequency of the aa genotype will decline. The final consequence will be fixation of A and a in different sublines and the loss of the a sublines. The rate of fixation will rise with either increasing selection or inbreeding intensities.

Underdominance

Single locus underdominance occurs if a heterozygous genotype (Aa) produces a phenotype (P_2) which is less fit than either of its homozygous alternatives ($P_1 = AA$, $P_3 = aa$). Under such conditions, inbreeding will increase the frequency of homozygous zygotes relative to parental genotype frequencies. Selection will increase the frequencies of homozygotes at a rate dependent on the selective differences among the three phenotypes ($P_1 > P_2 < P_3$). If $P_1 = P_3$, then both A and a will eventually fix in different sublines, since they are neutral with respect to one another, otherwise the fittest homozygote is expected to predominate and eventually fix. The rate of fixation with underdominance will also increase with the intensity of either inbreeding or selection.

With either dominance or underdominance, the genotypic consequences of inbreeding are identical to those predicted by the neutral model. Homozygosity will increase and, depending on fitness relations, one or more alternative alleles (and their homozygous genotypes) may be fixed in differentiated subpopulations. Inbreeding and selection are mutually reinforcing, increasing the rate of genotypic and allelic response to environmental selective pressures.

Overdominance

Single-locus overdominance (heterosis) occurs if genotype *Aa* produces a phenotype (P_2) which is fitter than either of its alternative homozygotes ($P_1 = AA$, $P_3 = aa$). (This model will also apply to other conditions which mimic single locus heterosis, e.g., marginal overdominance, Wallace, 1968b; frequency dependent selection, for review, see Berger, 1976). Inbreeding still reduces the frequency of *Aa* in the zygotes produced, relative to the frequency found in the parental generation. In this case selection acts to increase the frequency of *Aa* parents, relative to earlier zygotic frequencies. With overdominance, selection and inbreeding have opposing consequences, making the final result conditional. The intensity and balance of opposing selection and inbreeding will determine the genotypic consequences of that inbreeding.

Given a strong selective difference (i.e., P_2 >> either P_1 or P_2), heterozygotes will be maintained regardless of the intensity of inbreeding. The selective differences needed to maintain heterozygosity in the face of inbreeding are easiest to explore for selfers. Theoretically, a selfing group loses 1/2 of its parental heterozygotes during every bout of reproduction (homozygotes produce only homozygotes, heterozygotes produce 1/4 of each homozygote, and 1/2 heterozygotes). Heterozygosity will only be maintained if the homozygotes are less than 50% as successful as heterozygotes (i.e., $P_2 = 1.0$; $P_1 = P_3 = 0.5$; Table 4, Mather and Hayman, 1952; Hayman and Mather, 1953). The model can also be generalized to cases where homozygotes have unequal fitnesses (e.g., Wright, 1969). The equilibrium frequency of heterozygote genotypes will depend on the relative intensities of inbreeding and overdominant or diversifying selection.

The critical selective difference needed to maintain heterozygosity does decrease as the intensity of inbreeding decreases (Table 4). If inbreeding intensity is kept constant, increasing selection intensity will increase the heterozygote equilibrium frequencies. If selection is maximized ($P_1 = P_3 = 0$), then 50% of the zygotes produced will be heterozygous, even under the strictest of selfing (Fig. 11; Mather, 1973). Of course this is a balanced lethal system and can-

Table 4. Approximations of the phenotypic selection differentials[a] necessary to maintain heterozygosity in an inbreeding population (modified from Wright, 1969).

Mating	P(AA) = P(aa)
Selfing	.500
Full Sig–Full Sib	.763
Parent–Offspring	.750
Half Sib–Half Sib	.812
Double First Cousin	.855
N_e = 25	.974
N_e = 100	.994
N_e = 500	.998

[a]P(Aa) = 1; Homozygotes must be less successful by the tabled proportion, i.e., in a selfer, homozygotes must be less than 50% as viable as the heterozygote.

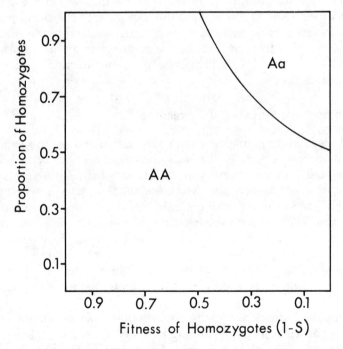

Fig. 11. The interaction between inbreeding and selection in a selfing organism. If the homozygotes are less than 50% as successful as the heterozygote, some heterozygotes will be maintained in the population. The proportion of heterozygotes remaining is a function of the intensity of selection above this critical value, reaching a maximum when s = 1 (see text for further details, redrawn from Mather, 1973).

not be expected to maintain multiple unlinked loci in heterozygous condition (Kimura and Ohta, 1971). Still, the number of heterozygous loci which can be maintained by selection is not enormously lower under inbreeding than under panmixia (Ch. 4; and for reviews, see Reeve, 1955; 1957; Reeve and Gower, 1958; Robertson, 1952; 1962; Carson, 1967; Hill and Robertson, 1968; Wallace, 1968b; Mather, 1973; Wright, 1977).

The consequences of mutation and migration on inbreeding's genotypic consequences are similarly conditioned by selection. If selection favors particular mutations, they are more likely to be assimilated into a population and so retard fixation. If, as is more likely, novel mutations are deleterious, then selection will oppose their assimilation and fixation will proceed apace. Similarly, if selection favors specific novel migrant alleles, or the novel combinations they produce, then fixation will be abated. If migrant alleles are disfavored, then the inbreeding effects will ensue at the rates expected on theoretical grounds. In the face of natural selection, the joint consequences of inbreeding, mutation, and migration on rates of fixation, and thus relatedness, in an inbred group cannot be predicted without knowledge of the direction and intensity of selection.

Genomic Consequences of Inbreeding

Besides affecting single-locus genotype frequencies, inbreeding has a marked effect on the total constitution of an organism's *genome* (all the alleles at every loci in an individual). Continuous inbreeding tends to increase allelic correlations *across* loci, whatever their linkage relations, and regardless of the action or inaction of selection. The one inevitable result of inbreeding is the production of this interlocus correlation, which will increase in magnitude with inbreeding intensity. In extreme cases inbreeding can produce significant "gametic phase disequilibrim," that is, nonrandom associations of alleles (e.g., Jain and Allard, 1966; Allard, 1975).

A diploid individual contains a maximum of two different alleles at any particular locus. Assuming no mutation and complete self-fertilzation, all of an individual's descendants will show high interlocus correlations. If we use Lewontin's (1974) binary notation to characterize a multilocus genome (e.g., $A_1A_2B_1B_2 = 0101$), then selfing by a 0101 individual will produce a limited number of genomes. In a neutral environment, 4 pure lines (reproducing only the parental genome) result, 0000, 0011, 1100, and 1111. If heterotic selection is intense enough 0101 may remain the most common parental genome, though all the segregants are expected (for an empirical example, see Jain and Allard, 1966). The major consequence is that a novel allele (e.g., A_3 or B_4) will never appear in the genome as a result of mating (though they could appear via mutation). All the original alleles are consistently associated with one another throughout an inbred line's reproductive history. This interlocus association will extend across the entire genome, so that all alleles at *every* locus (either one allele, or a maximum of two for loci subject to heterotic selection, ignoring, for the moment, multiple alleles) will share a common history.

Wright's (1965) F-statistics, if they are determined through genealogies or population size, may be suitable measures of such interlocus correlations. In this framework, F_{IT} could be considered an estimate of the proportion of an individual's genome which has shared a common ancestral history for at least two generations. Similarly, F_{ST} would measure the proportion of a subpopulation's gene pool which has been associated since a reference generation. Of course, high mutation rates would reduce the levels of association, as noted earlier. Both the association, and its mathematical estimate, should hold regardless of whether the environment is neutral or selective. For example, with heterotic selection, two alleles may be maintained at a single locus, but if inbreeding is intense enough, it will normally be the *same* two alleles. Thus, A_1 and A_2, either alone or together as a heterozygote, will remain associated with the same B, C . . . N locus alleles carried in the inbred individual's recent, and depending on inbreeding intensity even quite distant, ancestors. Increased inbreeding increases the probability that two alleles drawn at random from different loci in an individual have been associated in the past. Increased inbreeding intensities will, therefore, increase the proportion of an individual's genome that shares a common evolutionary history. In any inbred group a particular gene product is more likely to find itself in a familiar biochemical milieu than would be the case in a more outbred group.

Phenotypic Consequences of Inbreeding

In both neutral and selective envrionments, continuous inbreeding will affect the distribution of phenotypic variation resulting from genetic differentiation (Falconer, 1960; Crow and Kimura, 1970). Variability within families (zygotes produced by a single female during her lifetime) or subpopulations is usually reduced, while variance between families and subpopulations is increased by inbreeding. The megapopulation's (species) total variation is expected to remain the same.

Under neutral conditions, continuous inbreeding will produce families consisting of genetically (except for novel mutations), and therefore phenotypically, identical (ignoring gene-environment interactions) individuals (Fig. 12). This tendency for reduced

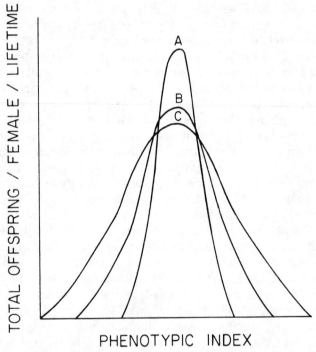

Fig. 12. Theoretical distribution of phenotypic variation under different inbreeding and selection conditions. All models assume that genetic contributions are additive and do not interact with the environment. A. Inbreeding in a neutral environment, within-family variation results only from mutation; B. Inbreeding combined with heterotic selection, within-family variation increases due to segregation; C. megapopulation panmixia, maximum within-family variance. Among population variance is greatest with C, declines under B and A.

phenotypic variation as a result of reduced genetic variation may in some cases be limited by reductions in developmental homeostasis in homozygous individuals (for review, see Lerner, 1954). Given enough heterotic selection to maintain heterozygotes in an inbreeding population, then the segregation of homozygotes will increase the within-family variance observed at particular levels of inbreeding, relative to conditions of neutrality. Limitations on the number of alleles per locus and continued associations of the same alleles across loci and across generations are still expected to reduce within-family variance relative to wider outbreeding (Fig. 12). The intensity of reductions in variability within families is expected to mirror inbreeding intensity.

Finally, within a large panmictic population, there are more alleles expected per locus, less constancy of interlocus associations, and each family is expected to contain a random sample of all the alleles in a megapopulation's gene pool. Under these conditions, variation among individuals within families is expected to be large (Fig. 12), while that among families is expected to decrease.

CHAPTER 4

The Disadvantages
of Inbreeding

Discussing the disadvantages of inbreeding is a time-honored tradition (for reviews, see Zirkle, 1952; Wright, 1977). Historical perspectives often trace the roots of the common judgement about the deleterious consequences back to Darwin's (1868; 1876) remarks that, "it is a law of nature that organic beings shall not fertilize themselves for perpetuity," and "The first and most important conclusion which may be drawn from the observations in this volume, is that cross-fertilization is generally beneficial and self-fertilization injurious." Although Darwin was primarily concerned with comparing uni- and biparental reproduction, Mendelism permitted generalization to biparental inbreeding and its similar genetic consequences. Through repetition, and much empirical support, the "detrimental" hypothesis of inbreeding has approached the status of law. So ingrained and widespread is the knowledge of inbreeding's injurious nature that Lerner (1954, p. 22) could say, "There is no particular need to discuss here the details regarding the reduction in fitness and viability occurring under inbreeding. Firstly, the deterioration of populations subjected to continued consanguineous mating represents a generally known phenomenon." Lerner is often cited in discussions of the consequences of inbreeding (e.g., Maynard Smith, 1978, p. 127) and his view is reiterated regularly in the literature of evolutionary biology: "It is an *almost* universal observation that severe inbreeding leads to 'inbreeding depression,' a serious reduction of fitness in its various components" (Mayr, 1963, p. 224, emphasis added), population genetics, " . . . inbreeding *usually* leads to a decrease in size, fertility, vigor, yield, and fitness" (Crow and Kimura, 1970, p.

61, emphasis added), and population biology, "But inbreeding lowers individual fitness and imperils group survival by the depression of performance and the loss of genetic adaptability" (Wilson, 1975, p. 80).

The modern concept of inbreeding depression is founded on a twin base provided by mathematical theory (Ch. 3 and summaries in Wright, 1969; 1977), and the empirical support of a vast store of practical experience with, and experimental investigation of, inbreeding. Most of this evidence comes, " . . . from domestic and laboratory animals and plants," in controlled situations (Lerner, 1954, p. 22). As Wright (1931) noted, half a century ago, mathematical consideration within the framework of the neutral model, in association with the fact of recessiveness, "gives the theoretical basis for the immediate degeneration which usually accompanies inbreeding." Though the neutral model of inbreeding's consequences explicitly assumes that alternative alleles and genotypes are selectively equivalent, it is consistently used to "explain" inbreeding depression in terms of an increased production of low fitness genotypes. Explaining selective effects with a nonselective model is logically inconsistent, and together with a reliance on evidence from "artificial" situations, appears, to have resulted in a potential misinterpretation of the consequences and importance of inbreeding in natural populations.

Genotypic Disadvantages

Discussions of inbreeding depression focus on the increased homozygosity resulting from inbreeding relative to more panmictic breeding systems. Depression is considered to be a direct result of this increased homozygosity owing to, (1) the unmasking of deleterious recessives (dominance effects), (2) the reduction in frequency of better adapted heterozygotes (heterotic effects), or (3) a combination of (1) and (2).

Whether dominance is the product of selection for modifiers capable of producing wild-type phenotypes in the face of recurring deleterious mutants (Fisher, 1931), or the chance inactivation of a mutant enzyme (Wright, 1977), recessiveness is usually a good indication that the recessive phenotype is detrimental in the current environment (Crow and Kimura, 1970). If the members of a breeding population carry a significant number of deleterious recessives in heterozygous condition, inbreeding will unmask them, resulting in an obvious depression in fitness for the individuals involved. Depression due to dominance effects is usually measured by the number of homozygous recessive individuals *lost*, compared to the number of individuals with dominant phenotypes *not lost* in a less inbred system (Falconer, 1960; Wright, 1977).

If a significant number of loci display heterozygote advantage, inbreeding's increased production of homozygotes will also depress individual fitness. The magnitude of depression due to heterotic effects can also be measured by the number of extra homozygotes produced and lost, versus the increased number of heterozygotes expected, and not lost, in a less inbred system.

The "detrimental" hypothesis predicts depression magnitudes that are a positive function of inbreeding intensity. Empirical support for this prediction abounds, with significant depression positively correlated with inbreeding intensity (usually measured by f or f_i) found in just about every cross-fertilizing plant and animal investigated (e.g., Fig. 13; for comprehensive reviews, see Falconer, 1960; Carson, 1967; Wright, 1977). As noted previously, most of this evidence comes from domestic or laboratory populations. Other than humans, the only animal subject of comprehensive studies of inbreeding in natural populations, appears to be the great tit (*Parus major*), studied by Bulmer (1973) and Greenwood et al. (1978). The latter interpret their results (which include Bulmer's data on the same population) as "the *first* detailed evidence of inbreeding depression in a natural population . . . ." The evidence, then, appears to be universal and nearly unanimous; inbreeding, especially if it is intense, lowers individual fitness relative to the alternative strategy of outbreeding.

Based on such considerations, many workers suggest that natural populations *should* outbreed. They also note that a "practical" outbreeding maximum, often approximated in nature, is random mating, though they rarely discuss how wide the panmixia really is (Falconer, 1960; Mayr, 1963; Wallace, 1968b; Crow and Kimura, 1970; Dobzhansky, 1970). As support for this conclusion, they cite many traits which they infer are adaptations promoting decreased levels of inbreeding. These include self-sterility and morphological characters promoting cross-fertilization in plants (e.g., Stebbins, 1950), single sex broods in some insects (e.g., *Sciara* flies, Metz, 1938), rare male mating advantages in some insects (Ehrman, 1970) and fish (Farr, 1977), and patterns of inbreeding

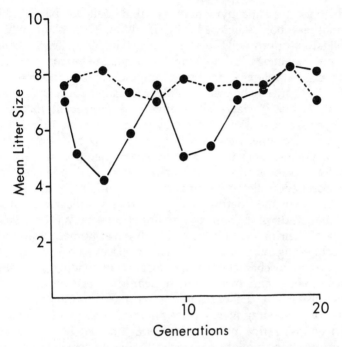

Fig. 13. Mean litter size in full-sib-mated lines of laboratory mice, *Mus musculus* (——), compared to outbred controls (----). Twenty inbred lines were begun, but only one persisted through generation 20 (redrawn from Wright, 1977, from the data of Bowman and Falconer, 1960).

avoidance in birds (e.g., Koenig and Pitelka, 1979), mammals (Hill, 1974) and in nonhuman (Itani, 1973; Packer, 1975; 1979) and human (Zirkle, 1952; Alexander, 1977) primates. Kalmus and Smith (1960) suggested that one function of sex, and equal sex ratios, is that they lessen inbreeding. As noted earlier (Ch. 2), some workers believed that the increased vagrancy of a few individuals in a normally philopatric species (e.g., Howard, 1960), or a general pattern of vagrant dispersal (e.g., Mayr, 1942; 1963) are beneficial because they promote wider outbreeding. More recently, Greenwood and his colleagues (1976; 1978; 1979a; 1980; see also Bengsston, 1978) suggested that the frequent sexual difference in absolute dispersal displayed by many philopatric species (Ch. 2) may function to prevent "*too close* inbreeding" (emphasis mine).

Supporters of the "detrimental" hypothesis must also explain the many species which are obviously and intensely inbreeding in

53

nature (e.g., parasitic hymenoptera which full-sib mate within their mothers' bodies before birth, Hamilton, 1967; plants which are obligatory or primarily self-fertilizing, Jain, 1976). They usually meet this challenge by making *ad hoc* adjustments to their hypothesis by referring to the genotypic consequences of inbreeding as a price to be paid for some associated advantage. Alexander (1974; 1977) views inbreeding as a price paid to obtain greater social cooperation (cf. Greenwood and Harvey, 1976). Plant biologists have long viewed selfing as a price paid for greater reproductive insurance in a sessile organism (i.e., pollen is always available) and for increased colonizing ability (i.e., one seed can start a population, Baker, 1959; and review in Jain, 1976).

The power of the "detrimental" hypothesis is illustrated in an interesting study of a group of rare ant species by Wilson (1963). Because of their rarity, he expected to discover numerous adaptations promoting outbreeding. When he discovered just the opposite, i.e., many characters promoting close inbreeding (including wingless males, and mating in or near the nest before mated queens dispersed), he concluded that the detrimental consequences of inbreeding were a price paid to insure mating in these species, whose rarity makes finding an "unrelated" mate a difficult proposition. It might have been simpler to conclude that the genotypic consequences of inbreeding are not all that detrimental. This is especially true since ants, unlike obligately sessile plants for which the reproductive assurance argument is plausible, can be quite mobile (given wings) and could conceivably locate mates through such potentially long-distance communication mechanisms as pheromones.

If the hypothesis is correct that inbreeding may be, on balance, advantageous for a wide variety of organisms, then, (1) traditional analyses of inbreeding depression must in some way be faulty, (2) inbreeding must have advantages that more than balance its obvious disadvantages, (3) the detrimental hypothesis is correct, but only for specific levels of inbreeding, while the semantic ambiguity surrounding exactly what inbreeding refers to has fostered an incorrect generalization which considers *all* inbreeding injurious, or (4) some combination of all of the above. Saving (2) and (3) for later (Chs. 5 and 6), perhaps inbreeding depression is less injurious than it appears to be.

Genotypic Disadvantages: An Alternative View

Dominance effects

The actual level of inbreeding depression resulting from the unmasking of deleterious recessives is expected to be a function of the magnitude of their disadvantage, and their frequency of occurrence in the group in question. Deleterious recessives accumulate to the highest possible equilibrium frequencies in panmictic groups and the larger the group the higher the frequencies. Each recessive arises as a single mutant in a single individual. Assuming complete dominance, it will proceed to spread throughout a panmictic unit (if it is not lost through drift), since it is masked, and therefore increases in frequency. Only when it is abundant enough that random mating will segregate a significant number of homozygotes can selection act to damp its increase. If a group at this panmictic equilibrium frequency is forced to inbreed more closely, the rate of homozygote production will increase, and the loss of such individuals can be measured as a fitness depression relative to the original panmixis. A switch from outbreeding to inbreeding will obviously depress fitness (Lerner, 1954).

In contrast, *continuous* inbreeding minimizes the equilibrium frequency of deleterious recessives. A deleterious mutant is not masked and dispersed throughout the breeding group, rather it is quickly reassorted into hymozygotes (e.g., in the generation after its original occurrence in selfers) and immediately placed at selective risk. If inbreeding is intense enough (e.g., selfing), a recessive behaves in the same manner as a detrimental dominant, but with a one generation delay in its selective loss (Haldane, 1932). The mutant's equilibrium frequency will be the lowest compatible with its recurrence rate and its selective disadvantage (see also, Livingstone, 1969; Bengsston, 1978).

While a switch to inbreeding from earlier outbreeding is likely to be maladaptive, continuous inbreeding is expected to be less harmful with respect to dominance effects. The much reduced frequency and magnitude of inbreeding depression in normally inbred organisms is consistent with this view (e.g., Jinks and Mather, 1955; Carson, 1967; Jain, 1976). The view is also consistent with the general rise in fitness after early and obvious depression observed in continuously inbred lines (e.g., generations 10–20, Fig. 13; and review in Wright, 1977). This increased fitness is thought to result from inbreeding's elimination of deleterious recessives from a group's gene pool (usually through subline extinction). Since inbreeding actually reinforces selection (Ch. 3), it might even be viewed as beneficial. It will increase the probability of the adaptive fixation of favored dominant alleles across the entire genome (inbreeding affects all loci simultaneously). East and Jones (1919, p. 140) made a similar point more emphatically and more colorfully,

> If undesirable characters are shown after inbreeding, it is only because they already existed in the stock and were able to persist for generations under the protection of more favorable characters which dominated them and kept them from sight . . . . If evil is brought to light, inbreeding is no more to be blamed than the detective who unearths a crime. Instead of being condemned it should be commended. After continued inbreeding a crossbred stock has been purified and rid of abnormalities, monstrosities, and serious weaknesses of all kinds.

Historically, it is just this consequence that plant and animal breeders rely on to eliminate unwanted ''sports'' and fix desirable characteristics (Falconer, 1960; Wright, 1977).

Heterotic effects

The magnitude of inbreeding depression resulting from heterotic effects depends on the intensity of selection and the number of alternative alleles at each heterotic locus. Under panmixis and with equal allele frequencies ($p = q = 0.5$), the number of heterozygous zygotes will equal the number of homozygotes produced. Adding alleles ($p = q = r = 0.33$) will increase the equilibrium proportion of heterozygotes (e.g., 3 alleles, 67% heterozygotes). If the selection coefficient (s) is less than the critical value needed to maintain heterozygosity at a given inbreeding intensity (Table 4, Ch. 3), then fixation will proceed and serious inbreeding depression will result. If selection is intense enough, heterozygosity will be maintained at some level betwen 0 and 50%. Any difference between the 50% heterozygosity expected under panmixia and lower levels resulting from inbreeding could then be considered a segregational load and a potential component of a true inbreeding depression.

Continuous inbreeding in the presence of selection gives an expectation of lower (but not zero) levels of fitness depression than is generally implied in print, or observed in experimental situations (e.g., Lerner, 1954; Falconer, 1960; Wright, 1977). It should not lead to the unmasking of enormous numbers of deleterious recessives and should only result if large and permanent declines in heterozygosity at relatively low selection intensities or at the highest inbreeding intensities. Yet observed levels of inbreeding depression appear to contradict this conclusion.

Many of the laboratory and domestic populations which provide the bulk of evidence regarding inbreeding depression are normally outbred. In many cases (e.g., Lynch, 1977; and for review, see East and Jones, 1919), this is deliberate with "unrelated" individuals or individuals from widely separated areas being mated randomly to create base populations. A subsequent switch to inbreeding will unmask any recessives which accumulated during the initial outbreeding, creating substantial depression. Of course, such conditions and their associated results have little bearing on the consequences of continuous inbreeding. It is more likely that organisms which inbreed in nature do so continuously, rather than switch between long periods of inbreeding and outbreeding.

The conceptual framework within which selection and fitness are defined, and the properties of the environment where they apply, are also important to interpretations of the consequences of inbreeding. Using a single-locus model, one representation of the logic of the "detrimental" hypothesis would still indicate that continuous inbreeding results in immediate fitness depression. Individuals which inbreed are expected to be less successful than those which outbreed. Consider organism A (genotype Aa). It selfs, producing 4 zygotes. One fails to develop because it is homozygous for a recessive lethal (a). Its competitor B (also Aa) outbreeds, producing 4 zygotes, all of which develop since none is homozygous for the novel lethal (a). Inbreeding is 75% as successful as outbreeding under these conditions of lethal dominance effects. Organism C (Aa) selfs, producing 4 zygotes, of which 2 die because they are homozygotes (AA, aa). Its competitor D (Aa) outbreeds, and 2 of its offspring die because they are homozygotes. Given large selection coefficients (here $s(aa) = s(AA) = 1$) inbreeding and panmixia have the same result. With multiple alleles, D can produce as few as 1 (3 alleles) or 0 (4 or more alleles) homozygotes by outbreeding. Even with intense selection, inbreeding is then 50–75% as successful as panmixis if there are multiple alleles and extreme heterotic effects. (This entire argument can be generalized to lesser inbreeding or selective intensities resulting in reduced depression). By this reasoning it is clear that whatever the selective environment, inbreeding is at an immediate disadvantage if there are dominance effects or heterotic effects and multiple alleles.

Perhaps this reasoning is only valid for the artificial environments where inbreeding depression is a fact of life. Both the reasoning and the empirical evidence associated with it do not, indeed cannot, apply to natural situations unless selective conditions in the two situations are identical. The major factors barring such an extrapolation are fundamental differences in how selective success is defined and in the properties of the environment in which reproductive success is determined. A primary source of confusion is the entirely different concepts of success associated with artificial and natural selection. The "detrimental" hypothesis appears to measure success in a currency of number of viable progeny *produced*. But, "it does not follow that an organism that produces a large number of progeny will also leave a large number of descendants" (Harper, 1977, p. 649). Descendancy is a truer measure of evolutionary success.

The "detrimental" hypothesis developed in a matrix of quantitative genetics for use primarily by plant and animal breeders. As a tool in applied breeding it serves its purpose well. The primary goal of breeders is to maximize the production of *viable* progeny, with little regard to descendancy. If evolutionary changes are desired, artificial selection is usually applied by altering fecundity (either increasing the number of offspring produced by favored individuals, or decreasing that of disfavored individuals). Rarely is selection performed by early culling. Rather breeders constantly attempt to maximize viability. The environment is actually designed to be hospitable, increasing the probability of survivorship even further. In this context, success (and therefore fitness) *should* be measured by the number of surviving progeny brought to *market*. The loss of subviable progeny before they can be marketed represents a tremendous economic cost (depression) for the breeder. Such progeny will be produced by inbreeding, and will be lost even in the benign environments that were designed to nurture survival.

However important to breeders, this economic inbreeding depression may be irrelevant to selection and evolution in natural environments. A natural environment is rarely benign. It usually limits the number of individuals surviving, with most progeny being lost before they can reproduce. Lacking economic investments or aesthetic values, natural selection does not distinguish between the viability and fecundity components of fitness. It invariably and opportunistically affects both in order to maximize the number of descendants, not the number of progeny produced. The harsh nature of natural environments usually imposes a population limit (carrying capacity) for any species. Since this is a limit on the number of individuals an environment can support, the average female in a species can expect to produce a *single* female descendant, regardless of the number of progeny she produces.

Reevaluating the earlier single-locus model by modifying the conditions to better approximate a natural environment results in an altered view of the immediate consequences of inbreeding. Organism A produces 4 zygotes by selfing. One fails to develop (lethal recessive), one is eaten by a predator, and one fails to obtain a nest-site, dying before reproducing. A leaves one descendant. Organism B outbreeds and produces 4 zygotes. All develop, one is eaten, and two fail to obtain nest-sites, dying before reproduction. B also leaves one descendant. I assume that only two nest-sites are available and ignore the possibility that both of B's "survivors" could gain one each leaving A's survivor none. This assumption is extreme but possible if, for example, it is a parental site that becomes available and prior residence establishes dominance.

In such an environment, inbreeding and panmixia can have identical success rates measured in descendants. The relative merits of either will depend on the harshness of the environment and the intensity of selection. Natural selection does not measure success in the fewest progeny lost, as assumed by the "detrimental" hypothesis. It only recognizes winners. Success is measured by the proportion of the next generation's parents represented by an individual's progeny (or other kin, Hamilton, 1964a and b). The number of progeny lost during the production of winners is not indicative of fitness, nor does it illustrate the direction of selection. To suggest otherwise leads to the untenable position of declaring an individual which is represented by 2 of its original 10 progeny in the next generation (80% loss) a loser relative to an individual represented by 1 of its 4 (75% loss).

If we accept the premise that selection rewards winners, the timing of loser production is probably less important than the number of losers produced. Rather than maximizing viability at every turn, and selecting primarily via fecundity, natural selection can be expected to increase the number of winners in any manner possible. If producing winners entails producing early losers, so be it. As Wallace (1968b; 1970; 1977) has noted, if intraspecific competition and normal population pressures insure death for a proportion of an individual's progeny for ecological reasons, earlier deaths due to genetic causes (i.e., a segregational load) may not be a liability.

The theoretical problem of a segregational load and the maintenance of genetic variability is not unique to discussions of inbreeding. It is a central point in current neutralist-selectionist arguments, and applies to all sexual reproduction (see Ch. 6). A number of models developed in the context of panmixis illustrate conditions, including various forms of truncation (Milkman, 1967; King, 1967; Sved et al., 1967), soft (Wallace, 1968b), or frequency-dependent (e.g., Clarke, 1979) selection, that can eliminate the problem of segregational load. If it turns out that any or all are actually occurring in nature, then segregational loads may be less important to sexual reproduction whether outbreeding or inbreeding.

I am not arguing that inbreeding depression as a result of increased segregational load does not exist. As a consequence of inbreeding and in laboratory and domestic populations it is certainly commonplace. I am arguing that the success of the ''detrimental'' hypothesis in this limited context should not lull us into accepting its truth for wholly different circumstances. In natural populations the depression, if any, resulting from inbreeding, may not be nearly as intense as many (Ch. 2) appear to suggest.

Inbreeding and Selection

There is a brief literature addressing interpretations of inbreeding depression as it relates to natural populations. Theoretical analysis by Franklin (1977) demonstrates that the proportion of loci expected to be identical by descent in any individual (estimated by f or f_i) is actually the mean of all individual f's in an identical reference population. Any individual in an inbred population, then, will have a realized homozygosity which varies about this mean. This variance is critically important, for it permits heterotic selection to act, favoring individuals more heterozygous than average. The end result could be a delay in the genotypic effects of inbreeding, which, as he notes, could help explain the fact that, "inbreeding coefficients overestimate the proportion of homozygous loci."

That inbreeding coefficients usually do overestimate homozygosity in a variety of organisms is widely recognized (for reviews, Lerner, 1954; Mayr, 1963; Crow and Kimura, 1970; Wright, 1977). Nowhere is this more obvious than in experimental populations of flour beetles (*Tribolium* spp.). Enfield (1977) has observed of them that, "No matter how long and hard we inbreed in our experimental material, we always have far more variation maintained than the inbreeding theory would predict." In the presence of natural selection neither homozygosis, nor its consequent depression, is a necessary correlate of inbreeding. An interesting example of the interaction of selection and inbreeding was reported by Zornoza and Lopez-Fanjul (1975) in a study of the effects of inbreeding on egg production in *T. castaneum*. In the presence of natural selection (implied by the extinction of many sublines), full-sib-mated lines ($f_4 = .594$) produced more eggs than their outbred controls ($f_4 = .010$; Table 5). Perhaps this could be called inbreeding enhancement.

Table 5. Inbreeding enhancement of clutch size in *Tribolium castaneum* at two ambient temperatures (data from Zornoza and Lopez-Fanjul, 1975).

| | Mean Clutch Size | | | |
| | 28 °C | | 33 °C | |
Generation	Inbreds	Outbreds	Inbreds	Outbreds
1	5.98	5.74	9.72	10.21
2	4.70	4.61	7.23	7.63
3	6.50	4.71	8.38	7.41
4	6.98	5.25	9.33	7.86

Wool and Sverdlov (1976) designed an elegant experiment to investigate the effects of inbreeding on *T. castaneum* in two different environments. One was "optimal and constant" (c) approximating a normal laboratory environment, the second was "suboptimal and unpredictable" (v) which I believe more closely simulates a natural environment. The inbred (v) lines produced more eggs and had a lower frequency of sterility than the inbred (c) lines. Both were depressed in these fitness components relative to the outbred controls in both environments. Wool and Sverdlov (1976) attributed the difference between the inbred lines to more intense heterotic selection on the (v) lines. Following Lerner (1954), they suggested that environmental variability would maintain more heterozygotes in the (v) lines because of their greater developmental homeostasis. The increased selection intensity in environment (v) would also be capable of maintaining heterozygotes, if the latter were advantageous, regardless of environmental fluctuations. Heterotic selection, then, may be capable of actively maintaining heterozygosity and reducing the depressive effects of inbreeding regardless of the environment.

That such a process is not impossible in relatively constant or predictable environments is indicated by King's (1918a-c; 1919) classic studies of inbreeding in laboratory rats. Her studies are often cited as the *only* example of a program combining inbreeding and artificial selection for vigor (e.g., Lerner, 1954; Wright, 1977). She began two inbred lines from a single litter of stock laboratory albinos, and maintained them both for over 90 generations of full-sib matings. The animal's environment was somewhat variable, and sometimes "harsh," with occasional food or nutritional deficiencies. After six generations, litters of "low" vigor were culled in both inbred and outbred lines (as expected such selection was not quite as intense in the outbred lines). The level of selection for the inbred lines was not especially intense as 468 first litters were produced by 936 adults of 6,825 (13%) young born during the first 25 generations. Tested at generation 25, the inbred lines showed no evidence of depression in fertility, age to maturity, growth rates, longevity, or variability in adult body weight. The inbreds actually exceeded the outbreds in fertility (mean litter; 7.45 vs. 6.70), indicating some enhancement. Contrary to expectations, the variability in adult body weight actually increased in the inbred lines during the course of the study. King's subsequent studies with Loeb (Loeb and King, 1927; Loeb et al., 1943) on histocompatibility relations indicated that the inbred lines had remained heterozygous at histocompatibility loci long after the neutral theory would have predicted fixation (the heterozygosity lasted at least to generation 67; theory predicts homozygosity by generation 25; Festing and Atwood, 1970). Although it is not conclusive, it appears that the full-sib lines remained heterozygous at many loci responsible for vigor (for a similar study on mice, with similar results, see Connor and Belluci, 1979).

While I agree with Wright (1977, p. 94) that, ''Two lines, both strongly selected for vigor, do not, however, provide as much information on this matter as 23 *largely unselected* lines'' (emphasis added), I also disagree with some interpretations of his implication. He is, of course, referring to his classic studies of inbreeding in the guinea pig (1921; 1922), which form the basis of most of the modern theories of inbreeding. But, as he notes, his study provides information on the matter of inbreeding depression for the plant and animal breeders who deal largely in unselected lines. For natural populations, where natural selection for vigor is inescapable, King's two lines provide more information than the thousands of studies of inbreeding in the absence of selection combined (see also, Franklin, 1977; Lande, 1977). The coincidence of considerable heterozygosity despite intense inbreeding is not limited to experimental evidence. In their extensive studies of extreme self-fertilizing (> 98% selfing) *Avena barbata*, Allard and his colleagues (Allard et al., 1968; Allard et al., 1972; Hamrick and Allard, 1975) reported much higher levels of individual heterozygosity than would be expected in the absence of some form of diversifying selection.

Investigations of inbreeding and its consequences for fitness in natural populations would provide critical information on the topic of the evolutionary importance of inbreeding. Unfortunately, both the number of such studies, and the samples on which those studies are based, are small for the animal kingdom. Certainly the largest and most consistent data base on the topic is that reported for humans. In one comprehensive review, for example, 12,779 still births and infant deaths were recorded among 335,710 outbred progeny, while 855 were recorded in the 13,763 born to first cousins or more closely related mates (35.9 vs 62.1/1000 births, Stevenson et al., 1966). In the same study the reported frequency of congenitally malformed young was higher in inbred than in outbred families (16.9 vs 12.1/1000 live births). Schull and Neel (1965) reported similar patterns of pre-infant and infant mortality in Japan, but extended the analysis by demonstrating significant depressions in important phenotypic characters (e.g., school performance, body size, muscular coordination) in the older ''child of inbreeding.''

In both of these cases, the populations under study were

relatively large and panmictic as is characteristic of many modern human cultures. Thus it is not surprising that the infrequent inbreeding on the background of regular outbreeding should result in obvious detrimental effects on infant viability. It is interesting, however, that a similar study of the "semi-isolated," and therefore presumably more inbred, population on the island of Kure in Japan demonstrated no inbreeding depression in the first 15 years of life (Schull and Neel, 1966).

Studies of nonhuman animals in nature are a rarer commodity. Packer (1979) reported on inbreeding depression in baboons (*Papio anubis*) with the offspring of "close relatives" suffering a 40% reduction in viability, based on his sample of a single individual and his female associates. In a more extensive study, Greenwood et al. (1978), continuing a study initiated by Bulmer (1973), have reported their measurement of "the relative frequency of inbreeding and the extent of inbreeding depression" observed in a natural population of the great tit (*Parus major*). Seventeen inbred matings (6 mother-son, 10 brother-sister, and 1 aunt-nephew) were compared to averages of outbred pairs with similar characteristics. They reported no significant inbreeding depression in clutch size or survival after fledging. Inbred pairs bred significantly earlier, a trait usually associated with increased reproductive success (Lack, 1966), but also produced significantly fewer fledglings than outbred pairs with identical clutch sizes (72% of the inbred eggs hatched and fledged vs. 83% of the outbreds). They concluded that for the great tit, inbreeding entailed a real fitness depression.

Van Noordwijk and Scharloo (1981) were also able to detect increased "juvenile" mortality (hatching reduced by 7.5% for every 10% increase in f), and reduced adult fertility as the result of relatively intense inbreeding in a European population of the great tit. In contrast to the average inbreeding study, however, they were also able to document an absence of depression and perhaps even an enhancement in *total* reproductive success, with recruitment into subsequent generations of inbred young equaling and even doubling that of outbred young. In the Netherlands, the real losses early in life apparently were more than compensated for by the later benefits associated with the relatively intense inbreeding characterizing their populations of the great tit.

Finally, in natural populations of normally cross-fertilizing plant species, the evidence is abundant. In almost every study of such species forced to self, signifiant inbreeding depression is observed (e.g., Price and Waser, 1979). Just as in the animal studies, however, the depression is normally documented for early developmental stages (e.g., decreased seed set vs. germination frequenecies, or increases in aborted seeds) rather than in terms of descendancy.

The evidence, though sparse, especially for animals, is consistent. Almost every investigator that has ever looked has been able to demonstrate significant depressions in ontogenetically early fitness components associated with relatively intense inbreeding. Most of those have also documented an increase in depression with increased inbreeding intensity. Yet the theoretical considerations explored above, King's (1918) experimental laboratory studies, and especially the occasional absence of depression in the presence of high natural inbreeding levels (e.g., Schull and Neel, 1976; Van Noordwijk and Sharloo, 1981; and see Chs. 7 and 8), imply that we must at least question the axiomatic standing of the notion that *all* inbreeding is injurious in nature.

I would not argue that the multitude of studies investigating inbreeding have not demonstrated depressions in important *components* of fitness. I would argue that most have not measured all of the components of fitness in natural conditions. I would especially question the general applicability of the inference, drawn from these partial results, that "it is obvious that conservationists ought to view inbreeding as anathema" (Soule, 1980, p. 158; see also Ralls et al., 1979). The question is, do such studies show an *overall* inbreeding depression, or might they demonstrate a partial cost of inbreeding without addressing potential benefits? Given a documentable depression in lifetime fitness, as has been documented in plants (for review, see Grant, 1971; 1975), which is the better description, *inbreeding* or *incest* depression? Even if inbreeding at some specified intensity (Ch. 7) is not as costly in terms of total fitness as conventional wisdom would imply, the question of the potential benefits of inbreeding is only raised and not answered by the caution to examine *all* fitness components.

CHAPTER 5

An Advantage for Inbreeding: Coadaptation and Outbreeding Depression

The modern epigenetic view of organismic development assumes that phenotypes result from a series of complex gene-gene and gene-environment interactions (for reviews, see Waddington, 1957; Wright, 1968). The genome is not an assemblage of independent genes acting additively, but rather an integrated and delicately balanced system compounded by selection because of its ability to produce well-adapted phenotypes through the interactive, as well as additive, effects of its allelic constituents (Chetverikov, 1926; Dobzhansky, 1937; 1970; Mather, 1943; Lerner, 1954; Mayr, 1954; 1955; 1963; 1975; Endler, 1977; Hedrick et al., 1978).

The initial stimulus for this view was the almost universal observation of such interactive properties as pleiotropy, defined as a single gene conditioning multiple phenotypic effects, and epistasis, in its modern sense of one gene conditioning the effects of a gene or genes at different loci. As our understanding of the biochemical mode of gene action has improved, our knowledge of the indirect and interacting paths between genes and phenotypes has increased. The biochemical bases of such phenomena as modifier-controlled dominance (Wright, 1969), and the importance of regulatory genes in the induction and suppression of gene activity (Fisher, 1931; Britten and Davidson, 1969; Davidson and Britten, 1973; Wilson, 1976) reinforced a view of the genome as a complex interacting system. Mayr (1963, p. 262) suggested that an accurate view of the genome could be illustrated, ''. . . in an obviously exaggerated form, in the statement: every character of an organism is affected by all genes and every gene affects all characters" (but, see Haldane, 1964).

If the phenotype is largely the product of nonadditive interactions (Mather and Caligari, 1976), then adaptation and fitness potential, in large measure, will also depend on such interactions. Given such conditions selection is expected to maintain allelic associations that interact well to produce well-adapted phenotypes. By favoring individuals with many harmoniously interacting systems, selection would produce, in Dobzhansky's words (1948), a "coadapted" genome.

Given a coadapted genome, arbitrary alterations in its make-up would have a high probabilty of reducing adaptation and fitness potential. This is nothing more than a reiteration of the traditional view of the likely effects of genetic mutation (Fisher, 1930). The more complex and interactive a system, the more likely a random alteration would disrupt it. In addition, Fisher (1930) demonstrated that the magnitude of disruption is theoretically expected to be positively correlated with the magnitude of associated alterations. In essence, if one tinkers with something which is complex and works well, one is more likely to reduce than improve its efficiency.

With minor modifications, the argument is also applicable to the effects of hybridization on coadapted genomes. Here, hybridization means the mating of genetically different individuals, with the degree of genetic difference determining the degree of hybridization. Mutation produces a genetic change in a genome that is random with respect to the state of the current environment including the remaining genetic background. Hybridization produces a series of *nonrandom* genetic changes in genomes. The magnitude of the total change would depend on the number of independent alterations made, which is itself a function of the degree of difference (i.e., unrelatedness) between mates.

Hybridization is nonrandom in that the genetic elements involved are not random samples of *all* the potential changes of alleles or chromosomes in question as is theoretically true of mutation. Instead, such altered elements have passed at least one selective test by being operative, at least in their native genetic milieu. As functional components of a successful genome they would individually, and on average, have a lower probability of depressing fitness potential than truly random mutations. Since an allele's selective history includes an association with a specific genetic background, it is expected to be especially well adapted to this background.

Since hybridization inserts alleles into novel backgrounds, they cannot as a rule be expected to function as well as they did in their native environment, nor as well as the native elements they ultimately replace. Thus, it should not be unusual for hybridization to depress fitness potential at least slightly.

From either parent's view, hybridization will alter a successful and coadapted genome by introducing a number of genetic changes in offspring. Even though the average change is expected to be less debilitating than an average random mutation, the greater number of changes associated with hybridization could result in much greater fitness depression than mutation alone would produce. The actual level of fitness depression associated with hybridization is likely to increase as the number of genetic differences between potential mates increases. This can never be a perfect correlation since the degree of disruption will also be a function of the type of change involved. For example, a single allelic substitution in the regulatory genome would normally have greater effect than a single substitution in the structural genome (Oliver, 1979). Similarly, there are single karyotypic differences that would produce greater disruption upon hybridization than almost any genic difference (White, 1978a). Whatever the mode of operation, and whatever the genetic systems altered, hybridization at least in extremis (e.g., interspecific mating) is expected to disrupt the "unity of the genotype" (Mayr, 1963; 1975), and potentially lead to a "swarm" of genetic endowments of low fitness (Dobzhansky et al., 1977, p. 180).

As the quotes imply, this is not a novel argument. Indeed, it is a basic assumption of *all* the currently accepted models of speciation (e.g., Mayr, 1963; Dobzhansky, 1970; Grant, 1971; Bush, 1975; Endler, 1977; White, 1978a). Nevertheless, I believe that the argument does have significant hidden implications. Given sufficient genetic differentiation, hybridization is expected to be maladaptive. Since genetic differences imply lesser relatedness (Ch. 3), we can conclude that outbreeding, at least at the level of extreme hybridization, will reduce fitness. If extreme outbreeding is maladaptive, then biological characters which promote or permit its occurrence should be selected against. Characters which promote mating between individuals with the same coadapted genomes (relative inbreeding) should be adaptive and positively selected. One potential advantage of inbreeding, then, is that its genomic consequence of maintaining interlocus allele associations

(Ch. 3) may permit more faithful transmission of coadapted genomes than would be possible with wider outbreeding.

In an absolute sense, the conservative effects of inbreeding will usually be imperfect. If, as appears likely (Ch. 4), natural selection maintains heterozygosity, even in intensely inbred groups, then the number of different genomes recombination would produce (2^N, with N = number of segregating loci assuming 2 alleles per locus) would insure each individual a unique genome. Nonetheless, because inbreeding limits ancestry, all of those alleles (barring recent mutations) are more likely to be associated in the present with the *same* subset of interacting alleles as they had been in the relatively recent past. Inbreeding is analogous to shuffling the *same* deck of varied cards over and over again, reproducing similar, though rarely identical combinations.

In contrast, wider outbreeding increases the probability of bringing together alleles that have not shared a recent evolutionary history. Unless selection has maintained the same alleles in the two less related lineages that produced outbred mates, then outbreeding will increase the likelihood that recombination will generate novel allele associations (with respect to recent history). Outbreeding, then, can be considered analagous to shuffling two *different* decks of varied cards, to produce truly novel combinations. The degree of outbreeding would be determined by the degree of difference between the decks. If novel combinations generated by outbreeding were less successful than the historically coadapted combinations better preserved by inbreeding, then the mating of differentiated individuals would entail an outbreeding fitness depression.

Two questions about the process of genetic differentiation and its relationship to outbreeding depression immediately arise: (1) What causes genetic differentiation?, and (2) How much differentiation is required to generate enough fitness depression to make inbreeding advantageous?

Genetic Differentiation and Outbreeding Depression

Ultimately, all genetic differences are the product of mutational events at either the genic or chromosomal levels of genetic organization. Differentiation can be defined as a process which produces genetically different individuals or groups of individuals from groups of originally identical individuals. If we assume for argument's sake that two individuals or groups are initially genetically identical, they can only become different by assimilating different mutations into their genomes or gene pools. At the level of a single locus, mutation is rare, but inevitable, owing to the imperfection of nucleic acid replication. Since immediate back mutation is improbable (Maynard Smith, 1978), each genetic novelty originating in a germ line is automatically assimilated by a gamete and any individual resulting from that gamete. The processes controlling accumulation of novel mutations in a gene pool are chance ("drift"), and if a mutant is favored by current conditions, natural selection.

A group will differentiate (one group becoming two), if either of two sets of conditions occurs. If novel mutations are selectively neutral, stochastic processes will tend to accumulate different mutants in different groups. If some mutations are favored in current environments, but different groups face different selective pressures, then groups will consist of individuals characterized by different favored mutations. If unopposed, both drift and selection, either independently or jointly, could result in groups and their constituent individuals becoming increasingly more different with the passage of time.

There are conditions which oppose, and conceivably could balance, the forces of differentiation. Either selection or drift can prevent the differentiation of individuals within groups. If a particular mutation is disfavored by current environmental conditions, selection can remove it from a group by discriminating against its bearer. This will oppose genetic differentiation within the group by limiting the number of variants in the group and maintaining the genetic *status quo*. Sampling error can also eliminate a novel mutant regardless of its selective value especially shortly after its origin while it is still rare (for review, see Kimura and Ohta, 1971). Given a group of differentiated individuals, division into differentiated subgroups can still be prevented by free interbreeding among group members. The resulting gene flow will carry a random sample of all the variants present in a group's common gene pool. As the argument implies, genetically similar subgroups of differentiated individuals are not characterized by absolute genetic identity among all members. Rather they consist of individuals which, as a group, carry identical variants at similar frequencies, with the result that variance in allele frequencies between "subgroups" is less than or equal to the variance among individuals within subgroups (Nei, 1972).

Both the rate and degree of subgroup differentiation depend on the balance between these opposing factors (for summary reviews of mathematical treatments, see Wright, 1969; 1978). The primary factor limiting subgroup differentiation is likely to be gene flow. Given complete panmixia, differentiation is only possible if selection discriminates between different variants in different areas, or between different patterns of mating within an originally interbreeding group. If interbreeding is limited in some way, increased mutation rates, allelic neutrality, or varied selective conditions could all increase the probability and rate of subgroup differentiation. Once initiated, the degree of differentiation would be positively correlated with the time since panmixia ended and the degree of difference between the selective conditions associated with each semi-isolated subgroup. The question remains, what conditions are needed to initiate subgroup differentiation in the face of the gene flow engendered by initial panmixia?

Geographic Differentiation

Two contrasting, but not mutually exclusive, models are available which predict a sufficient reduction in gene flow to initiate subgroup differentiation. The traditional "geographic" model was originally proposed as an explanation of how differentiation could proceed far enough to produce reproductive isolation and initiate speciation (Dobzhansky, 1937; 1970; Mayr, 1942; 1963; Stebbins, 1950; Grant, 1963; 1971; White, 1978a). The model suggests that the cohesive force of gene flow can be reduced or eliminated if an initially panmictic group is physically divided into isolated subgroups by a geographical barrier. For example, an advancing glacier could divide an interbreeding group into two isolates, each in their own refugium. The model assumes that the extrinsic physical barrier is large enough that the species' normal dispersal will not permit mixing of the subgroups (Mayr, 1963). Mayr (1963) also assumes that such distances are often less than a species' mobility would imply, especially in groups with localized and philopatric dispersal (Ch. 2).

Once a population is subdivided by an extrinsic barrier, resulting subpopulations would be free to differentiate. If they were isolated for sufficient time, and their respective environments were different enough, they could accumulate enough genetic differences that incipient reproductive isolation might have developed. Should contact between such groups be reestablished, gene flow between the subgroups would entail significant hybridization and resulting outbreeding depression could reduce the level of effective gene flow. If the outbreeding depression were severe enough, it would act as a positive feedback in maintaining the genetic isolation despite sympatry. This would permit further differentiation, resulting in greater levels of outbreeding depression (I will use outbreeding depression and postmating reproductive isolation synonymously), *ad infinitum.* The feedback process would only end when the possibility of gene flow had ceased completely and each subgroup had become an independently evolving lineage. In the end two species would exist where before there was one.

Speciation is not an inevitable consequence of geographical isolation (e.g., Mayr, 1963). If allopatric populations have failed to differentiate enough to induce significant reproductive isolation, then secondary contact could reduce whatever differences had arisen through the homogenizing effects of subsequent interbreeding. A number of conditions could influence the path of differentiation. For example, if isolated populations were not separated for very long, or if their gene pools resisted reorganization via genetic homeostasis (Lerner, 1954), or if they lived in similar environments (Mayr, 1963), they might not have accumulated enough genetic differences to initiate speciation. An implicit assumption of this argument is that a minimal (threshold) level of differentiation is necessary to produce the critical level of outbreeding depression.

Proponents of the geographical model suggest that this critical reproductive isolation is the major distinguishing character of taxonomic species groups. "Species are groups of interbreeding natural populations that are reproductively isolated from other such groups" (Mayr, 1969a). "Species are, accordingly, systems of populations; the gene exchange between these systems is limited or prevented by a reproductive isolating mechanism or perhaps by a combination of several such mechanisms" (Dobzhansky, 1970, p. 357; also, see Bigelow, 1965; Grant, 1971; White, 1978a). While isolation between species is normally accentuated, some also stress the free interbreeding within species (e.g., Dobzhansky, 1970, p. 375). Mayr (1963, p. 177) explicitly suggests that, "Depending on the species, as many as 30 to 50 percent of the members of a deme may be such newcomers in every generation.'' He suggests that it is such gene flow which normally prevents a continuously distributed species from differentiating enough to induce reproductive isolation. The presumed absence of significant reproductive isolation within relatively panmictic species is certainly consistent with the assumption that substantial differentiation (often referred to as a genetic revolution, e.g., Mayr, 1954; 1963; Carson, 1959; 1975) is necessary to induce outbreeding depression intense enough to qualify as reproductive isolation.

If the geographical model of differentiation and speciation is correct in all of its particulars, it implies that outbreeding at the level of interspecific hybridization is maladaptive. Selection, then should favor secondary mechanisms which prevent such wide outbreeding and its consequent fitness depression. We expect characters to evolve which promote inbreeding, at least at the level of limiting interbreeding to within species. Of course this is the classic argument which implies that postmating isolation, including reduced F_1 viability or fertility, or F_2 hybrid breakdown, having initially developed as ''the accidental byproduct of genetic divergence'' (Dobzhansky et al., 1977, p. 180) can be (and has been) a sufficient selective force to cause the evolution of less ''wasteful'' premating isolating mechanisms after secondary contact (Grant, 1963; Mayr, 1963; Dobzhansky, 1970). Grant (1963, p. 503) has pointed out that this fine-tuning process was first discussed by A. Wallace and has christened it the ''Wallace Effect.''

Mutational Differentiation

The geographic model of differentiation and speciation relies on numerous assumptions about the genetic changes associated with speciation. Yet, as Lewontin (1974, p. 159) has noted, ''. . . we know virtually nothing about the genetic changes that occur in species formation.'' This ignorance offers an opportunity to replace the geographic model's assumptions in order to investigate an alternative model of differentiation. I propose the alternative based on an assumption that significant outbreeding depression can result from the hybridization of individuals with a small number of genetic differences, rather than the large number assumed necessary by the geographic model. The altered assumption leads to a model which reverses the order of cause and conse-

73

quence implied by the geographic model. This mutational model leads to a conclusion that the process of group differentiation can be initiated by the relatively low-level outbreeding depression associated with mutational differentiation of individuals in an originally panmictic group.

Depending on focus, mutation can be considered either a rare or fairly common event. At the level of a single locus, conservatively estimated mutation rates range from 10^{-9} to 10^{-6} per generation in prokaryotes and many unicellular eukaryotes, and from 10^{-6} to 10^{-4} per generation in most metazoans and higher plants (Dobzhansky et al., 1977). At the level of an individual organism, mutation is more common. If metazoans possess from 10^4 to 10^5 functional loci, then with an average mutation rate per locus of 10^{-5}, the average gamete will carry 0.1-1.0, and the average diploid individual, 0.2-2.0 newly arisen mutations (Dobzhansky et al., 1977).

Given that mutations are independent events, two individuals chosen at random from the same family, population, or species are not likely to carry identical newly arisen mutations (though a large enough population will insure that identical mutations are likely to arise in different individuals, Dobzhansky et al., 1977). Sexual reproduction will normally replicate such parental mutations (m_1) and transmit them to half of each individual's offspring (on average). Simultaneously, each gamete will also carry its own complement of novel and often unique mutations (m_0). Each offspring can be characterized as consisting of an ancestral genome (G) (in a panmictic group, G will be a random sample of the variants in the group's gene pool), a set of parental mutations (m_1 which occur in nonrandom, familial (i.e., a parent and some of its offspring) associations, and its own set of newly arisen mutations (m_0). A second round of mating will break up the familial associations of m_1 alleles, dispersing them throughout the panmictic group. In essence, they become a part of the ancestral genome by being distributed randomly into a third generation of offspring. At the same time, the m_0 mutations are replicated and assorted into new families and a different set of noval mutations (m_2) occur. It is the dispersal of parental mutations throughout a group in the second generation after their occurrence that prevents subgroup differentiation. In the first generation after their appearance such mutations are not distributed randomly. Rather, they are assorted into differentiated family subgroups. At this level group differentiation is an inevitable consequence of independent mutation during

74

gametogenesis and the small sample of individuals from a total population actually belonging to any family. The level of differentiation observed is a function of mutation rates, with higher rates being associated with a greater number of differences between individuals in the first generation and between family groups in the second. It is in the third generation that random mating can reduce the level of mutational microdifferentiation produced by the genetic correlations within families.

Karyotypic microdifferentiation will follow an identical course. Karyotypic mutations include paracentric (not involving the centromere) and pericentric inversions, translocations, intrachromosomal deletions and duplications, and changes in arm or whole chromosome numbers owing to fission or fusion (for review, see White, 1973; 1978a). If all rearrangement types are considered, then in organisms as different as plants and humans about one of every 500 individuals is observed to carry a newly arisen and truly unique structural mutation. When they occur, such rearrangements produce individuals different from all their fellows. If such a differentiated individual reproduces successfully, the rearrangement will be assorted into families which differ from other families. Only if the next generation is panmictic can this initial level of differentiation be diminished as the rearrangement is dispersed throughout the panmictic group. Although a static picture is presented here, it should be obvious that the process of microdifferentiation, at both the genic and chromosomal levels, is a continuous process. In every generation in a panmictic group one group of mutations will be assorted into differentiated families, while a second group is dispersed throughout the population.

If we assume that inevitable family microdifferentiation resulting from mutation can induce outbreeding depression, then geographical isolation is no longer *necessary* to initiate microdifferentiation and speciation. Random mating implies that some individuals will mate within differentiated families (inbreed), while others will find mates in other families. If inbreeders are more successful, then selection will have reduced effective gene flow between families. At the same time, selection will favor any characters causally associated with the adaptive inbreeding. Such characters will increase the probability of intrafamily inbreeding, depressing gene flow below that produced by the initial outbreeding depression. This would permit further interfamily differentiation resulting in potentially increased outbreeding depression should individuals continue to hybridize. Any increased postmating depression raises the selective pressure for more efficient premating mechanisms which promote increased inbreeding.

This entire argument is logically equivalent to the "Wallace Effect" argument about speciation and adaptive reproductive isolating mechanisms (e.g., Dobzhansky, 1970). However, it does add a crucial assumption that the positive feedback between postmating isolation and increasing differentiation associated with speciation can be (but not necessarily is) *initiated* by a smaller number of mutational differences than implied by the geographic model. The essential difference between the geographic and mutational models is their view of the relation between postmating isolation (outbreeding depression) and quantitative measures of genetic differentiation. The geographic model assumes that, on average, isolation is a step function of the level of differentiation, with a large minimal level of difference needed to induce *significant* outbreeding depression (Fig. 14). For example, in discussing the *Drosophila willistoni* fruit fly complex, Ayala (1975; Dobzhansky et al., 1977; Table 6) suggested that the similar levels of differentiation observed between subspecies and between semispecies did not imply that the development of sexual (reproductive) isolation was independent of differentiation. Rather, he concluded that given sufficient differentiation (that characteristic of subspecies), only minor additional changes were necessary to induce specific isolation. In contrast, the mutational model assumes that *significant* outbreeding depression can occur with minimal genetic differences, and that the level of depression observed is likely to be some *continuously* increasing function of differentiation (Fig. 14).

Table 6. Nei's (1972) genetic identity (I) and distance (D) coefficients among taxonomic groups in the *Drosophila willistoni* complex (data from Ayala et al., 1974).

Taxa Compared	(I)	(D)
Local Populations	0.970	0.031
Subspecies	0.795	0.230
Semispecies	0.798	0.226
Sibling Species	0.563	0.581
Full Species	0.352	1.056

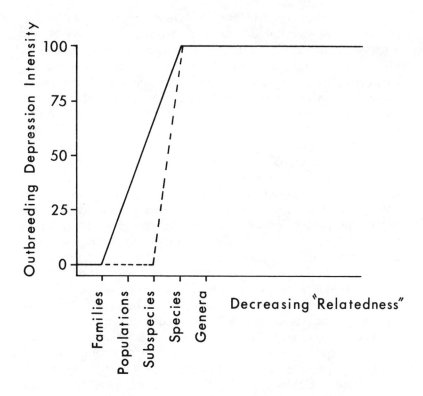

Fig. 14. The presumed relationship between decreasing relatedness (increasing differentiation) and outbreeding depression (reproductive isolation), for the mutational (——) and geographical (----) models of genetic differentiation and speciation. The latter postulates an abrupt "step" increase in isolation at the level of species. The mutational model postulates a gradual and continuous increase, even within populations and species.

I believe that the models reflect different interpretations of what *significant* depression is, rather than incompatible views of the process of differentiation. In the context of the geographical model's species definitions, significant depression must provide 100% isolation. In many cases such extremes will only appear after considerable differentiation (Mayr, 1963; Dobzhansky, 1970). This emphasis on a total absence of gene flow in species definitions does not necessitate a denial of intermediate levels of outbreeding depression at intermediate levels of differentiation. Indeed, the architects of the geographical model of speciation make note of, and discuss extensively, intraspecific outbreeding depression (e.g., Mayr, 1963; and especially Dobzhansky, 1970, pp. 303–7). However, their "populational" perspective, and its tacit emphasis on population level consequences, does promote explanation via arguments of species benefit (e.g., speciation is an adaptive process because it maintains species integrity; e.g., Mayr, 1963; Dobzhansky, 1970; 1972; Bush, 1975). This concentration on population consequences has tended to obscure the possibility that intermediate levels of outbreeding depression may be important for species members rather than species.

By ignoring species definitions and focusing on individuals the mutational model defines significant outbreeding depression as that level which can act as a selective force conditioning the evolution of individual characteristics. Since outbreeding depression is defined as an immediate fitness reduction, it is expected to be an effective selective force regardless of its absolute intensity. Even in an infinite and panmictic population, a selection coefficient (s) of 1.0 (outbreeding depression = 100%) is not necessary to effectively drive the evolutionary process. A selection coefficient of 0.001 (outbreeding depression = 0.1%), though difficult or impossible to measure empirically, can do the job, though at a much slower rate (Fisher, 1930; Haldane, 1932). The end result is the same, the ultimate fixation of the genetic substrate controlling the more adaptive character state in the current environment. In this case, such adaptive characters are expected to promote inbreeding, since this will reduce the level of outbreeding depression at every stage of differentiation.

Origin of Outbreeding Depression

The major assumption of the mutational model is that numerically insignificant genetic differences between families within an initially panmictic population can produce outbreeding depression. The two modes of genetic differentiation are: (1) karyotypic, and (2) genic. It is relatively easy to demonstrate intuitively that outbreeding depression will develop simultaneously with the assimilation of most chromosome rearrangements. With the exception of paracentric inversions, such rearrangements normally reduce the fertility of their heterozygous bearers. In such carriers, including the original mutant, the processes of meiosis and gametogenesis are disrupted. The resulting loss in fertility usually insures that the novelty will be eliminated owing to the selective elimination of its bearers. Should an individual carrying such a novelty mate with another carrier (inbreed), then offspring homozygous for the novelty may be produced with unimpaired fertility. If such homozygous mutants are in any way better adapted to current conditions than ancestral homozygotes, then rather than being eliminated they could increase in frequency. Should they somehow manage to continue inbreeding, positive selection will continue. Eventually, they will have formed a new population which has outcompeted and replaced the ancestral type in at least part of the original range (James, 1970).

Regardless of associated genic differentiation, at every stage of karyotypic evolution the outbreeding depression resulting from fertility declines in heterozygotes will continuously favor inbreeding in *both* mutant and ancestral populations. This simultaneous development of a genetic difference and intense postmating reproductive isolation has been defined as "stasipatric" (White, 1968), or "quantum" (Grant, 1963) speciation. Depending on where within an ancestral species (or subspecies) range such adaptive novelties are assimilated, the process might be further classified as parapatric (range margins) or sympatric (range interiors) speciation. White (1978a) contends that sympatric is not an appropriate appelation in this case, because the two groups do not coexist in the same area for an extended period of time. Nonetheless, it is true that mutant and normal individuals are initially within range of each other's dispersal, meeting the necessary criterion for sympatry (Mayr, 1963). The current distribution of chromosome races and species in various groups of plants, insects, reptiles, and mammals (for review, see White, 1978a) is consistent with a conclusion that karyotypic differentiation can, and has in the past, induced enough outbreeding depression to initiate and complete speciation. For many groups (e.g., Morabine grasshoppers, White, 1974; some *Sceloporus* lizards, Hall and Selander, 1973; the *Thomomys* pocket gophers, Thaeler, 1974; Patton, 1972; and the plant genus *Clarkia*, Lewis, 1973), it appears to have been the sole or, at the very least, a primary force in speciation. Since karyotypic differentiation tends to generate instant species, it usually cannot produce conditions which continuously favor intraspecific inbreeding. Therefore, any answer to the question Why inbreed?, probably lies with genic factors.

Origin of Coadapted Genomes

The production of allelically differentiated families during every bout of reproduction is, on average, likely to result in less severe fitness reductions in hybrids than is characteristic of karyotypic mutation. The important sterility effects of the latter are likely to be reduced or absent. Thus, the 25–100% outbreeding depression associated with karyotypic hybridization should also be considerably reduced (< 5%?). Unlike karyotypic mutation, the assimilation of one or two allelic novelties will rarely, if ever, produce an instant species. Assuming low levels of outbreeding depression, however, does not imply that low levels of hybridization are of no importance to individuals within species. Any fitness depression is likely to be a powerful force in shaping the character of individuals over time.

Genic differentiation results from nonrandom association of novel mutants with a familial subsample of a population's gene pool. For example, in a panmictic group, each individual contains a random sample of all available alleles. Since a diploid organism is limited to two alleles per locus, any polymorphism will produce an ancestral genome G that can be represented as a set of different subsamples (e.g., G', G'', . . . G^N). Assume that G' contains a relatively rare allele, A, at a specific locus. At a second locus, assume that a novel mutation (B → b) has occurred in one of the gametes producing G'. If the association of A and b shows positive epistatic effects such that it has a higher fitness potential than any alternative association (e.g., AB, __B, etc.), then G's is likely to count among its successful offspring a number of individuals carrying the newly favored combination. It is expected to have greater reproductive success than G'' or G^N. If the Ab individual and its offspring outbreed (mate with individuals outside the Ab family), b will be dispersed throughout the larger group with little chance of being reassociated with the rare A. If the new b combinations (__b) are less fit than Ab, then the outbreeding will result in a fitness depression owing to the disruption of the Ab association. If instead of outbreeding, Ab individuals were to breed among themselves (e.g., parent-offspring or full-sib mating), then the probability of transmitting the Ab combination to subsequent offspring would increase, thereby raising their fitness potential. During this process, selection would concurrently favor characters which were causally associated with the increased inbreeding. Lesser inbreeding intensities would increase the probability of disrupting the novel association until with random mating in very large pupulations, the probability of reassociation would approach zero.

If genes interact epistatically, a *single* novel mutation can, if it is coadapted with a low frequency variant or complex of variants at other loci, induce enough outbreeding depression to favor intraspecific inbreeding. The substrate variant (or variants) must be rare, for if it were common, outbreeding would *not* disrupt the novel association and little fitness depression would result. For carriers of such novel combinations, the advantage of inbreeding will increase with the intensity of positive epistasis. If the novel mutation interacts poorly with alternative genetic backgrounds available in the group (i.e., negative epistasis), the disadvantage will increase for carriers and extend to nonfamily members which would suffer their own outbreeding depression should they hybridize with Ab family members.

If fitness does depend on epistasis, then a novel allelic mutation will occasionally, and by chance, produce conditions which favor relatively intense inbreeding. Why inbreeding? As a first approximation, because fitness potential is increased and adaptation is fine-tuned when *novel* combinations of harmoniously interacting alleles are preserved and transmitted together, rather than being broken apart as a consequence of wider outbreeding.

There is little empirical evidence about the frequency of the conditions necessary to promote increased inbreeding. The model does suggest that increased numbers of epistatically interacting mutations, as well as increased levels of positive epistasis, will independently raise the frequency. In the context of traditional concepts of inbreeding depression (Ch. 4), the disadvantages of inbreeding stem from intralocus interactions (i.e., dominance and overdominance). Since one major advantage of inbreeding appears to depend on interlocus interactions, perhaps we can view the overall selective value of inbreeding as resulting from a balance of its genotypic costs and opposing genomic benefits. If for any organism, fitness is primarily a consequence of additive (or multiplicative) genetic effects, then relatively intense inbreeding may be maladaptive. The more pronounced such effects, the more maladaptive the inbreeding. If, on the other hand, epistatic interactions are the primary determinants of fitness potential, then inbreeding, even if it is intense, may be adaptive, and the more pronounced the epistasis, the more adaptive the inbreeding. Since inbreeding is not expected to depress fitness in the absence of dominance and overdominance (e.g., Crow and Kimura, 1970, p. 80), ''pure'' epistasis should be associated with relatively intense inbreeding. Considering potential breeding systems as a continuum that ranges from selfing to species-wide panmixia, each species might be expected to have an ''optimal'' level of inbreeding (Fig. 15). Given two broad classes of loci: (1) those affecting fitness primarily through dominance or overdominance (D), and (2) those affecting fitness primarily through epistasis (E, though members of each class are likely to produce both types of effect, e.g., Powers, 1944; Jinks, 1955), their relative importance could determine optimal levels of inbreeding. Their relative mutation rates and the average magnitude of their fitness effects will contribute to the optimum by determining the frequency and magnitude of selection favoring a particular level of inbreeding.

If Mayr (1953; 1975) is right about the ''unity of the genotype,'' and modifiers truly make the species (Harland, 1936), then intragenic interactions will often be less important than epistasis in determining fitness potential for individuals in natural populations (Mather, 1943; 1953; Wigan, 1944; Soule, 1973; Hedrick et al., 1978). Conditions which favor increased intraspecific inbreeding would be expected to recur at an appreciable frequency.

Maintenance of Coadapted Genomes

Given the proper initial conditions, epistasis and inbreeding can coevolve, reducing gene flow among family groups. If this initial isolation is combined with a recurrence of suitable conditions, then the probability that each group will continue to differentiate via the assimilation of new and *different* combinations will also increase. If the process continues, each extended family's genome will come to consist of a series of coadapted and interacting gene complexes. The end result will be two internally cohesive genomes which are incompatible with each other with respect to interbreeding.

Genic differentiation, then, resulting from mutational pressures within an initially panmictic population appears to be as capable of initiating the positive feedback of speciation as karyotypic differen-

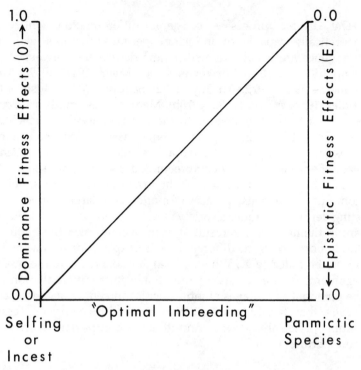

Fig. 15. Hypothetical optimal inbreeding level as a function of the balance between intragenic (dominance and heterotic) and intergenic (epistatic) interactions in determining overall fitness potential. As the latter increase in relative importance, the favored level of inbreeding also increases.

tiation. The major difference between these two modes is one of temporal scale. Karyotypic differentiation produces extreme reductions in fitness which foster instant speciation. The degree of depression resulting from allelic differentiation is likely to be smaller and changing conditions could more easily reverse the process. Even if the trend continues, each bout of reproduction is expected to increment the degree of fitness depression by a small amount approximately equal to the original value. If, as is likely, the conditions necessary to assimilate favored combinations (favorable mutant and rare substrate) are rare, then such increments are likely to be infrequent as well as minor. The process will grind on, but the fitness depression driving the system will initially be hard to demonstrate. In the end, it will usually take many generations to produce enough outbreeding depression (or associated premating isolation) that *two* species will be clearly recognizable.

The diverse processes of genic differentiation which are theoretically capable of inducing speciation without allopatric divergence are usually termed parapatric (clinal or area-effect) or sympatric speciation (for reviews, see Mayr, 1947; 1969b; Dobzhansky, 1970; 1972; Murray, 1972; Scudder, 1974; Bush, 1975; Endler, 1977; White, 1978a; 1978b). Many of these models are coincident, or at least analogous to the mutational model developed here. They differ primarily in the genetic assumptions made and in focus (e.g., disruptive selection at a single locus is often used in place of epistasis to model outbreeding depression, but see Endler, 1977). They concentrate not on the origin of outbreeding depression, but on the consequences of moderate to large degrees of existing depression under a variety of initial conditions. While important in themselves, the resulting controversies over the frequency and importance of the different modes of speciation and what each should be called (e.g., White, 1978a) are not crucial to the present argument. In the context of mutational microdifferentiation and the potential advantages of intraspecific inbreeding, a general consensus that family differentiation and outbreeding depression within species are possible, and in many groups demonstrable, is more pertinent.

Intraspecific Differentiation

The recent application of electrophoretic techniques to indirectly analyze genetic variation in natural populations has demonstrated that high levels of group and individual variability are a general rule (for reviews, see Selander and Johnson, 1973; Lewontin, 1974; Powell, 1975; Ayala, 1975; Avise, 1976; Nevo, 1978). This information reinforced the judgment of many systematists who had already concluded that variability was characteristic of the living world (e.g., Mayr, 1942; 1963; Stebbins, 1950). Analysis of morphological and electrophoretic data indicated that variability was not distributed randomly throughout species groups. More often discontinuous patterns of similarities and differences were observed within as well as among species. The common pattern was hierarchical, with individuals within a population more similar than those from different populations, and populations within subspecies more similar than those from different subspecies, and so on (Table 7 and Ch. 8). Often the variability was distributed clinally (regular spatial changes in the frequency of specific variants), while in other cases the variation was distributed into differentiated groups but without spatial regularities (i.e., a mosaic distribution, for examples of both clines and mosaics of different traits in the same species, see Highton, 1977; Hedgecock, 1978; for general reviews, see Endler, 1977; White, 1978a).

Table 7. Average genetic identity (similarity[a]) between closely related taxonomic groups in various animals (Data from Avise, 1976, and White, 1978a).

Organism	Populations	Sub- or Semispecies	Species	Genera
Drosophila				
D. willistoni	0.97	0.79	0.47	–
D. obscura	0.99	0.82	–	–
D. repleta	1.00	0.88	0.78	–
D. bipectinata	–	0.91[a]	0.79[a]	–
Fishes				
Lepomis	0.98	0.84	0.54	–
Cyprinidae	0.99	–	0.90	0.59
Salamanders				
Taricha	0.95	0.84	0.63	0.31
Lizards				
Anolis	–	–	0.21	–
Sceloporus	0.89[a]	0.79[a]	–	–
Rodents				
Dipodomys	0.97[a]	–	0.61[a]	0.16[a]
Sigmodon	–	–	0.76[a]	–
Mus	0.95[a]	0.77	–	–
Peromyscus	0.95[a]	–	0.65	–
Thomomys	–	0.84[a]	–	–

[a]Indicates Roger's (1972) similarity index (S). All other values use Nei's (1972) genetic identity (I). A value of 1.0 indicates that two groups have same alleles at same frequency.

Regardless of the fine points of spatial organization, species that consisted of differentiated subgroups were something of a conundrum for those who assumed that species were "freely interbreeding groups" (e.g., Mayr, 1963). In a truly panmictic species, gene flow should limit the possibility of such local differentiation. The actual levels of differentiation observed in nature could only be explained if species were less than panmictic, or selection strongly favored different genetic variants in different groups, or some combination of the effects of reduced gene flow and disruptive selection. The existence of intraspecific genetic variation is consistent with, if not supportive of, the mutational model of differentiation. The support is weak since there are many other potential explanations for such patterns which are also consistent with the data (e.g., heterogeneous environments selecting for different allele complexes).

Intraspecific Outbreeding Depressions

As the major champion of the "balance" school of thought about levels of genetic variation observed in nature, Dobzhansky (1937; 1951; 1970) has repeatedly stressed the importance of heterosis in determining fitness (for reviews of balance and classical schools, see Lewontin, 1974). He suggested that individuals carrying different alleles at the same locus, or different inversions on homologous chromosomes, were more likely to reproduce successfully than homozygous individuals (a view shared and supported by many, e.g., Lerner, 1954; Gowen, 1952; Wallace, 1968b; 1977; Berger, 1976). It was this stress on heterozygote advantage which provided one line of theoretical credence to the conclusion that inbreeding was likely to depress fitness (Ch. 4; Crow and Kimura, 1970).

Despite his focus on the advantages of heterozygosity, Dobzhansky (e.g., 1970) also stressed the fact that fitness was not associated with heterozygosity *per se*, but rather with population specific heterozygotes compounded into coadapted complexes of interacting alleles at different loci during a common selective history. Experimental interpopulational matings indicated that such complexes differed among populations and often were incompatible after recombination in hybrid offspring. While the wide outbreeding expected from interpopulation mating theoretically increased individual heterozygosity, it also resulted in varied forms and degrees of outbreeding depression in many plant and animal species.

For example, Dobzhansky and Spassky (1968) examined the problem by determining the conditional fitnesses of second chromosomes extracted from two geographically separated (Arizona and California) populations of *Drosophila pseudoobscura*. Chromosomes that were lethal or quasi-normal when homozygous were made heterozygous on their native and then on foreign genetic backgrounds. When compared to the quasi-normals, lethals were equally viable or even slightly heterotic on their native backgrounds. The same chromosomes were slightly deleterious on foreign backgrounds indicating a lack of common selective history. Similar results were reported by Watanabe (1969) for *D. melanogaster* from Japan. He tested homozygous second chromosomes in both native and foreign environments with respect to the remaining chromosomes. The frequencies of lethals (1) and semilethals (s) increased on the foreign backgrounds (native, $1 = 0.15$, $s = 0.07$; foreign, $1 = 0.17$, $s = 0.19$). Both studies are consistent with a hypothesis that fitness (for heterozygotes and homozygotes) was conditioned by epistatic effects of modifying alleles on other chromosomes that had accumulated in native genomes during a common selective history and which differed among populations.

A second line of evidence illustrating the importance of the differentiation of interacting gene combinations has emerged from the detailed studies of balanced polymorphism, especially in natural populations of Lepidoptera and Gastropoda (for review, see Ford, 1964). The case of the lesser yellow-underwing moth (*Triphaena comes*) is especially relevant, because the homogeneity in phenotypic variation observed across its range is the product of varied genomes, rather than of genetic homogeneity as is often assumed (e.g., Mayr, 1963; Emlen, 1978). Throughout most of its range, *T. comes* is monomorphic in wing color. In central and northwestern Scotland, as well as on many offshore Scottish islands, a melanic phase (*curtisii*) is often abundant. Experimental breeding of individuals from a single population indicated that wing color was controlled by a single locus (or supergene) and that the melanic mutant was almost completely dominant (only 6 or 749 heterozygotes with intermediate phenotypes). Surveys of the populations of Barra and Orkney islands (160 km apart) indicated identical levels of polymorphism, and breeding experiments confirmed that the melanic mutant was identical in both populations. Nonetheless, when Orkney and Barra heterozygotes were crossed, the resulting offspring showed little phenotypic discontinuity, with every imaginable intergrade between the homozygous phenotypes emerging. The conditional dominance of the melanic allele had been disrupted. Thus, the same phenotypic polymorphism was controlled by the same major gene in two populations of the same species, but utilized different coadapted complexes of modifiers to produce identical phenotypic results. Moreover, interpopulation hybridization resulted in the disruption of the entire system.

Philopatry, Inbreeding, and the Evolution of Sex

That such disruption can adversely affect fitness potential is perhaps better illustrated by the tropical swallowtail butterflies, *Papilio dardanus* and *P. memnon*. Females in these palatable species mimic members of other distasteful species. They will mimic different model species, often more than one in a single locale, resulting in polymorphic populations. The various female morphs in such a population are controlled by series of closely linked genes which normally produce clear-cut dominance with each female mimicking an appropriate model. Interpopulational crosses produce diverse progeny lacking this dominance as the differentiated modifier systems present in each population are disrupted by hybridization. The end result is reduced efficiency in mimicry and a likely fitness depression in the hybrids that are at greater risk to predation (Clarke and Sheppard, 1960; Clarke et al., 1968; Ford, 1964; for similar dominance modifiers in vertebrates, see Gorden and Gorden, 1957; Avise, 1975; Highton, 1975).

Direct investigations of the relative viability, fecundity, and longevity of intraspecific hybrids (including those resulting from intersubspecific and interpopulation matings) in a wide variety of organisms suggests that outbreeding depression is fairly common, and most likely results from the disruption of epistatically coadapted genomes (for comprehensive reviews, see Wallace, 1968b; Dobzhansky, 1970; and especially Endler, 1977, Ch. 4). A particularly detailed series of investigations of various *Drosophila* species followed Dobzhansky's (1948; 1950) initial exposition of the problem of coadaptation. With a single exception (McFarquhar and Robertson, 1963), they were all consistent with the hypothesis that the disruption of interacting loci eventually resulted in hybrid breakdown (Brncic, 1954; 1961; Ehrman, 1960; Vetukhiv, 1954; 1956; 1957; Wallace, 1955; Wallace and Vetukhiv, 1955; Anderson, 1968; 1969; Zouros, 1973; Dobzhansky, 1974; Ayala et al., 1974).

When compared to intrapopulation progeny, F_1 hybrids typically showed increases in the fitness components measured (luxuriance or hybrid vigor). This increased fitness, however, was transient as the F_2 progeny or backcrosses displayed significant fitness depression relative to intrapopulation controls (Table 8). The depression had greater adaptive significance than the luxuriance owing to its greater persistence. The general consensus emerging from these studies was that hybrid vigor or luxuriance resulted from the increased heterozygosity of the F_1 progeny, acting to mask deleterious recessives from both populations, increase their genetic

88

(biochemical) versatility, or both. The subsequent F_2 breakdown was attributed to the recombinational disruption of *both* parental genomes during F_1 gametogenesis which resulted in negative epistatic interactions reducing fitness.

Table 8. Comparison of viability, fecundity, and longevity of intra- and interpopulation hybrids of *Drosophila pseudoobscura* and *D. willistoni*. Intrapopulation values of measured fitness components are standardized at 1.00 (after Wallace's (1968b), summary of Vetukhiv's data).

Species	F_1	F_2
Viability		
D. pseudoobscura	1.18	0.83
D. willistoni	1.14	0.90
Fecundity		
D. pseudoobscura	1.27	0.94
Longevity		
D. pseudoobscura (16°)	1.25	0.94
D. pseudoobscura (25°)	1.13	0.78–0.95

This conclusion was supported by more detailed studies which used manipulation to "construct" flies with homologous chromosomes known to be (1) intact and from the same population, (2) intact, but one from each population, (3) one intact, one a product of recombination between populations, and (4) both recombination products of two populations (Brncic, 1954; Wallace, 1955). With little variation, the results indicated that relative fitness declined from (2) > (1) > (3) > (4). The increased disruption of parental combinations during hybrid gametogenesis increases the level of outbreeding depression indicating that there may be an "optimal" level of outbreeding (Wigan, 1944; Mather, 1953: Bateson, 1978).

Supporting studies with interpopulational crosses resulting in F_1 luxuriance followed by F_2 breakdown, or in some cases immediate hybrid dysgenesis, have been reported for many plant species (e.g., Clausen, 1951; Kruckeberg, 1957; Vickery, 1959; Grant and Grant, 1960; Grant, 1971; Gottlieb, 1971; Hughes and Vickery, 1974; Price and Waser, 1979), a snail (Paraense, 1959), arthropods other than Drosophila (Goldschmidt, 1934; Ford, 1949; Blickenstaff, 1965; Oliver, 1972; 1977; 1979; Balashov, 1975), amphibians (e.g., Moore, 1950; 1975; Callan and Spurway, 1951; Spurway,

1953), a reptile (Hall and Selander, 1973) and perhaps a bird (Van Noordwijk and Scharloo, 1981). In most of these studies, and in lesser detail for many other organisms (for review, see Endler, 1977), a consistent relationship between fitness and relatedness emerges (Fig. 16). Means and variances of many fitness components (e.g., fecundity, fertility, viability) appear to be a function of the time since two populations have diverged (e.g., Hedrick, et al., 1978). By adding data from the inbred end of the mating continuum (Chs. 3 and 4), a general relation between fitness and mate relatedness, itself a function of time since divergence, can be produced (Fig. 16).

At extreme inbreeding intensities, F_1 and F_2 means and variances are expected to be relatively low (incest depression). At intermediate levels of relatedness, no difference in parental and offspring means and variances are expected (optimal inbreeding). As relatedness decreases, the F_1 mean increases relative to the parental, and the variance decreases (hybrid vigor or luxuriance). Simultaneously, F_2 means are expected to decrease and variances increase, as a result of recombination in the F_1 generation (hybrid breakdown—outbreeding depression). Finally, as relatedness decreases even further, direct incompatibility is expected to result in immediate decreases in F_1 means and increases in F_1 variances (Fig. 16, e.g., hybrid inviability—severe outbreeding depression). A major unresolved question is whether hybrid vigor can appear at some level of differentiation without a concomitant decrease in F_2 fitness. If possible then this permanent heterosis, versus a transient luxuriance, would shift the optimum level of inbreeding to the right (Fig. 16).

Reports of undiminished intraspecific interfertility, even between widely separated populations, have appeared with some regularity (e.g., Dice, 1933 and for reviews, see Stebbins, 1950; Ford, 1964), but at a much lower frequency than cases of dysgenesis. With few exceptions (e.g., Jewell and Fullager, 1965) they were limited to examination of single components of F_1 hybrid fitness (usually fertility). In such studies, the pertinent studies of F_2 or backcross progeny were rarely performed, and in the larger vertebrates sample sizes were often too small to distinguish any but extreme differences. Some of these studies overlooked strong evidence of incompatibility of one type while emphasizing undiminished fitness at a second level. For example,

Dice (1933) is cited as reporting that subspecific crosses of mice in the genus *Peromyscus* were completely interfertile. While he did emphasize an apparent absence of postmating barriers to such crosses, he also noted in a less cited sentence that, "fighting does occur between some newly mated individuals, especially when members of the pair are of different races, and sometimes one or both animals may be injured or killed." Despite the apparent success of interracial pairs that do manage to mate, the probability of success will be reduced relative to more peaceful intraracial pairs because of the behavioral incompatibility.

Most direct evidence of intraspecific outbreeding depression results from the hybridization of individuals from geographically distant populations or morphologically differentiated subspecies (but see below). There is no compelling reason, logical or empirical, to believe that the same processes and resulting incompatibilities could not occur in more closely related, but still differentiated forms (i.e., between families within a group). The resulting outbreeding depression would often be less intense, and therefore harder to measure, but could still be a potent selective force. Laboratory investigations have shown that coadaptation can develop quickly (< 10 generations, King, 1955; Johnson, 1974), and does not require external isolation to produce significantly different coadapted lines from a single initial population (e.g., Palenzona et al., 1974; 1975). Further support for the possibility of extensive intraspecific outbreeding depression emerges from the many theoretical studies which have demonstrated (usually via simulation) that a wide variety of initial conditions analogous or equivalent to those underlying the mutational model can produce genically differentiated subpopulations partially isolated by outbreeding depression. This can occur in the absence of geographical isolation, indeed even in the face of considerable gene flow (e.g., Thoday and Gibson, 1962; 1970; Jain and Bradshaw, 1966; Pimental et al., 1967; Crosby, 1970; Slatkin, 1973; 1975; Endler, 1973; May et al., 1975; Caisse and Antonovics, 1978; and for comprehensive reviews, see Thoday, 1972; Endler, 1977.

I assume that epistasis is important in determining individual fitness (see also, Soule, 1973; Mayr, 1975; Wright, 1977; Hedrick et al., 1978; Hartung, 1981), and that this theoretical and empirical network can be applied to the mutational model of family differentiation. If interfamily hybridization does, at least occasionally, lead

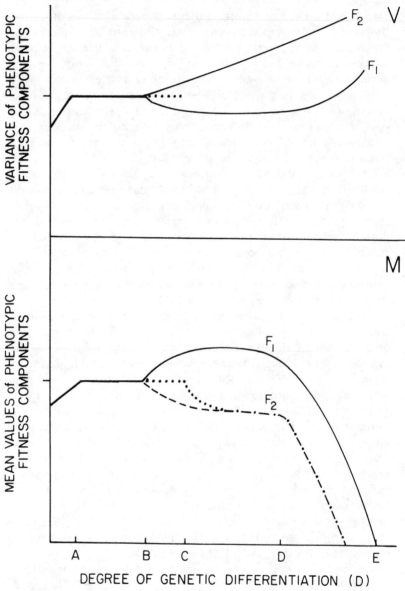

Fig. 16. Hypothetical model of a general relationship between the mean and variance values of various quantitative fitness components (e.g., fecundity and viability) and the degree of relatedness of mates. Extreme inbreeding ($d < A$) is expected to produce an incest depression. Less intense inbreeding ($A < d < B$) is not expected to produce major changes in either F_1 or F_2 fitness. As the level of outbreeding increases, $B < d < D$), F_1 hybrid vigor is expected to occur. If there were no change in F_2 fitness (...., $B < d < C$), the increased F_1 fitness would be con-

to significant outbreeding depression, then I can offer a more detailed and precise hypothesis in answer to the original question, Why philopatry? The occurrence of differentiated families with cross-incompatible, but internally coadapted, gene complexes can produce selective conditions which favor intrafamilial inbreeding. This inbreeding is advantageous because it more faithfully transmits favored gene combinations, initially compounded via chance mutation and the sexual lottery, that wider outbreeding would necessarily have broken apart.

Origin and Maintenance of Philopatry

The important relationship between dispersal and gene flow, and therefore, differentiation, has long been recognized. As with so much in population biology, it was Wright (1931; 1940) who first emphasized the notion that members of a geographically widespread species were likely to be "isolated by distance," owing to limited dispersal resulting in reduced panmixia. Refinements and extensions of his early work (e.g., Wright, 1943; 1951; 1978; Malecot, 1948; Kimura and Weiss, 1964; Weiss and Kimura, 1965; Maruyama, 1969; 1970; Kimura and Ohta, 1971; Spieth, 1974; Nagylaki, 1976) have produced a number of mathematical models relating dispersal patterns (gene migration) and expected differentiation of neutral alleles in space and time. All agreed that the more limited an organism's dispersal, the more likely that a megapopulation would fission into partially isolated subpopulations. These would then be free to differentiate through the stochastic processes grouped under the rubric of drift. They also suggested that minor levels of effective gene flow (equivalent to effective size $N_e > 10,000$ or the immigration of a single individual drawn randomly from the megapopulation into each subpopulation every generation) would prevent neutral differentiation. As more realistic assumptions were derived from the dispersal patterns observed in nature (e.g., Kimura and Ohta, 1971; Felsen-

---

Fig. 16.(*continued*)

sidered stable (heterosis). At some level of differentiation (either B or C), increased outbreeding is expected to result in a monotonic decline in F_2 fitness (hybrid breakdown). At that point, F_1 vigor would be considered transient (luxuriance), and outbreeding would entail a net fitness depression. At greater degrees of differentiation ($D < d < E$), F_1 fitness would begin a monotonic decline finally reaching zero (species level reproductive isolation). The model is a modification of one presented by Hedrick et al. (1978).

stein, 1975; Wright, 1978), the modern "stepping stone" models indicated that greater, but certainly not extreme, rates of migration were probably necessary to prevent neutral differentiation.

Simultaneously, parallel *selective* models of the relation between gene flow and differentiation were being developed. They assumed that ecological conditions varied within a megapopulation's (species') range (e.g., Fisher, 1930; Huxley, 1938; 1942; Thoday, 1958; Slatkin, 1973; 1975; Endler, 1973; 1977, Caisse and Antonovics, 1978; White, 1978a). They demonstrated that disruptive selection was capable of producing marked subpopulation differentiation in spite of massive levels (including levels greater than panmixis) of gene flow. These theoretical models were supported by a number of observations of natural populations of plants and animals subject to disruptive selection (for reviews, see Jain and Bradshaw, 1966; Ehrlich and Raven, 1969; Antonovics, 1971; Thoday, 1972), in which differentiation was observed.

All the models converged on a view that actual levels of gene flow will wholly (neutral models), or in part (selective), determine the levels and patterns of genetic differentiation observed in nature. As Wright (1940; 1943) noted, this meant that comprehensive investigation of population structure and geographic differentiation required estimates of gene flow. It now appears that considerations of the phenotypic homogeneity observed in many species (e.g., Mayr, 1942; 1963; Emlen, 1978), their members' obvious mobility, possible bias against "inbreeding" (Chs. 3 and 4), and the mathematical tractability of panmixia, all conditioned a view that many species were both potentially and actually panmictic (e.g., Dobzhansky, 1937; 1970; Mayr, 1942; 1963; 1975; Wallace, 1968b; Crow and Kimura, 1970). Gene flow was assumed to result from fairly high levels of intersubpopulation dispersal. Since most adherents of the high gene flow models were also strong supporters of the unity of the genotype and the importance of epistasis and coadaptation (see above), they were faced with something of a challenge. Mayr's (1954; 1963; p. 284) ingenious solution was a hypothesis that the massive gene flow observed within species would act to select for "those genes that have a maximum fitness in the greatest possible number of combinations," or so-called "good mixer" genes. He perceived the *species* as a genetically cohesive and coadapted unit that would resist assimilating novel mutations unless they interacted harmoniously on the species-wide genetic background.

94

But as Mayr noted (1942; 1963), and Ehrlich and Raven (1969) emphasized, when individuals are marked and tracked, dispersal is often localized and philopatric (Ch. 2). In an elegant analysis of the relationship between gene flow and genetic differentiation, Endler (1977; Ch. 2) independently reviewed much of the literature I reviewed in chapter 2 reaching a conclusion that philopatry was common in a wide variety of plant and animal groups. In addition, he made the important point that gene flow does *not* necessarily equal dispersal. Lowered reproductive success associated with longer dispersal distances often reduces effective gene flow below the already low levels implied by philopatry alone. Perhaps gene flow is more a trickle than a brook (Endler, 1979)?

Endler concluded that the gene flow characterizing many natural populations was not likely to swamp local adaptive differentiation, itself a response to spatial variation in the environment. He concluded that parapatric genetic divergence, and ultimately speciation, were likely events rather than theoretical possibilities. White (1978a) concurred, explicitly invoking low vagility (philopatric dispersal), again and again, to explain the fixation of genetic novelties, especially chromosomal rearrangements, that were expected to be detrimental as heterozygotes. Even Mayr (1963) invoked philopatry when he discussed "microgeographic" isolation, as when a founder group is isolated just beyond the normal dispersal range of a species' main population. If dispersal were limited only by mobility, such founder groups would often be less than isolated in mobile animals. Only when a rare long-distance propagule, of a normally philopatric species, reaches a new environment is isolation likely to result.

Meanwhile, the modelers modeled, varying gene flow in order to determine the quantitative domain of its potential consequences. For example, Caisse and Antonovics (1978) were able to demonstrate that a heterogeneous environment divided into two regions, each selecting for an alternative allele at a particular locus, could produce a step cline at that locus with many combinations of selection and gene flow values. They also showed that a second locus controlling premating isolation (e.g., different flowering times) could also differentiate as a result of the outbreeding depression generated by the disruptive selection at the first locus. The conditions for inducing this Wallace Effect were more stringent than those permitting differentiation at the first locus. More intense selection and necessarily moderate gene flow were required.

As might be expected, massive gene flow swamped any differentiation, but if gene flow were too limited, premating isolation failed to evolve as well, since too few low-fitness hybrids were produced to effectively select for secondary isolation.

Of course this is exactly the point. In almost every investigation of the relation between gene flow and differentiation (but, see Karlin and MacGregor, 1974; Kempton, 1974; Teague, 1977), gene flow enters the picture as an *independent* variable. It is a given. Either panmixis or philopatry, something in between, or an arbitrary selection of migration values are used to reach conclusions about the consequences of gene flow. Following Cain's (1977) rule, perhaps it is better "to ask questions of the animals, not of the pundits." What happens if gene flow can evolve? What if we examine its causes as well as its consequences? More precisely, assuming that epistasis and outbreeding depression are facts of life, and given genetic variation in the substrates controlling dispersal mechanisms, how will natural selection shape dispersal?

As we have already seen, if epistasis is important and outbreeding depression common, then intrafamilial inbreeding can be adaptive. If a particular family has a genetically based tendency to disperse philopatrically, their probability of inbreeding will increase (Ch. 2). The increased inbreeding associated with philopatry will increase their fitness relative to similar individuals with tendencies to disperse more widely and suffer the resulting outbreeding depression. Given time, and the recurrence of novel epistatic combinations, then the genetic substrate associated with philopatry will eventually fix in such a family. Any favorable combinations arising after philopatry is the rule will be assimilated more quickly and with less waste (in maladapted progeny), while reinforcing the entire process. When a major portion of each genome consists of coadapted complexes of alleles (as I assume to be the case for most organisms), it will no longer be necessary for novel combinations to appear to drive the system. Disruption of already assimilated combinations will cause sufficient outbreeding depression to maintain the selective pressure favoring philopatry and its consequent inbreeding. In essence, I believe philopatry is a primary reproductive isolating mechanism, which evolves in response to postmating isolation (outbreeding depression) resulting from the disruption of coadapted gene complexes after interfamilial outbreeding. Philopatry would be the result of a Wallace Effect in miniature, occurring within a single species.

Ultimately, it permits subgroup differentiaiton, and because the conditions favoring it are continuous, once the process is initiated, it is likely to grind on until the positive feedback produces differentiation, hybrid dysgenesis, or both, at levels high enough that analagous models focusing directly on speciation become appropriate. From this perspective, and at least for mobile animals, the evolution of philopatry might be considered the evolution of allopatry. Only then does the "isolation" of two bird species by the Amazon River (Mayr, 1942), or an invisible barrier between different morph ratios in the butterfly *Maniola jurtina* (Ford, 1964) and similar "area effects" become explicable (for reviews, see Cain, 1973; White, 1978a).

Philopatry, then, can be an adaptation to heterogeneity in the *genetic* environment. In a sexually reproducing species, sufficient conditions for its evolution would be genetic variation in dispersal mechanisms (Ch. 2), and conditions which produce spatially separate individuals which carry different and incompatible genomes. There are at least two processes which could produce such a genetic environment. The most obvious, and perhaps most common in nature, is ecological heterogeneity. Selective differences in the external environment are expected to occur in spatial associations, and will, therefore, favor the assimilation of different alleles and allele combinations in geographically separate areas. This is equivalent to the ecogenetic hypothesis of the function of philopatry, applied to metal stressed plants and up-and-downstream salmon (Ch. 2). It is just such conditions, with externally controlled disruptive selection at one locus, conditioning selection at a second locus controlling migration, that has been successfully modeled. Under such conditions, a novel migration modifier allele will be positively selected only if it *reduces* the level of migration (Karlin and MacGregor, 1974; Teague, 1977).

A second process offers a potential explanation for those species (e.g., Laysan Albatross) which are philopatric in seemingly homogeneous environments. The key may be that genetic heterogeneity does not require ecological heterogeneity for either its initiation or maintenance. Given a large but homogeneous environmental patch, we would still not expect a *single* mutation favored in that environment to arise independently in two or more individuals (unless the population were extremely large). More likely, two different mutations (or sets of mutations), each favored in the current environment, but each currying that favor through different proximate means, would be assimilated by two individuals and hence their families. Should these novel complexes be reproductively incompatible, selection would favor inbreeding, and thus philopatry, even though the ecological environment was homogeneous. This process would be driven by the opportunism of natural selection and the randomness and independence of mutation.

A series of laboratory experiments on the development of genetic adaptation in novel (changed) environments demonstrates the feasibility of this strictly genetic process (e.g., King, 1955; Johnson, 1974; Palenzona et al., 1974; 1975). King (1955) performed a series of crosses designed to elucidate the genetic bases of newly evolved DDT resistance in *Drosophila melanogaster* flies. He varied the selection intensities, and the life stage subjected to the poison (larvae, adult), and was able to increase resistance in all lines. He also discovered that crosses between such lines, which originally were from the same stock, even when subjected to identical selective conditions, disrupted the resistance adaptation with F_2 hybrids displaying reduced resistance. He concluded (1955, p. 317) that, ". . . different lines stemming from the same original stock can build different systems within a dozen generations." The hybrid dysgenesis indicated that the systems were not just different, but also incompatible, at least with respect to one character making a significant contribution to fitness in the experimental environment.

Genetic heterogeneity, then, whether it arises in response to ecological heterogeneity, or results from the assimilation of different mutations by spatially separated families in a homogeneous environment, can favor inbreeding. Therefore, it can be considered one of the ultimate causes of philopatry. If this hypothesis is true, then in philopatric species the intensity of outbreeding depression should be positively correlated with the geographical distance separating mates. This prediction is based on an auxiliary hypothesis that the degree of genetic differentiation will also be positively correlated with distance in philopatric species. Although the majority of studies of genetic differentiation and outbreeding depression are not detailed enough to examine the prediction, those few that are tend confirm it, offering some support for the hypothesis. Selander and Kaufman (1975) reported that relatedness (estimated electrophoretically) dropped sharply between individuals separated by 20–30 m in the philopatric snail

Helix aspersa, and continued declining at increasing distances (Fig. 17). Similar correlations have been reported in a wide variety of organisms but usually on a larger geographic scale (e.g., in a riverine fish, Merritt et al., 1978; an amphibian, Hedgecock, 1978; birds, Baker, 1974; 1975; and various mammals, Selander and Yang, 1969; Patton and Yang, 1977; see also Ch. 8).

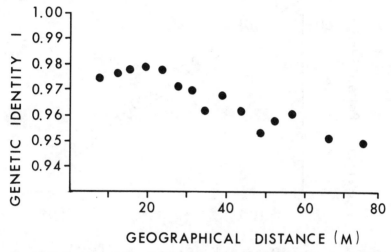

Fig. 17. Nei's mean genetic identity between pairs of colonies of the snail, *Helix aspersa,* as a function of the mean geographic distance between those colonies illustrating the expected decrease in relatedness with increasing distance (after Selander and Kaufman, 1975).

When investigated in similar detail, outbreeding depression also appears to be correlated with geographic distance between hybridizing parents (e.g., Kruckeberg, 1957, Fig. 18; Paraense, 1959; Oliver, 1972; Price and Waser, 1979). With respect to outbreeding depression, the broad hypothesis of a geographic association can be narrowed to produce a more specific and therefore more powerful test. If philopatry evolved to prevent outbreeding depression, then the magnitude of philopatric dispersal should be roughly correlated with the spatial boundaries of panmictic and inbreeding families (in this case inbreeding because of dispersal-limited population size). Some critical distance, between the median and maximum dispersal characteristic of a species, should be associated with the first appearance of low-level outbreeding depression. If true, then individuals from areas more distant than the critical outbreeding distance should display reduced reproductive success, if mated, relative to pairs taken from within this distance. This prediction is amenable to test via experimental manipulation of mates.

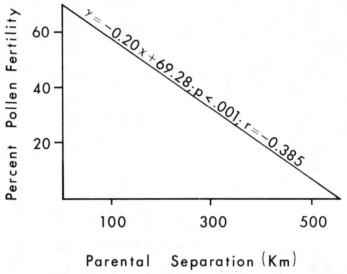

Parental   Separation (Km)

Fig. 18. The relationship between pollen fertility and geographic distance between parent plants within subspecies of the plant species *Streptanthus glandulosus* illustrating increased outbreeding depression with increasing distances (data from Kruckeberg, 1957).

While I (Shields, 1979) generated this specific prediction, *a priori*, that is, in the absence of any concrete evidence of its truth or falsehood, chance has since provided data with a direct bearing on its validity from an elegant and detailed study by Price and Waser (1979). Independently, and through a different line of reasoning, they generated the hypothesis that there might be an optimal balance between intense inbreeding and overwide outbreeding. To test their hypothesis, they chose a small montane perennial wildflower (*Delphinium nelsoni*). Their design artificially crossed individuals living arbitrary distances apart. They reported statistically significant outbreeding depression if mates were separated by more than 10 m, and significant inbreeding depression if they selfed or were less than 1 m apart (Fig. 19). Both sorts of depression resulted from significant reductions in the numbers of seeds set per flower, and more importantly in the number of plants surviving from those seeds to breed in the next season. They controlled for ecological contributors such as sib competition and overcrowding, and concluded that the most likely explanation for the reduced success of mates from the more distant locales was genetic incompatibility, as demanded by the outbreeding depression hypothesis. In the context of dispersal, the critical outbreeding distance (> 10 m),

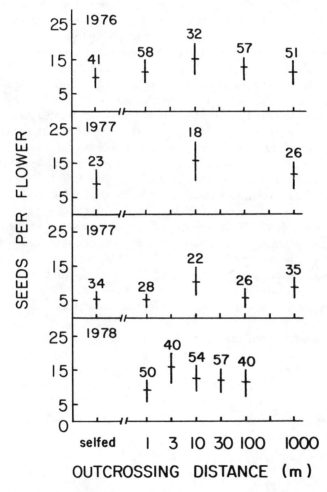

Fig. 19. The number of seeds set per flower in *Delphinium nelsoni* as a function of the geographical distance separating parent plants illustrating significant outbreeding depression at rather short distances (from Price and Waser, 1979).

was correlated with maximum dispersal (> 95% of pollinator moves < 10 m from parent), and was greater than median dispersal ($\simeq 1$ m, pollen; $\simeq 0.15$ m, seeds), again consistent with the hypothesis. Although the median dispersal distances observed appear to be less than the theoretical optimum, this may not be the case. Pollen dispersal is likely to be greater than reported because presentation of only pollinator movement ignores pollen carryover to second and third plants (Schaal, 1980). In addition, the optimal dispersal distance may be less than 10 m, since the highest seed set occurred in the sole replicate at 3 m (Fig. 19), though the difference between 3 and 10 m was not statistically significant. Thus, Price and Waser's (1979) data appear to be broadly consistent with my predictions, and did lead them to similar conclusions. Unfortunately, Price and Waser's study is unique with respect to its microgeographic scale. The hypothesis that philopatry evolved to prevent outbreeding depression is placed at greatest risk by its prediction that similar results should emerge from like studies of other species of philopatric plants and animals.

The evidence about differentiation, outbreeding depression, and geographical distance currently available fails to falsify the optimal inbreeding hypothesis as outlined in the preceding chapters. The evidence does offer sufficient support for the argument that further examination of its structure and implications are warranted. I began by asking Why philopatry? and answered, Because it promotes inbreeding. I asked, Why inbreeding? and answered, Because it is less disruptive of coadapted allele combinations than wider outbreeding. Embedded in these questions and their answers is an unasked and therefore as yet unanswered question. As Crow (1956; also, see Muller, 1958; Malmberg, 1977) has noted, if epistasis were important in determining fitness potential, it would most likely be so in asexual organisms. Because of their clonal reproduction, they are expected to be better at transmitting coadapted genomes without disruption than are sexual organisms. As these considerations imply, embedded in the question, Why inbreed? is a more fundamental question, Why sex? (Shields, 1982b).

CHAPTER **6**

Inbreeding and Sex: Paradox Lost?

In diploid eukaryotic organisms, sex can be defined as the production of offspring by the fusion of gametes (syngamy), which themselves are the recombination products of parental meiosis during gametogenesis. Prokaryotic sexual processes include genetic exchange (again recombination), but usually do not entail syngamy. Any process which lacks recombination of, or insertion into, an individual's genome is usually considered asexual. As defined, the ubiquity of sexual reproduction in nature has produced "a kind of crisis" in evolutionary biology (Williams, 1975, p. v). The crisis emerges from a consensus that while sex's obvious consequences appear to benefit the "group" or species in the long run, they also appear to result in significant and immediate detriment for the individuals engaging in the practice. The apparent dominance of group benefit over individual cost has stimulated a variety of hypothetical and hotly debated explanations of the function of sex.

Accepting the obvious, a number of schools have proposed a complex of often complementary hypotheses explaining sex as a truly biotic adaptation. Focusing on the effects of syngamy, the Fisher-Muller School (Fisher, 1930; Muller, 1932; 1958; Crow and Kimura, 1965; 1969; Kimura and Ohta, 1971) suggested that the primary function of sex was to increase the rate of adaptive evolution by increasing both the rate and probability of combining two independent and favorable mutants into a single individual. Focusing on the consequences of recombination, the "reassortment" (Thompson, 1976) school (Darlington, 1932; 1958; Dobzhansky, 1937; 1970; Lewis, 1942; Mather, 1943; 1953; Stebbins, 1950; 1957;

Dodson, 1953; Mayr, 1963; Felsenstein, 1974) also suggested that sex functioned to increase evolutionary rates, but emphasized the increased genetic flexibility resulting from the generation of novel allelic combinations from variants already present in a group's gene pool. Reinforcing each other, both schools concluded that sex was ubiquitous because sexual species were: (1) less likely to go extinct, (2) more likely to speciate, (3) or both (1) and (2), owing to their increased flexibility and evolutionary potential (see references above, also Stanley, 1975; Van Valen, 1975; Treisman, 1976) relative to asexual species. Fisher (1930, p. 50) went so far as to suggest that sex might be the *only* character "evolved for the specific rather than for the individual advantage." In his excellent review (from which my conceptual organization is derived), Thompson (1976) agreed that sex was probably a biotic adaptation. However, his interpretation of the admittedly sparse experimental evidence (e.g., Thompson, 1977), suggested that sex actually slowed the rate of evolution. He concluded that sex might prevent a group from wastefully depleting its genetic variance by tracking unimportant environmental fluctuations too closely.

Dissatisfied with reliance on biotic adaptation and its implication of effective group selection in general, a third school (Williams, 1966; 1971; 1975; 1980; Maynard Smith, 1968; 1971a; 1971b; 1974; 1976; 1977; 1978; Ghiselin, 1969; 1974; Williams and Mitton, 1973; Levin, 1975; Nyberg, 1975; Treisman and Dawkins, 1976; Felsenstein and Yokoyama, 1976; Glesener and Tilman, 1978; Shields, 1979; Bremermann, 1979a; Charlesworth, 1980a and b; Hartung, 1981; Case and Bender, 1981; Moore and Hines, 1981) spent a great deal of time and energy exploring the individual consequences of sex in search of advantages that would more than balance the obvious disadvantages.

With some drift, each of the schools followed an intuitive argument first expressed in detail by Weismann (1891) that the crucial consequence of sex was the generation of genetic novelty. They were also unanimous in inferring from this that sex must function to meet changed or changing environmental conditions (see also Bonner, 1958). In the end, the primary differences between the various schools were in their detailed explanations of what kinds of novelties (mutational or recombinational) were important in maintaining sex, who (individual or group) benefited from those consequences, and when (immediately or in the future).

The entire problem of sex was attacked on a broad front by

a host of investigators using comparative evidence, intuitive and mathematical analyses, and computer simulation, in order to determine what factors controlled the adaptive value of sex, and how such factors determined the sign (i.e., adaptive or maladaptive) of that value. Detailed results of these studies have fueled a series of comprehensive and synthetic reviews (e.g., Ghiselin, 1974; Williams, 1975; Thompson, 1976; and especially, Maynard Smith, 1978). Fortunately, these details are not as important for the arguments developed here, as are some of the general conclusions emerging from them. Instead of reviewing details again, I will rely on the earlier reviews to summarize pertinent conclusions and evidence when needed.

There is a growing consensus that the conditions that would favor the Fisher-Muller explanation of sex are not likely to be frequent or efficient enough to maintain sex (fusion) as a strictly biotic adaptation. The process of bringing favorable mutants together is expected to contribute to that end. The primary difficulty is that what sex brings together more quickly, it breaks apart just as quickly (Thompson, 1976). Evidence for within-population genetic variance for recombination is unequivocal in contradicting any hypothesis of sex that relies solely on arguments of group benefit (Turner, 1967; Williams, 1975; Maynard Smith, 1978). So the extreme individual selectionists (Ghiselin, 1974) were probably correct in exploring the individual benefits of sex in order to balance individual costs. Unfortunately, though they have succeeded in producing a number of partial or potential answers, all such explanations are restricted by a lack of generality, a reliance on admittedly unrealistic assumptions, or on infrequent conditions as primary selective forces. In the end, they are unable, either singly or jointly, to explain the maintenance of sex in many regularly, or obligately, sexual organisms. Sex then, is a paradox, a contradictory thorn in the sides of those, including myself, who view natural selection as a process operating through the reproductive success of individuals (Williams, 1980).

The Disadvantages of Sex

Syngamy

The dual nature of sex allows an independent analysis of the detrimental consequences of both its normal component processes (syngamy and recombination). The primary disadvantage of syngamy can itself be viewed in two different ways, either as a significant ecological (Maynard Smith, 1978), or genetical (Williams, 1975; 1980) "cost" associated with *biparental* reproduction. Maynard Smith (1978, p. 2) succinctly described the former as, "the twofold disadvantage of producing males," while Williams (1975, p. 9) described the genetic cost as, "the 50% cost of meiosis." Maynard Smith argued that in a sexual species, with equal numbers of males and females, sex is not an "evolutionarily stable strategy" (Maynard Smith and Price, 1973), being susceptible to invasion by parthenogenesis. In this situation, the putative value of parthenogenesis is an immediate increase in the *relative* fecundity of a parthenogenetic female. Such a female produces only daughters, but in numbers expected to equal the total output of a sexual female (whose progeny will usually consist of equal numbers of females and males). Thus the proportion of parthenogenetic females in a total "population" consisting of both sexual and parthenogenetic females will increase, actually doubling in the early generations when they are still rare. If there is to be a cost of producing males, or investing in male function, then "males" must function solely as sperm donors. As both Williams (1975) and Maynard Smith (1978) have pointed out, the ecological cost does not apply in situations where male parental care is necessary to produce successful progeny, nor, perhaps, to organisms with isogamous gametes and no clear distinction between the sexes (see also, Manning, 1976a; but see Charlesworth, 1980a). It also applies with less force to hermaphroditic organisms, if they can reduce their investment in male function without reducing reproductive success. Such asymmetric investment is expected to be most easily attained in self-fertilizing organisms (Maynard Smith, 1978), a prediction amply confirmed in selfing plants which often show predicted reductions in pollen investment (Cruden, 1977).

The genetic argument of a cost of meiosis implies that a major disadvantage of syngamy results from sexual parents discounting their genetic representation in descendants by 50% because they "share" offspring with unrelated individuals. A sexual parent produces haploid gametes which fuse with another individual's gametes to produce progeny. Thus, half of each sexually produced offspring's genome is maternal, half paternal, so that a sexual female that produces 10 offspring can claim only 50% of their genes, or 5 offspring equivalents. In contrast, a parthenogenetic (or otherwise asexual) individual's offspring carry only their mother's genes. If she produced 10 offspring, they would equal 10 offspring equivalents, or twice the total genetic representation of a sexual female. Recently, Williams (1980) has suggested that this cost can be viewed in the context of inclusive fitness and kin selection. A sexually reproducing female invests in relatives (offspring) with lower relatedness ($r = 0.5$) than similar asexual females (parent-offspring $r = 1.0$). Inclusive fitness theories of kin selection (e.g., Hamilton, 1964a; West Eberhard, 1975) suggest that beneficence, including parental investments, should be dispensed preferentially to closer kin. This implies that sex can entail a genetic cost, in that individual donors are not maximizing the relatedness of their most direct beneficiaries, regardless of fecundity effects.

Maynard Smith (1978) and others have suggested that the ecological and genetical costs of sex are the same problem. In most instances, they are indeed two sides of the same coin. Yet this practical symmetry does not imply a logical equivalence between the two. For example, the genetic argument could apply with equal force to outbreeding hermaphrodites, even if they limited investment in male function obviating any ecological cost. Theoretically, an internally fertilized and crossbreeding hermaphrodite would be capable of reducing its investment in male function until its relative fecundity approximated that of an asexual individual (Maynard Smith, 1978, p. 40; Charlesworth, 1980a). The perhaps unrealistic assumption in this case is that each individual is guaranteed one mating (but, see Fischer, 1980). If true, the sex ratio would be 1, there would be no competition for mates, and asymmetric investment in sexual *function* would be evolutionarily stable (Maynard Smith, 1978).

Such individuals might produce 9 fecund progeny for every 10 produced by an otherwise equivalent asexual individual. This would occur, for example, with a transfer of 80% of initially male investment into female function, and result in a reduced 10% (vs. the normal 50%) ecological cost of sex. If such organisms outbred, they would produce 9 offspring with an $r = 0.5$, for 4.5 genetic offspring equivalents. When compared to 10 asexual progeny ($r = 1.0$), and their undiscounted 10 offspring equivalents, the genetic cost in inclusive fitness to the sexual individual is readily apparent.

Both the ecological and genetic models of the disadvantage of syngamy imply at least a two-fold advantage for asexuality. For that advantage to apply, progeny produced asexually should be equally fit relative to sexual progeny. Since asexuality is *not* replacing sex in the wide variety of obligately sexual organisms, and since asexuality and sex appear to occur in equilibrium in many heterogonic species which alternate between the two strategies, then any hypothetical equivalence between sexual and asexual progeny fitness is likely to be untrue. The explanation most often advanced to explain this paradox is that sexual progeny, for some reason, are more than twice as fit as asexual progeny in applicable environments.

Recombination

The disadvantage of recombination is as easy to conceptualize as that of syngamy, but at present it is essentially impossible to quantify. The origins of the argument can be traced from Fisher (1930), and is perhaps best expressed by Maynard Smith (1978, p. 78), who notes, "More generally, one can simply say that since surviving individuals have genotypes of higher than average fitness, they only stand to lose, in a uniform environment, by producing recombinant offspring." The cost of recombination can be measured as a "load" (Williams, 1975) corresponding to the average reduction in progeny fitness resulting from the disruption of favored coadapted genomes during gametogenesis. The end result of sex is that demonstrably successful parents will, on average, produce less adapted progeny because they will possess genomes that are likely to be significantly different from those of their parents. In essence, recombination reduces the heritability of fitness, so that there will be less correlation between the fitness of a parent and its offspring. In contrast, asexual reproduction theoretically allows a successful parent to transmit an exact duplicate of its successful genome to its progeny (Maynard Smith, 1978). In a uniform environment, then, natural selection will favor individuals with reduced (or zero) recombination, because fitter parents will produce fitter offspring in such conditions *only* in the absence of recombination. The argument implies that in a relatively constant or uniform environment, sexually produced progeny are more likely to be less, rather than more, fit than asexual progeny, increasing the already considerable disadvantage of sex.

A large measure of theoretical and observational evidence supporting this view of recombinational load has accumulated over the past 50 years (for review, see Maynard Smith, 1978, Ch. 5). Indeed, recombinational load has generally been proposed as a driving force behind the evolution of such diverse characters as, chromosome linkage groups in general (Fisher, 1930; Wright, 1931; Darlington, 1932; 1958), the reorganization of separate loci into closely linked supergenes (Ford, 1964; Turner, 1967b), and the maintenance of balanced chromosomal inversion polymorphisms in flies, especially *Drosophila* (Dobzhansky, 1937; 1970). In each of these instances, the characters are thought to have evolved specifically to reduce the levels of disruptive recombination. Following the logic of these arguments to their ultimate conclusion led to Turner's (1967a) seminal question, "Why does the genome not congeal?" Why does recombination (and syngamy) not give way to nonrecombinational asexual reproduction?

The Advantages of Sex

The search for sex's advantages was facilitated by the occurrence of within-population variation in recombination, which automatically focused attention on sex's consequences for individuals. It was made even simpler by the "apparently unanimous" (Daly, 1978, p. 771; also, see Williams, 1975; Maynard Smith, 1978) conclusion that the primary consequence of sex, and therefore its function, was to increase the genetic diversity of one's offspring (so that siblings differed among themselves *and* from their parents) in response to changed or changing environmental conditions (but, see Manning, 1976b). Williams (1975, p. 7) stated the paradigm for investigating sex quite explicitly, "it is easier to reason from a set of premises to a valid conclusion if you know the conclusion in advance." Many followed his lead, and the search for an explanation of sex became a search for the proper premises, that is, for the initial conditions, types, and degree of environmental fluctuation which would favor sexual reproduction. Within this model two distinguishable (though some believe that they are operationally identical) classes of models evolved. The ecological models focused on the consequences of varying environments and the genetical models focused on the consequences of randomly generated linkage disequilibria in finite populations (the Hill-Robertson effect). Without entering the discussion of whether they are all subsets of a single model (e.g., Felsenstein, 1974; Felsenstein and

Yokoyama, 1976) or truly independent (e.g., Maynard Smith, 1978), I will treat them separately.

Ecological models: Varying abiotic environments

All the ecological models rely on environmental conditions which vary in such a manner that offspring face qualitatively different environments than those faced by their parents. For the most general models of simple abiotic spatial and temporal variation, Maynard Smith (reviewed in 1978) has shown that if two or more loci are important in adapting an individual to a single state of any of an environment's variable features (e.g., features = temperature and rainfall, states = hot or cold, wet or dry), or if the states of different features are correlated (e.g., hot areas are wet, cold areas dry), then recombination will almost always be maladaptive (occasionally neutral). Only in the unlikely event that correlations between the states of different features change sign from generation to generation (e.g., generation 1 = hot-dry, cold-wet; generation 2 = hot-wet, cold-dry), would selection favor increased recombination (Maynard Smith, 1979).

Varying biotic environments

Since the abiotic environment is unlikely to vary in the necessary manner, the focus of these models has changed to biotic components of the environment that could so vary (e.g., Levin, 1975; Jaenike, 1978; Glesener and Tilman, 1978; Bremermann, 1980; Hamilton et al., 1981; Lloyd, 1980; Moore and Hines, 1981). The basic rationale is that other organisms, including predators, prey, competitors, and especially pathogens, are also evolving. Varying via mutation and recombination themselves, they might generate sufficient temporal variation in selective conditions in every generation to favor sex in other competitors, predators, prey, or host organisms. In this context, sex would be a necessary tactic in a *coevolutionary* war.

While such models may be more appealing at an intuitive level than the abiotic models, they too suffer from being rigorously applicable only under a narrow range of conditions. Analytic treatment and computer simulation (e.g., Hamilton et al., 1981; Moore and Hines, 1981) indicate that only when 2 or more loci are each being selected by independent aspects of a temporally varying environment (e.g., 2 loci fighting 2 different pathogens), will sex regularly be favored. In order for this effect to emerge, the sexual population must be large and highly polymorphic at the appropriate loci. Given all of these conditions, then sex can be maintained, but the selection regimes and associated necessary conditions certainly imply that ". . . it appears unlikely that a viable one locus model for maintenance of sex based on fluctuation of environment can be devised" (Hamilton et al., 1981). This agrees with Moore and Hines (1981), who "concur with this conclusion for two or a few loci, although the realization that the advantage of asexuality decreases as the number of [independently] selected loci increases gives the random temporal uncertainty hypothesis plausibility not hitherto recognized." Thus, while the simple varying environment pressures may, in special circumstances, contribute to the value of sex, they are not likely to explain its ubiquity (Hamilton et al., 1981; Moore and Hines, 1981).

A third less general, but more plausible, model combines a specific pattern of dispersal and spatial heterogeneity in the environment to produce positive selection for higher recombination (Maynard Smith, 1968; Slatkin, 1975). This model requires two differentiated populations living in selectively different and geographically separated areas, each contributing migrants to a third ecologically unique area. If members of the two parent populations only meet in the third area, and if selection in that area favors a novel genotype which consists of alleles drawn from each parent population, then selection can favor recombination in the novel environment (Fig. 20). In the illustrated case, a linear habitat is sharply divided into a central novel region (linear extent = Z) in which haploid genotype Ab is favored, while the original environments favored the fixed genotypes AB and ab. If $Z > \delta / \sqrt{s}$ (where δ = average dispersal distance; s = selection intensity against the parental genotypes and alternative recombinants), there would be no selection on recombination. If $Z < \delta / \sqrt{s}$ (Case C), selection will favor increased recombination in the small central region but reduced recombination in the much larger parental regions. Finally, if $Z \approx \delta / \sqrt{s}$ (Case B), recombination will be neutral in the parental regions and positively selected in the novel environment. While this model does indicate that there are plausible conditions which would select for increased recombination, it is unlikely that such conditions occur frequently or widely enough to explain recombination universally (see also, Case and Bender, 1981). Maynard Smith (1978) also noted that it

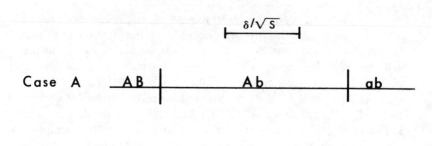

Case A

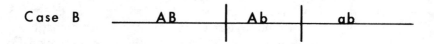

Case B

Case C

Fig. 20. Relation between characteristic dispersal distance (d), selection (s) and the distance between environmental discontinuities (Z) which will determine the selective value of recombination in the central environment (from Maynard Smith's treatment, 1978, of Slatkin's 1975 model).

was equally easy to conceive of similar conditions which would favor reduced recombination (e.g., if two loci switch selective states at the same spatial location, or the states of different features are spatially correlated).

Sib-competition models

A third class of ecological models have developed from Williams's seminal discussions which rest on an assumption that intense selection coupled with fluctuating environments could produce conditions favoring sexual reproduction in a wide variety of organisms (Williams and Mitton, 1973; Williams, 1975; 1980). Williams expressed the essence of his argument in an elegent gambling metaphor. A heterogeneous, fluctuating environment may be viewed as consisting of a series of lotteries (patches), each having a single winning ticket (number) imposed by selection. An asexual parent, then, buys 100 tickets, only to discover that all have the same number. A sexual parent may be able to afford fewer tickets, owing to the cost of males (Maynard Smith, 1978), but each will have a different number, increasing the possibility that at least one of them will win one of the lotteries.

Expanding on a graphic model developed by Emlen (1973), Williams (1975) saw this advantage of sex as resulting from the production of progeny with a broader probability distribution of fitness potential than would result via asexuality. Given this difference, sex would be favored if selection were intense enough that only those progeny with extremely high fitness (sisyphean) genomes would be likely to survive (Fig. 21A). Decreased selection intensities would decrease the advantage of sex, until asexuality regained its former favor (Fig. 21B). The necessity of extreme selection intensities led Williams (1975) to conclude that the model was limited to organisms producing enormous numbers of progeny which could meet the selective pressure. In the end he concluded that his models could explain sex in high fecundity ($> 10^7$ offspring/female/lifetime), and perhaps some medium fecundity (10^3 - 10^7 OFL) species, but they could not explain sex in low fecundity ($< 10^3$ OFL) organisms (including most of the vertebrates). Extending his gambling analogy, low fecundity organisms would not be expected to have a large enough stake (fecundity) to insure the production of sisyphean genotypes, and so for them sex appears to remain maladaptive (Williams, 1980).

In a formal, mathematical simulation of Williams's basic model, Maynard Smith (1976b; 1978) detected the predicted trend. Sex produced an advantage only when 30–40 individuals competed for a single patch, implying that the parents contributing competing

113

offspring to each patch produced many progeny. He also cautioned that his numerical results (lower than Williams's intuitive estimate) were possibly an artifact of the arbitrary conditions of his simulation (e.g., each patch consisted of 5 different selective features). More realistic conditions might increase the association between high fecundity and an advantage of sex, confirming Williams's conclusion that sex appeared to be maladaptive in the majority of low fecundity organisms.

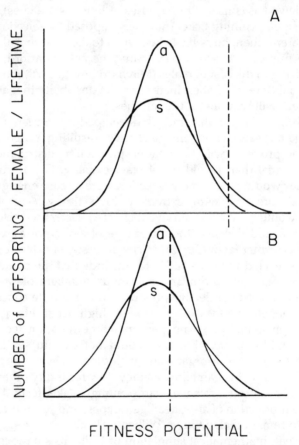

Fig. 21. The relationship between selection intensity (i) and the probability distribution of fitness potential associated with the progeny produced in a single female's lifetime via asexual (a), and sexual (s) reproduction. A. High selection intensity favors the more variable sexual progeny. B. Low selection intensity favors the less variable asexual progeny.

114

Maynard Smith (1978) went further, questioning the applicability of William's "sib competition" model to many high fecundity organisms. He based his critique on what he perceived was both a crucial assumption, and a crucial weakness of Williams's Elm-Oyster model, the necessity that sibs compete in environments, which differ from that of their parents. If offspring were dispersed randomly into a heterogeneous environment, one to a patch, there would be no sib competition and the advantage of sex would disappear. Extending the gambling metaphor, Maynard Smith (1978, p. 100) suggested that the comparison would be with an asexual parent buying 100 identically numbered lottery tickets, but entering them in 100 different lotteries (each with a different winning number) so that the asexual strategy is at no disadvantage. He concluded that the Elm-Oyster model is not as general an explanation as Williams had hoped, indeed was not likely to apply even to its illustrative organisms. The elm is problematic because most seeds fall very short distances from their parent, and therefore may face conditions similar to those faced by that parent, and the oyster because its dispersal is so vagrant that sibs are unlikely to compete in the same patches.

Williams (1975) offered yet another model, the cod-starfish hypothesis, which contained a kernel of the argument to answer Maynard Smith's objections (Williams explicitly noted that the cod-starfish model could apply to the elm and especially to the oyster), because it did not require sib competition for unitary patches in a heterogeneous environment. It does assume intense selection (and therefore applies primarily to high fecundity organisms), and that the primary advantage of sex results from increased variability in progeny with a resulting increase in the number of offspring blessed with sisyphean genomes (Fig. 21). The novel approach of this model was a switch from a coarse to a fine-grained environment. In addition, progeny were dispersed randomly throughout parental habitat, rather than as sib groups into discrete and variable patches. Sib competition still occurred, but the arena was no longer discrete subdivisions, but rather had expanded to the entire parental environment. Taken together the models imply that sex will have an advantage, regardless of the spatial structure of the environment, as long as selective conditions change over time, and if selection is intense enough to insure that *only* sisyphean genomes can expect success.

I have not presented most of the details or supporting evidence, which suggests that jointly, Williams's (1975) and Maynard Smith's (1978) models, along with those relying on similar logical structures (e.g., Taylor, 1979; Bulmer, 1980; Hartung, 1981), do provide reasonable explanations of the maintenance of sex in environments which vary in plausible ways. They appear to be generally applicable to species with sufficient excess fecundity to afford the sexual gamble. But the paradox is not resolved for low and medium fecundity organisms, which, at least theoretically, cannot afford the gamble. Williams's (1975, p. 102) answer for them was that sex is "a maladaptive feature . . . for which they lack the preadaptations for ridding themselves" (see also, Treisman, 1976; Williams, 1980). Maynard Smith's (1978) more "hopeful" conclusion was that the genetic, rather than the ecological, models offered the best hope for a general and universal (applying to low and high fecundity organisms alike) explanation for recombination (if not for syngamy).

Genetic models: linkage disequilibrium and the Hill-Robertson effect

Recombination produces all of its consequences, both good and bad, through a single mechanism of reducing linkage disequilibrium. By definition, disequilibrium exists if gamete genotype frequencies do not reflect independent assortment. In the simplest case of a two-locus haploid genome with 2 alleles at each locus (the argument can be generalized to the diploid multilocus case), there are 4 gamete genotypes (AB, Ab, aB, ab). If the frequency of these gametes (genotypes) are g_{AB}, g_{Ab}, g_{aB}, g_{ab}, then D, a coefficient of linkage disequilibrium (Lewontin and Kojima, 1960; Lewontin, 1974) can be calculated by comparing the frequencies of coupling (AB, ab) and replusion (Ab, aB) gametes by,

$$D = (g_{AB} \times g_{ab}) - (g_{Ab} \times g_{aB}) \qquad 7$$

If the loci are segregating independently (free recombination between them), and Hardy-Weinberg conditions apply, then the gamete frequencies will equal the crossproducts of their constituent allelic frequencies and the population will be in linkage equilibrium (D = 0). A population of gametes in disequilibrium will contain an excess of coupling (D > 0) or replusion (D < 0) gametes. Such a population, then, consists of gametes which carry, as a group, a *nonrandom* association of alleles, such that, for example, a gamete carrying A is more likely to carry B than b. Since the only genetic consequence of recombination is to reduce such disequilibria, (i.e., the disruption of nonrandom allele associations), any advantages or disadvantages of recombination must stem from this effect.

Viewed in this manner, the disadvantage of recombination is obvious. One of the primary forces expected to produce linkage disequilibrium is natural selection (for review, see Lewontin, 1974). Whenever selection favors an individual because it possesses harmoniously interacting (i.e., coadapted) alleles, then linkage disequilibrium is expected, because it will simultaneously reduce the frequency of less favored "random" associations. Selection generates the nonrandom state we call adaptation, recombination alters that state, producing a significant depression in fitness (recombinational load) relative to tighter linkage which would have permitted a combination to pass from parent to offspring unchanged.

To demonstrate a potential advantage for recombination, then, it is only necessary to demonstrate selectively disadvantageous linkage disequilibria which could profitably be reduced. Obviously, the conditions responsible for such disequilibria must be nonselective, making chance factors likely candidates. In a masterful synthetic review of the consequences of recombination, Felsenstein (1974; Felsenstein and Yokoyama, 1976) suggested that all the models claiming an advantage for recombination (and sex), from Fisher and Muller, through Maynard Smith and Williams, ultimately can be expressed in terms of the Hill-Robertson effect. Hill and Robertson (1966) discovered (via simulation) that randomly generated disequilibria coupled with linkage could limit a group's response to selection. They suggested that the decreased response resulted from linked alleles interfering with each other's selective increase and ultimately fixation. Given a randomly generated disequilibrium, recombination has two potential advantages. On average, it is expected to, (1) increase the probability of fixing newly favored alleles (composer effect), and (2) decrease the probability of fixing newly disfavored alleles (editor effect). The alleles in question can "originate" in two distinct ways. In a changed environment, the selective value of some alleles, currently segregating at equilibrium frequencies, will change sign. In any environment, alleles with novel selective values will originate in every generation via random mutation. Such mutations can be either favorable or unfavorable, but the latter is far more likely. Thus the raw materials are normally present. If chance factors do produce nonrandom associations including such novel alleles, then linkage will reduce the efficiency of selection in producing adaptive evolution. The question remains, are these composer and editor effects, either independently or jointly, significant enough factors to outweigh the disruptive effects of recombination?

A novel favorable mutation, or a previously deleterious allele favored by a recently changed environment, initially occurs at relatively low frequencies. In a finite population, they are unlikely to occur with all the alleles segregating at other loci, and so will not be in linkage equilibrium. At least part of the time such alleles are likely to originate in association with other *less* favored alleles. In such an association, they are less likely to increase in frequency and more likely to be lost as a result of drift, as the poor linkage relation interferes with positive selection on the novel allele (Hill-Robertson effect). The composer effect of recombination increases the probability that the newly favored allele will, sooner or later, become associated with the more successful genetic backgrounds available in the population. Complete linkage (or asexuality) limits *all* novel favorable alleles to their original associations. By shuffling the deck in every generation, recombination increases the likelihood that combinations of favorable alleles will get together. This argument applies whether the "population" in question is a local deme, or the population of progeny (sibs) produced by a single female. Therefore recombination's composer can be favored by both group and individual selection, as has been demonstrated by computer simulations (Felsenstein, 1974; Felsenstein and Yokoyama, 1976).

Maynard Smith and his colleagues (Strobeck et al., 1976; Maynard Smith, 1977; 1978) visualize the same process from a conceptually (but not mechanistically) different perspective. Emphasizing the utility of the concept of "gene" or "replicator selection" (Dawkins, 1976; 1978), they view a gene for recombination as primarily affecting its own replication rate, rather than its bearer's individual fitness. From this framework, the concept of "hitchhiking" (e.g., Maynard Smith and Haigh, 1974; Maynard Smith, 1978) becomes useful. An allele which increases recombination will be associated with novel favorable allele combinations at other loci more often than an alternative allele for lower recombination. Positive selection will act to directly increase the frequency of such favorable combinations which will, therefore, indirectly increase the frequency of the high recombination allele. The latter increases by hitching a ride with the favorable combinations it helps produce. Computer simulation (Strobeck et al., 1976) has indicated that such hitch-hiking would only be important if the locus for recombination was tightly linked to the loci at which favorable combinations were produced.

Whether viewed from the perspective of hitch-hiking, the Hill-Robertson effect, or even the original intuitive arguments (e.g., Fisher, 1930; Muller, 1932), it is obvious that for the composer effect to be of major and general significance in maintaining recombination, favorable mutants must occur at fairly high rates. Maynard Smith (1978) concluded that such limitations made it likely that the composer effect of recombination might be a sufficient explanation of why the genome does not congeal *completely*, but it was inadequate as an explanation of why recombination occurred at the levels actually observed in nature. The composer was, at best, a partial answer to the question why sex.

A second consequence of recombination which Felsenstein (1974) explored in detail was the decreased likelihood that a group would accumulate and fix newly disfavored alleles owing to an automatic editor associated with the composer. The editor effect was the obverse of the composer, and also operated by reducing randomly generated linkage disequilibria. Rather than increasing the efficiency with which selection could operate on favorable alleles and combinations, the editor increased selective efficiency against deleterious alleles and combinations. Muller (1964, p. 8) introduced the problem by pointing out that an asexual species "incorporates a kind of ratchet mechanism, such that it can never get to contain, in any of its lines, a load of mutations smaller than that already existing in its at present least-loaded lines." More importantly, he also noted that such least-loaded lines could "become more heavily loaded by mutation." Expanding on Muller's original argument, Felsenstein (1974) concluded that owing to the greater genomic frequency of deleterious (vs. favorable) mutations, recombination's editor effect was possibly of greater importance than the composer effect.

One can illustrate both the ratchet and the editor which functions to prevent the ratchet from operating by considering a population of individuals, each carrying a unique and newly arisen mutation. Any allelic combination which includes such a mutation will be in linkage disequilibrium with alternative genotypes generating the Hill-Robertson effect. At times, and by chance, even an otherwise most favored genome will contain a novel and deleterious mutant. Such a genome's positive selective value will interfere with the selective elimination of any deleterious mutants associated with it. If the individuals within such a population reproduced asexually, then the deleterious mutants would tend to accumulate in the group's gene pool (via the ratchet), so that succeeding generations of individuals will carry them in ever increasing numbers (Fig. 22A) at an ever increasing cost in fitness. On the other hand, if two of the novel mutants are actually favored (e.g., A and B in Fig. 22A) but arise in different individuals, they cannot be brought together into a single individual unless one recurs in an individual which carries the second from a previous ancestor. Asexuality's lack of a composer is entirely due to its inability to reduce linkage disequilibria between such favorable mutants. In this case, immediate fitness is not reduced, but a potential for increasing fitness is missed.

If the individuals in such a population reproduced sexually, recombination would reduce the linkage disequilibria associated with novel mutations, so that both the composer and the editor would be more (the ratchet less) likely to operate, thereby maximizing fitness potential. Depending on mutation rates (see below), recombination can produce offspring carrying fewer, more, or an equal number of mutations as each parent. If these are generally deleterious, sex can limit, or even reduce a group's mutational load, by reassorting independent parental mutations into a single "waste" gamete or individual (ii in Fig. 22B), which can, then, be eliminated by natural selection. Complementing this process, a second gamete or offspring (i in Fig. 22B) will be produced which will be selectively favored owing to its reduced mutational load (Muller, 1964). This editing process can continue, generation after generation, obviating the ratchet, and helping to maintain the lowest mutational load consistent with characteristic mutation rates and selection operating in the group.

If two favorable mutations (A and B, in Fig. 22B) have originated in two different individuals, then the "waste" gemete of the editor becomes the favored individual (ii in Fig. 22B). Under such conditions recombination will have brought novel favorable mutations together into an adaptive association. In any case, recombination does possess a potential advantage over asexuality, and its capacity

120

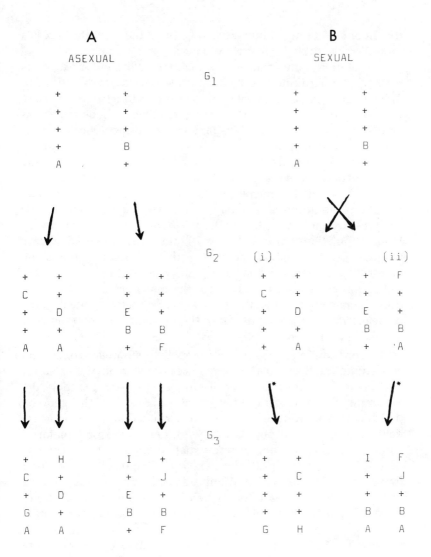

Fig. 22. A comparison of asexual and sexual reproduction illustrating, A., the ratchet effect of asexuality, and B., the editor (i) and composer (ii) effects of recombination. Each haploid genome is the product of replication (asexual) or recombination of replicated parental genomes (sexual), over three generations (G). Progeny produced in the third generation via sex are the product of interbreeding (*) between two individuals loaded with a single mutant (i.e., more than one zygote is present in each class of sexual progeny), while selection only permits one class (either i or ii) to survive and reproduce (for further details, see text).

to edit and compose simultaneously affirms the view that sex is a more flexible strategy than asexuality.

To explore the importance of sexuality's editor and asexuality's ratchet, Maynard Smith and Haigh (in Maynard Smith, 1978, Ch. 3) have initiated quantitative studies of the factors likely to control their operation. These included the rate of deleterious mutations arising in a genome per generation (U), the average selection coefficient against such mutations (s), and the size of the population. Their admittedly preliminary results indicated very roughly ("within an order of magnitude") that for progeny produced asexually, if $U/s \leqslant 1$, the ratchet would not operate (i.e., deleterious mutations would not accumulate so that recombination would be unnecessary), if $U/s \geqslant 10$, the ratchet would operate in all but very large populations, and if $U/s \geqslant 20$, the ratchet would always operate. Similar analyses suggested that for sexual groups the editor would operate as long as roughly $U < 1$ (though increasing individual fecundity would increase the threshold U needed to induce the ratchet), but that this would only be useful if "the majority of deleterious mutations are only slightly deleterious" (s is very small, Maynard Smith, 1978, p. 36).

Maynard Smith's (1978, p. 36) compelling summary conclusion concerning the theoretical consequences of recombination's editor effect was, ". . . for a given error rate per site per replication, the maximum amount of essential genetic material in the genome which can be reproduced without steady deterioration is substantially greater for a population with genetic recombination." Although this is couched in terms that could be misconstrued as group benefit, and has been explicitly simulated in such a framework (Felsenstein, 1974), the advantage also applies to a female which produces a "population" of progeny in her lifetime, since her individual success is measured by comparing her population of progeny with those produced by others. A female which reproduces sexually, then, benefits by producing *some* offspring with a reduced load of deleterious mutations when compared to the load carried by *all* the offspring produced by her asexual competitor.

Though limited, there is empirical support for the hypothesis that asexuality can incorporate a ratchet, resulting in an asexual group's steady accumulation of harmful mutations and an associated reduction in fitness. The most extensive studies have involved heterogonic species which normally alternate sexual and

122

asexual generations. When such a species is experimentally prevented from engaging in sexual reproduction (e.g., conjugation in protozoa, syngamy and recombination in arthropods) a gradual, and then accelerating decline in vigor, fertility, or some other fitness component usually accompanies the forced asexuality (for reviews, see Geddes and Thompson, 1914; Wright, 1977, Ch. 5). The end result was often the extinction of entire asexual stocks (reproducing exclusively by fission or parthenogenesis). This characteristic pattern of declining vigor associated with ultimate extinction led Wright (1977, p. 147) to conclude that as an explanation of the observed decline, "that of gradual accumulations of unfavorable mutational effects seems preferable in the case of decline under parthenogenesis." In the only comparable study of a vertebrate, Leslie and Vrijenhoek (1978; 1980) presented indirect evidence based on genetic comparison of clones of the obligate parthenogenetic fish, *Poeciliopsis monacha-lucida*, "suggesting that deleterious genes may accumulate in genomes sheltered from recombination."

Though far from conclusive, the combined weight of the theoretical considerations and the data supporting them, suggests that the ratchet may be the most harmful consequence of asexuality. This implies that the editor may be the most important beneficial effect of sex and recombination. If true, the often mentioned association between obligate asexuality and higher risks of extinction (e.g., Stebbins, 1950; 1971; Dobzhansky, 1970; Stanley, 1975; Maynard Smith, 1978) may not result from asexuality's lack of genetic flexibility or evolutionary potential. Rather, given a sufficient mutation rate an asexual group may court extinction because it is actually unable to *prevent* evolutionary change, as its ratchet steadily accumulates deleterious mutations and reduces the group's level of adaptation.

Together, then, the ecological and genetic models of the evolution and maintenance of sexual reproduction have clearly succeeded in outlining the problem. Just as clearly, all of their partial and potential answers to the question, Why sex?, whether considered singly or in concert, have failed to explain sex in *all* of its manifestations (see also, Williams, 1975; 1980; Maynard Smith, 1978). While many (myself included) consider Williams's sibling competition and progeny diversification models reasonable explanations of the maintenance of sex, they can only apply to relatively high fecundity organisms (> 10,000 offspring per lifetime) which can afford the gamble of sex. For most low fecundity organisms, including the *Drosophila* flies and vertebrates studied most extensively by biologists, the occurrence of sexual reproduction remains a puzzling anomaly.

Inbreeding and Sex: A Resolution?

Until very recently (e.g., Maynard Smith, 1978; Shields, 1979; 1982b; Charlesworth, 1980a; Williams, 1980), discussions of the problem of sex either implicitly or explicitly equated sex with biparental outbreeding (random mating in large, $N_e > 10,000$ populations). Current representations of the cost of syngamy, whether measured in males produced or as a genetic cost of meiosis, are presented in a calculus which obviously relies on an assumption of perfect outbreeding (Ch. 3). Only if mates have zero alleles identical by descent would the cost of meiosis equal 50%. Most of the theoretical treatments of recombination have also assumed large, random mating (= outbreeding) populations. For whatever reasons, the relativity of relatedness, the continuous nature of inbreeding, the operation of inbreeding via either nonrandom assortative mating *or* random mating in limited populations, and the absolute impossibility of perfect outbreeding (Ch. 3), have failed to enter discussions of sex except in the most rudimentary fashion. Exploration of the consequences of sex, both beneficial and detrimental, in a framework which explicitly includes inbreeding and outbreeding as alternative modes of sexual reproduction, may generate novel conclusions (also, see Charlesworth, 1980a and b).

Cost of syngamy

In a perfectly outbreeding species, the cost of meiosis will be a 50% loss in genetic representation in offspring which are shared with an *unrelated* mate. In terms of inclusive fitness and kin selection, it is obviously better to invest parental resources in progeny that are closer ($r = 1.0$, asexual) than more disant ($r = 0.5$, outbreeding) relatives. But as Williams (1980) has also noted, asexuality is not the only mechanism which will increase r between a parent and its offspring. Since relatedness is an increasing function of the level of inbreeding (Eq. 2, Ch. 3), increasing the relatedness of parents will also increase relatedness between parents and their offspring. Obviously self-fertilizing organisms do not share off-spring (parent-offspring r $\simeq$ 1.0). Less obvious perhaps, but none-theless true, any level of fairly continuous inbreeding, whether nonrandom (e.g., full-sib mating) or random (N_e < 1000), will increase r, and given sufficient time is expected to produce the r = 1.0 characteristic of asexuality (for a quantitative treatment, see Ch. 8). In a regularly inbreeding species, there may be little or no genetic cost of meiosis, and any level of inbreeding will reduce any such cost below that expected in outbreeders. If, in the earlier example of a cross-fertilizing hermaphrodite, mates were related (e.g., siblings with an $r \simeq$ 0.5), then progeny would be more closely related to their parents (r = 0.75 vs 0.5 with outbreeding). This would yield a parent 6.75 offspring equivalent vs. the 4.5 associated with wider outbreeding, and the genetic cost of sex would have been reduced considerably. As inbreeding intensity in-creased, the cost of meiosis would be expected to decrease, finally disappearing with continuous self-fertilization.

Recently, Dawkins (1979) has criticized this view as a fundamen-tal misunderstanding of kin selection. For argument, he assumes that a species is monogamous, and that a female has a choice of outbreeding (producing a progeny with an r = 0.5), or mating with her brother (producing a "super-child" with an r = 0.75). The er-ror, he suggests, is failing to consider brother's reproductive suc-cess independent of sister. If both outbred, brother would produce a nephew or niece with an r = 0.25 for her, that when added to her own progeny (r = 0.5) would yield genetic representation equal to the single progeny of incest. Dawkins (1979; also see Bengsston, 1978) did note that the proposed advantage of inbreeding, of bring-ing "extra close relatives into the world," would apply to many polygynous species where incestuous matings would not deprive "brother" of opportunity for mating elsewhere.

Hidden in his critique is the assumption that the gene is the only replicator and primary unit of selection. Dawkins (1979) does sug-gest that the argument can be rephrased to "genes for inbreeding are propagated at the expense of genes for outbreeding, having a greater probability of getting into each child born." To a gene, it is irrelevant whether its transmission probability is 0.75 in one relative or 0.5 + 0.25 in two. But the applicability of the criticism relies entirely on the gene selection view.

Consider the same situation, but make the perhaps more realistic assumption that the trait in question (e.g., sex) requires substitution at 2 independent loci (i.e., asex is $A_1A_1B_1B_1$ while sex is $A_2\_B_2\_$) and the conclusion will change. The probability of such a genetically complex trait being transmitted will be the probability that both alleles (A_2 and B_2) will be found together in at least *one* of the progeny produced. For the inbreeding pair, the probability that the trait will be transmitted would be 0.75 (i.e., 12/16 of progeny of siblings carrying the pair would also carry the pair). For outbreeding siblings, however, this probability falls to 0.50, as male and female each would have a 0.25 transmission probability for the pair (4/16 of each sib's progeny). As the genetic basis for any trait becomes more complex, with substitutions at more loci controlling phenotypic differences, the disparity in the genetic cost of meiosis between inbreeding and outbreeding, and therefore inbreeding's relative advantage, would become more pronounced.

Regardless of the relation between the genetic cost of meiosis and the ecological cost of producing males, will inbreeding affect the problem of investment in male function? Both Maynard Smith (1978) and Williams (1975; 1980) suggest that inbreeding sex will still entail an ecological cost if parents expend equal resources on male and female function. If males function *solely* in the fertilization of females, and if conditions are such that inbreeding will occur, then only sufficient sons should be produced to insure that all of a female's daughters will be fertilized. Since, in many cases, a single son will be sufficient to inseminate all his sisters, an overproduction of males can lead to wasteful "local mate competition" (Hamilton, 1967; Alexander and Sherman, 1977), with closely related males competing among themselves for mating rights. Females which reduce such wasteful competition by biasing the primary sex ratio of their progeny in favor of more productive females are expected to be more successful. The female-biased sex ratios observed in many inbred or incestuous arthropods (especially *Hymenoptera*, for reviews, see Hamilton, 1967; 1972; Alexander and Sherman, 1977), and the decreasing male investment (measured by a pollen/ovule ratio) associated with increasing inbreeding intensities in hermaphroditic plants (Cruden, 1977), are both consistent with a view that inbreeding, coupled with sex-ratio adjustments, can, and in a variety of organisms, has reduced or eliminated the ecological cost of syngamy. Thus, inbreeding sex may entail substantial reductions in *both* the genetic and ecological costs of meiosis.

Inbreeding and Equal Sex Ratios

Williams (1980, p. 374) has stated that even in inbred groups, if parents "continued to spend resources equally on the production of sons and daughters, they would be equally (as compared to out-breeders) wasteful of resources" (see also, Maynard Smith, 1978). The consensus his statement represents is that inbreeding *per se* generates female-biased sex ratios, and that the combination of inbreeding and female-biased sex ratios is a necessary condition for reducing the ecological costs of sex. Williams (1980) also concluded that since most vertebrates do not show biased sex ratios, they are not inbreeding and must be suffering the full cost of meiosis. If inbreeding is not the direct cause of unequal sex ratios, then an equal sex ratio would not necessarily imply that a particular organism is outbreeding.

I (Shields, 1979, 1982b) have suggested that if males function solely to fertilize females, and inbreeding is assured, then reduced investment in male function should, and apparently does, follow. If males have additional roles, beyond sperm donation, or parents cannot be sure that close inbreeding will occur, then equal investment may be the rule regardless of average inbreeding intensity. For example, there is a consensus (e.g., Williams, 1975; 1980; Maynard Smith, 1978) that if an organism mates monogamously, and males behave parentally (e.g., most birds), equal investment will be the rule regardless of the mating system.

What is apparently overlooked in such discussion is that parenting is only one of the potential roles a male may fill in order to insure successful reproduction. Regardless of the mating system or male parental disposition, if males compete among themselves for the control of resources necessary to raise offspring (e.g., nest sites, food, predator or weather refuges including hibernacula; for review, see Emlen and Oring, 1974), then equal investment could be favored even in polygynous systems and in the absence of paternal care. Since females in such systems are likely to be incapable of defending resources against the often larger and more aggressive males, the latter would be necessary for successful reproduction. This means that male investment would not necessarily be wasteful in a variety of mating systems.

A crucial factor in determining whether male investment will be wasteful, and therefore whether there will be an ecological cost of sex, might not be the presence or absence of paternal care, but the occurrence of any form of paternal investment whether directed at obtaining mates or parenting. Adaptive sex ratios may actually be determined by the degree of intrasexual competition for reproductive resources (including members of the opposite sex) combined with the patterns of competitor relatedness characterizing a particular organism. For example, if dispersal were extremely limited, by choice or low mobility, then the high relatedness of neighboring males would result in inbreeding (Ch. 2) and in wasteful local mate competition (Hamilton, 1967; 1972). In such circumstances, it could pay to reduce male investment resulting in a female-biased sex ratio. Indeed, many of the parasitic hymenopterans parasitize hosts singly (for review, see Hamilton, 1967), while some mites actually mate within their mother's body (e.g., Elbadry and Tawfik, 1966). Either behavior almost guarantees full-sib incest and therefore limits potential male competition for mates to full siblings. It is such species that do show the expected female bias in primary sex ratios (e.g., 1:6 to 1:9 in the *Adactylidium* spp. mite, Elbadry and Tawfik, 1966).

A question remains as to whether it is the inbreeding *per se* or the sib competition that favors the biased sex ratios. One school has emphasized the importance of inbreeding (e.g., Hamilton, 1967; Williams, 1980; and especially Maynard Smith, 1978) and predicts that female-biased sex ratios will *always* be associated with inbreeding. I (Shields, 1979) have suggested that the occurrence of less related males competing with sons for daughters might force a female to produce more sons than predicted by the average level of inbreeding, in order to compete successfully and insure inbreeding. I concluded that inbreeding could, but not necessarily would, contribute to and be associated with biased sex ratios.

More recently, Taylor and Bulmer (1980), using various mathematical analyses and simulations, demonstrated more rigorously that sib competition was more important than inbreeding in controlling adaptive sex ratios. They suggested that whenever competition among sibs (or other close kin) of *one* sex was more intense than among members of the other sex, the sex ratio should be biased away from the high competition sex. Symmetrically, they showed that even if competition were intense among same-sex kin, if the competition were of equal intensity in both sexes (e.g., in a finite, random mating, and completely inbred deme), the favored sex ratio would be one-to-one. Taylor (1981) concluded that, "Sib-mating (or selfing in hermaphrodites) or more generally mating between relatives, often contributes to these factors, but the inbreeding which results, in itself, has no role in determining sex ratio."

The ecological cost of males, then, may be overrated as a problem in explaining the adaptive value of sex. For the many organisms in which some form of male investment is required for successful reproduction, potential costs should be small or nonexistent. In organisms with minimal paternal investment, the costs will apply, but given the appropriate population structure (e.g., Taylor and Bulmer, 1980; Taylor, 1981), costs can be reduced by adjusting the ratio of investment in different sex offspring. Inbreeding *will* reduce the genetic costs of syngamy by increasing the relatedness of parents and their offspring, and may, but need not, be associated with documented biases in primary sex ratios. In the latter case, the association is not likely to be directly causal.

Recombinational load

In a sexual population, recombination will generate a potential genetic load by breaking up associations of harmoniously interacting alleles from different loci. By reducing the nonrandom genotypic disequilibria generated by selection, recombination may show a fitness depression relative to a more perfect asexual replication. The degree of potential recombinational load is expected to vary with inbreeding intensity (Shields, 1982b). Theoretical analyses and computer simulations of relatively intense or extreme inbreeding (e.g., Jain and Allard, 1966; Weir and Cockerham, 1973; Nei and Li, 1973; Li and Nei, 1974; Charlesworth, 1976; Charlesworth et al., 1977), as well as empirical study of animals (e.g., Allard and Wehrhahn, 1964) and especially plants (e.g., Allard et al., 1968; Weir et al., 1972; Hamrick and Allard, 1972; Schaal, 1975; Jain, 1976), all indicate that both random and nonrandom inbreeding can increase allelic correlations across loci, whether the loci are linked or not, and in the presence or absence of epistatic selection (for general review, see Allard, 1975). In the end, a major consequence of relatively intense inbreeding (and perhaps a primary function?) can be viewed as, "organizing the entire populational genotype into a sort of giant supergene . . . to increase the frequency in the population of genotypes which confers [sic] high fitness and hence to increase adaptation to the local environment" (Allard, 1975, p. 124).

For example, in an inbred group fixed at each of two interacting loci (e.g., both parents AABB), recombination can *never* disrupt the allelic associations at those loci. The problem becomes more complex in the more realistic case when a population is segregating at some, or even many, loci, and individual heterozygosity is being selectively maintained. If the favored genotypes at interacting loci are heterozygotes (e.g., both parents AaBb), intense inbreeding will increase the probability that A and a will be associated *only* with B and b, an association that has already proven itself in successful ancestors. Inbreeding, then, in combination with natural selection, would be capable of increasing the likelihood of producing favored AaBb genomes.

In contrast, wider outbreeding increases the field of allelic variability ($A_1A_2B_1B_2$ x $A_3A_4B_3B_4$) permitting a wider variety of progeny genomes. In some, or all, of these, allele combinations will be produced that have never been found in successful ancestors, and so have a lower probability of interacting well, and a greater probability of generating a significant recombinational load.

What has been described here as recombinational load is a major component of outbreeding depression (Ch. 5). Sex, whether inbreeding or outbreeding, will produce a recombinational load in segregating populations. By limiting potential mates to close relatives, inbreeding can minimize the maladaptive consequences of recombination. This would occur because the probability that alleles which are brought together in offspring have proven their compatibility in a successful ancestor increases with inbreeding intensity. At a multilocus level, inbreeding tends to preserve successful and coadapted genomes, with the degree of preservation positively correlated with the continuity and intensity of inbreeding. "By contrast, an outbreeder is ill-equipped by virtue of its mating system to perpetuate specific genotypes adapted to specific niches" (Allard, 1975, p. 124).

The same point can be made phenotypically. Williams's (1975) and Emlen's (1973) suggestion that sex functioned to increase the variance of the probability distribution of a single female's progeny's fitness potential (Fig. 21) assumes that sex is equivalent to wide outbreeding. Continuous inbreeding tends to mimic the theoretical effects of asexuality by producing a family of progeny with a narrower distribution of fitness potential (Fig. 12, Ch. 3). As the intensity of inbreeding increases, the genotypic (and presumably phenotypic) resemblance between parent and offspring is expected to increase. Should environmental factors interact with a species' biological properties to induce low selection intensities (e.g., Fig. 21B), then inbreeding might be favored over outbreeding, and for the same reasons as asexuality.

Inbreeding, then, will ameliorate, and can eliminate, all of the disadvantages of sexual reproduction. If it is continuous and intense enough, it will reduce, and can eliminate, the genetic cost of meiosis, and if there is one, the ecological cost of producing males as well as reduce the degree of recombinational load. With a single exception it can do everything that asexual reproduction does. If fitness potential and adaptation depend in any measure on any form of heterotic selection, then sex, whether inbreeding or outbreeding, will entail a segregational load. Segregation implies that any heterozygous locus will invariably produce progeny which are homozygous for its constituent alleles. Since such homozygous segregants are defined as less fit than their heterozygous parents, sex entails a fitness depression owing to their production (Wallace, 1968b; 1970; Dobzhansky, 1970; Crow and Kimura, 1970). Given inbreeding's genotypic consequence of reducing zygotic heterozygosity (Ch. 3), segregational load may be greater for an inbreeder than an outbreeder. This is one of the theoretical components of inbreeding depression. As it is, only asexual reproduction is capable of transmitting diploid heterozygous genomes without a segregational load. Given this, and the fact that asexuality appears to do everything that inbreeding does, only more efficiently, the question remains, Why would asexuality not replace sex, even if the latter were inbreeding? If we equate sex and inbreeding for the sake of argument, then we are no longer limited to discussions of sex's traditional function of generating variable progeny in changed or changing environments. Since the traditional argument necessarily assumed outbreeding, the question evolves to: Is there a potential function of sex, compatible with the consequences of inbreeding, that predicts the occurrence of sex in place of asexuality in any appropriate organism or environments?

Inbreeding Versus Asexuality: A Question of Fidelity

Traditionally, and with little disagreement (e.g., Mather, 1973; Williams, 1975; Maynard Smith, 1978), the major advantage of asexual reproduction has been considered its copying fidelity. In one form or another, individual, kin, or group selection was viewed as favoring a balance between the enhancement of immediate fitness (via asexuality), and the flexibility required to meet future environmental flux through genetic change (via sexuality). Given a set of information (a DNA blueprint) that has controlled the development and activity of an individual that has met the environmental challenge by surviving and reproducing more successfully than individuals with alternative blueprints, what is an appropriate strategy for maintaining that adaptive success in that individual's descendants? In stable and uniform environments, a reproductive mechanism that permitted precise duplication of such a successful blueprint should be favored. Previous workers (e.g., Stebbins, 1950; Williams, 1975; Maynard Smith, 1978) have suggested that this is precisely the consequence and one of the benefits of asexual reproduction. The logic of their arguments led to a necessary reliance on an assumption that sex (= outbreeding) must be associated with environments which varied in ways that prevented successful genomes in one generation from being successful in the next. Without that assumption, it followed that many organisms would be reproducing asexually, a conclusion at odds with much of the evidence (Williams, 1975; 1978; Maynard Smith, 1978).

If, for the moment, we assume that there are a broad range of environments and associated conditions that would favor precise replication of successful parental genomes (e.g., uniform and stable environments), then the usual inference would be that organisms in such environments *should* be asexual. Yet for a variety of situations such a conclusion would be wrong. That it remains a consensus can perhaps be attributed to a failure to consider the reproductive consequences of mutation, and a usually hidden, and perhaps blinding, assumption that sex is synonymous with outbreeding.

Sex versus asexuality

Reproduction can be divided into two component processes, (1) replication of parental DNA, and (2) fusion and transmission of replicated DNA during progeny production. Whether asexual or sexual, reproduction's components of replication and production are usually spatially and temporally independent. For a wide variety

of organisms, mutation might be an *inevitable* biochemical consequence of replication (Ch. 5). For such organisms, replication itself
could never transmit *successful* parental genomes with perfect
precision. Asexuality would endow offspring with *perfect copies*,
but of *imperfectly replicated* parental genomes, and so would not
transmit the sucessful genome, but one altered by an unspecified
number of novel mutations. In the face of significant mutation
pressure, asexuality would be incapable of transmitting parental
genomes with perfect fidelity. Asexuality's ratchet would cause the
assimilation of such mutations in every generation (given a sufficient mutation rate), making the production of progeny genetically
identical to their parents impossible. Because of the ratchet, the
process might also be cumulative, so that any difference between
an initially successful ancestor and a particular set of its lineal
descendants, would increase with each bout of reproduction
separating them (Fig. 22). Ever equitable, asexuality would
distribute this parental *mutational* load into *all* of an individual's
progeny, with each offspring suffering, on average, equivalent
fitness reductions.

With respect to recent mutation, sex should be capable of greater
fidelity in transmitting successful parental genomes. Recombination is expected to edit parental mutations into waste gametes or
progeny (Fig. 22B, ii). Simultaneously, some progeny would be
produced that in the extreme would resemble their parents at all
but their own newly mutated loci (Fig. 22B, i). This conservative
aspect of sex should theoretically apply regardless of the relatedness of mates (Felsenstein and Yokoyama, 1976; Bernstein, 1977;
Shields, 1979; 1982b; Bremermann, 1979a; Bernstein et al., 1981).

Recently, however, Heller and Maynard Smith (1979) have
argued that selfing, and by implication lesser levels of inbreeding,
may suffer a ratchet similar to asexuality's ratchet. Their argument,
while valid, is questionable in this context, because it depends on a
special condition. In their analysis, selfing suffers a ratchet, if and
only if, the deleterious mutations in question are *fixed* in
homozygous condition in a finite diploid population. They suggest
that the ratchet operates, ". . . because an individual homozygous
for i mutations cannot, by selfing, produce offspring homozygous
for fewer mutations" (Heller and Maynard Smith, 1979, p. 290).
Because of the small population size associated with selfing
($N_e = 1$), such conditions may occur with some frequency in selfers.
Yet the ratchet will also operate in any size population, regardless

of inbreeding intensity, as long as the loci in question are fixed in the entire population.

While their models are interesting, they may be less relevant to a comparison of sex and asexuality. I have (Shields, 1979), and am here, arguing that sex can edit deleterious parental mutations *immediately* after their origin. In contrast, given a sufficient mutation rate asexuality is powerless. For example, if one mutation can be expected to arise in *every* individual in *every* generation, then each of those mutations will be transmitted to *all* its progeny, which will also have their own personal mutations. In the absence of recombination, selection cannot effectively eliminate such mutations except by extinguishing the *entire* line. If each mutation is somewhat deleterious whether alone in haploid species, or in heterozygous condition in diploids, then sex will have an immediate benefit (for similar arguments and conclusions, see Bernstein, 1977; Bremermann, 1979a; Bernstein et al., 1981; Moore and Hines, 1981).

Since novel mutations are almost invariably going to be present in parents as members of heterozygous loci, recombination will edit, regardless of inbreeding intensity. In Heller and Maynard Smith's words, (1979, p. 289) even in selfers, "no ratchet operates on the heterozygous loci, because by selfing a heterozygote can give rise to a normal homozygote." I would add that if an ancestral locus were normally heterozygous (e.g., A_1A_2), then a selfer newly loaded at that locus (e.g., A_1A_4) could not transmit the ancestral heterozygote. Selfing would still maintain the perhaps more important interlocus associations (A_1 with rest of the genome). However, relatively intense breeding, coupled with cross-fertilization, would permit maximum editing efficiency and maintenance of interlocus associations. If mates are close kin, but members of different nuclear families (i.e., possess no common parents), then the parental mutations each carries will have arisen independently. The likelihood of two independent mutations at the same locus in two parents is low, so parental heterozygotes are more likely to be reconstituted while editing parental mutations when mates are drawn from different nuclear families.

This reduced fidelity may be at least part of the reason for the relative rarity of selfing and other forms of extreme incest in nature. Based solely on genetic considerations, editing is more efficient and less wasteful when mates are close but nonfamily kin (e.g., first cousins, Shields, 1982b). Similar considerations may explain the relative rarity of automictic forms that result in complete homozygosity (e.g., embryonic doubling, or premeiotic doubling and fusion of sister chromatids) that cannot transmit adaptive heterozygotes at all. The other forms of automixis (e.g., fusion of primary pronuclei, or secondary nonsister chromatids) at best mimic the effects of selfing (i.e., some recombination potential with significant segregational loads; for review, see White, 1978a, p. 288).

Sex will obviate the ratchet, minimizing mutational loads, while asexuality is incapable of doing the same in the face of significant, but not unrealistic, mutation pressure (Bernstein, 1977; Bernstein et al., 1981). With respect to the variation potentially generated by mutation, sex can reproduce successful parental genomes more faithfully than asexuality. This will be as true of extreme inbreeding as it is of any level of outbreeding. The hypothesis that sexual reproduction in the form of inbreeding may serve to preserve adaptation by increasing the resemblance of progeny and their parents is consistent with the "reasonably well-established" generalization "that the frequency of recombination tends to be higher in selfing or inbreeding species or varieties than in related outbreeding ones" (Maynard Smith, 1978, p. 120; see also Stebbins, 1950; Darlington, 1958; Grant, 1958; Charlesworth et al., 1977). Given the obvious terminological differences, perhaps the true association is between increased inbreeding intensity and increased levels of recombination (usually estimated by recombination indices = number of chromosomes + number of chiasmata per genome; see Darlington, 1958). As the continuity and intensity of inbreeding increase, reaching a maximum at obligate selfing, the field of allelic variability available for recombination is expected to decrease. This could reduce to nil the probability of disrupting extant coadapted allele complexes. At the same time, mutation will continue unabated, so that increasing recombination, by increasing crossover opportunities, will increase the efficiency of both editor and composer with *wholly* beneficial consequences. If, on the other hand, inbreeding intensity were reduced, then the probability of disrupting coadapted complexes would increase, unless the level of recombination also declined. The observed correlation, then, is compatible with a primary function of inbreeding of preserving that which has proven itself.

Inbreeding versus outbreeding

Wide outbreeding is even more likely to produce progeny with genomes significantly different from their successful ancestors than is asexuality. Though the editor would operate, minimizing mutational change, the genetic differences between mates would generate a diversified progeny. Few or none would be expected to closely resemble either of their parents (Ch. 5). The cost of such diversification would be a significant recombinational load (outbreeding depression), which would outweigh any benefits gained through the editor.

For example, if the ancestral and coadapted portion of an individual's genome were indicated by pluses (e.g., Fig. 22), then outbreeding would entail mating (+) individuals with others carrying alleles from different complexes (e.g., minuses, so + − + − + a, Fig. 22). Parental mutations could be edited, but the resulting progeny would carry potentially maladapted mixtures of pluses and minuses, never before associated in a successful individual. To continue the blueprint analogy, outbreeding would be like taking two *different* blueprints, for two different structures, cutting them into pieces and reassorting them into entirely novel combinations. While the new structures might function, they would not be likely to resemble the originals in any but a cursory way.

If conditions existed that favored relatively precise transmission of parental genomes, then inbreeding could be favored over both asexuality and outbreeding. Inbreeding's favor would stem from its versatility, as it reduced (or eliminated) the disadvantages associated with both asexuality and outbreeding, and managed to gain their respective benefits. By reducing the field of allelic variability available for recombination, it would reduce or prevent the disruption of coadapted genomes. By reducing effective population size and reducing the number of different individuals in a deme's ancestry (Ch. 3), inbreeding would produce a *family* of genetically homogeneous (and not necesarily homozygous, Ch. 4) individuals. The homogeneity would only become apparent upon inspection of the large ancestral genome (all loci except those with recent mutations), at which *all* deme members are expected to carry similar arrays of previously associated alleles. For this ancestral genome, that which recombination broke apart, syngamy would reunite, since true novelties would be unavailable. Of course, if there were segregating loci in such a deme, even intense inbreeding would entail some diversification of progeny. By limiting the field of recombination, inbreeding cannot produce *exact* duplicates of parental genomes, but it will reduce the number of expected differences and the probability that such differences will entail *untried* associations of alleles likely to produce outbreeding depression. Inbreeding would not be expected to produce perfect reproductive fidelity, but it will do a more efficient job than outbreeding which, by definition, is a diversifying influence.

In the same inbreeding population, recombination would act to reduce the detrimental gametic disequilibria generated by the occurrence and transmission of rare deleterious mutations. The editor increases the potential efficiency of selection against such mutations with immediate benefit. Since most mutations are likely to be deleterious (Fisher, 1930), the effect of the editor may be a primary function of recombination, especially when it is associated with mating of relatively close kin (also see, Daugherty, 1955; Felsenstein, 1974; Manning, 1976b; Bernstein, 1977; Bremermann, 1979a; Bernstein et al., 1981).

As an added bonus, and perhaps a secondary function, inbreeding sex also facilitates composition of novel but favorable allele combinations with greater frequency than asexuality, just as the Fisher-Muller school has long maintained. In contrast to outbreeding, the limited field of alternative alleles in potential mates associated with inbreeding makes it less likely that, ". . . a successful combination of characteristics is attained in individuals only to be broken up in the next generation by the mechanism of meiosis itself" (Wright, 1931). In the end, fusion of related gametes, themselves the product of recombination of the previous generation's chromosomes, is a flexible, and yet a conservative process, "affording an opportunity for new departures and in tending to secure a holding fast of that which is good" (Geddes and Thompson, 1914; see also Grant, 1958; 1963; 1971).

The relative costs postulated to be associated with the alternative reproductive strategies (Table 9) suggest that if the mutational load of asexuality is greater than the combined segregational and recombinational load of sex, then sex can be favored by individual selection for its immediate benefits. Similarly, if inbreeding's greater segregational load is more than balanced by a reduced recombinational load relative to a specific level of outbreeding, then inbreeding will be favored. As with any system with costs and benefits, then, different conditions may favor different choices and different optimal levels of inbreeding or outbreeding in different species (for review, Shields, 1982a and see Ch. 7).

That sexual reproduction may act to preserve adaptation, at least if mates are relatively close kin, is consistent with Crow's (1966) in-

Table 9. The relative values of the genetic costs hypothetically associated with alternative reproductive strategies.

Potential Costs	Reproductive Strategy		
	Outbreeding	Inbreeding	Asexuality
Cost of meiosis	high	low	none
Cost of males	high or none	low or none	none
Recombinational load	high	low	none
Segregational load	low	high	none
Mutational load	low	low	high

tuitive, and I believe correct, view that "the bulk of selection is concerned with maintaining conditions as they are." Williams (1966, p. 54) expressed the same view more forcefully, "I regard it as unfortunate that the theory of natural selection was first developed as an explanation for evolutionary change. It is much more important as an explanation for the maintenance of adaptation." If the arguments developed here are true, they may help to resolve the paradox of sex. Inbreeding can have immediate positive effects on *individual* reproductive success relative to alternative mating strategies (outbreeding and asexuality). If conditions exist whereby inbreeding's segregational load is less than outbreeding's recombinational load and asexuality's mutational load, then inbreeding sex could have originated and be maintained in a variety of organisms as a result of individual selection. If true, it may no longer be necessary to invoke future needs or goals, species benefit, or an inability to evolve a more adaptive asexuality to explain the ubiquity of sex.

CHAPTER 7

The Who and How of Inbreeding: Predictions and Evidence

If inbreeding does function primarily to preserve successful genomes during reproduction, more specific predictions concerning who should inbreed are possible. Inbreeders should occur in environments in which successful parental genomes have a high probability of being successful in subsequent generations. Extending Williams's (1975) gambling analogy once more, if winning lottery numbers (i.e., well-adapted, high-fitness genomes) remain relatively constant from generation to generation, rather than changing haphazardly, then it will benefit a current winner to bequeath to its progeny tickets with numbers as similar to its own as possible. What have been called uniform, constant, or stable environments would be expected to favor inbreeding. Characterized by improbable spatial homogeneity and temporal stability, such environments are expected to be rare. However, these only generate sufficient and not necessary conditions for inducing or maintaining inbreeding's favor.

Overlooked in the search for changing environments that might favor progressive (i.e., sexual) reproduction was the selective relevance of the stability or constancy of the association between particular genomes and particular environments. Adaptation to ecological conditions need not be limited to allelic substitution in response to every environmental fluctuation. One common alternative appears to be the *fixation* of complex epigenetic systems that adaptively respond to environmental flux phenotypically rather than genetically. Characters like developmental and genetic homeostasis, switch genes controlling phenotypic expression in heterogeneous environments, canalization, and experiential modification of behavior (learning), all permit and promote development of favored phenotypes in the face of considerable environmental perturbation (for review of genetic "buffering," see Lerner, 1954; Waddington, 1957; Wright, 1977; for review of learning, see Mason, 1978; Pulliam and Dunford, 1980).

The distribution of adaptive epigenetic systems suggests a possible phylogenetic trend, with the higher complexity that results in genetic independence of ecological (both biotic and abiotic) change being associated with a more advanced state (e.g., vertebrates). An ideal example of a complex adaptive system might be the vertebrate immune response. If a host genetic response were required to deal with every change in potential pathogens, most vertebrates would have lost the war to their parasites long ago. Owing to their short generation times, and large population sizes, the average bacteria or virus is constantly generating genetic novelty. Because of their longer generations and much lower fecundity, the average verebrate host could not possibly respond with genetic changes in the germ plasm to every novel pathogen. Such a race would be expected to go to the reproductively swifter pathogen (Bremermann, 1980). Given this challenge, the favored strategy appears to have been the evolution of a complex and phenotypically plastic immune system.

In protecting organisms against pathogens, the vertebrate immune system performs two separate functions: (1) a general capacity to discriminate self from nonself, and (2) a capacity for recognizing, matching, and mobilizing an attack on specific pathogens (for reviews, see Jerne, 1974; Burnet, 1975; Bremermann, 1979b; 1980; Till, 1981). Variation, either genetic, phenotypic, or both is required for the efficient operation of either function. Since the patterns and kinds of variation characterizing each function differ, as do the proximate mechanisms generating it, it is possible to reach conflicting conclusions about the relationship between host-pathogen wars and the relative value of inbreeding, outbreeding, and sex.

By concentrating on the self-discrimination role of the major histocompatibility loci of the immune system, Bremermann (1980) provided a sound and more explicit version of the hypothesis that a *biotically* varying environment can favor outbreeding sex because of its diversifying effects (for the more general versions, see Ch. 6). Bremermann's (1980) elegant suggestion was that we view host-pathogen interactions as a coevolutionary war. In order to generate an adaptive immune response, an organism must label itself as self to provide its cells with immunity from attack. This requirement sets up a selective pressure for counteradaptation by pathogens to camouflage their identity by carrying the self-identity badge of their prospective hosts. Given a genetic identifier, like the H-2 major histocompatibility locus in a host, the war's conditions are set. If the self-identifying proteins were fixed in a particular host, then its pathogens could easily come to match these proteins because of their higher rates of evolution. This would dangerously increase the probability of vertical transmission of a pathogen from a host to all of its progeny, as well as increase the probability of horizontal transmission to the host's contemporary collateral kin (Bremermann, 1980), both producing significant reductions in inclusive fitness.

Bremermann (1980) concluded that an optimal and evolutionarily stable host strategy would be to assimilate numerous mutations at the identity locus (loci) via frequency dependent selection and constantly reshuffle these variants via sexual recombination, so that all individuals would carry almost unique identifiers. In this way, the probability of a pathogen matching both parent and progeny or any group of contemporary kin would become vanishingly small. For Bremermann (1980), sex was favored by individual selection because the sharing and shuffling of alleles at a major histocompatibility locus would sufficiently limit the casualties in the host-pathogen war, thus outweighing any other costs (see also Lloyd, 1980).

In contrast, examination of the attack function of the immune system can provide a rationale for perceiving sex's favor in the conservative consequences of inbreeding (Shields, 1979; 1982b). The modern "network theory" and "clonal selection hypothesis" of the immune system postulates a regulatory substrate with low or moderate germ-line variation that nonetheless produces enormous amounts of phenotypic variation in pathogen attacking antibodies (millions of different clones in every individual) without the need of genetically anticipating or tracking pathogen changes (for reviews, see Jerne, 1974; Burnet, 1975; Bremermann, 1979b; Till, 1981).

The germ line DNA for antibody proteins is split into a number of constant and variable gene loci coding for different subunits of the final protein. Each of these loci also carries a variety of alleles, but many fewer per population than the histocompatibility identifier. A finished antibody is assembled by selecting different variable and constant subunits. By assembling subunits in different combinations and permutations, a wide variety of stem-line clones are generated. The basic diversity at this level is then enhanced by *somatic* mutations in the structural genes in antibody producing stem lines. Such stem cells even appear to possess unique, "sloppy" replicases that actually function to increase their somatic mutation rate. The end result is that each individual will carry an enormous number of waiting antibodies many of which will be novel and some unique.

On the appearance of a pathogen, the clone producing an antibody that, by chance, can neutralize it, will be selected to increase its rate of proliferation and antibody production. The result is increased survivorship. Because of the enormous diversity in stem cells, the response is expected to occur whether the pathogen in question is a mutational or geographical novelty to a host and its ancestors or not. Prior experience with a particular pathogen, however, will facilitate subsequent host responses to the same pathogen via a phenotypic priming effect.

At the attack level, the immune response appears to be a complex epigenetic phenomenon controlled by a nearly invariant regulatory, and midly variable structural, germ line DNA. The entire substrate produces high antibody diversity as a phenotypic response to a constantly changing environment. Both the complexity and the sensitivity of the underlying regulatory substrate to change are indicated by the ease with which one or a few mutations can result in severe immune deficiencies or autoimmune diseases (Burnet, 1975). On this level, the immune system is a flexible adaptation, fine-tuned by many generations of selection to meet the challenge of evolving pathogens by somatic and phenotypic adaptation rather than through the maintenance and recombination of heritable variation. Because of this fine-tuning and intrinsic complexity, this portion of the immune system as the product of a highly interactive and coadapted epigenetic substrate is likely to be susceptible to the costs of outbreeding depression.

These nearly opposite views of the relevance of the immune system and the function of sex are not mutually exclusive or logically incompatible. Bremermann (1980) and Lloyd (1980) suggest that the need for continuous change at a *single* locus with major fitness effects is of paramount importance. Thus, outbreeding and sex are selected even if it disrupts the remainder of the genome. The two strong assumptions implicit or explicit in their view is that epistasis and coadaptation are less important in conditioning individual fitness than their major gene, and that inbreeding sex is incompatible with maintaining the diversity required at the major gene.

My view (Shields, 1979; 1982b), in contrast, presumes that inbreeding sex is compatible with both requirements and perceives coadaptation and epistasis as the more important contributors to fitness. By inbreeding, an organism can maintain the coadapted complexes of alleles so important to regulating the attack function. Since inbreeding is sexual, recombination can also generate and maintain significant diversity at one or a few critical loci. All that is required is that diversifying selection (i.e., frequency dependent or heterotic selection) maintain such variability in the face of the variance erosion characteristic of inbreeding. Inbreeding can provide the best of both, maintaining allele associations where warranted and simultaneously allowing major gene diversity in concert with selection. Outbreeding, in contrast, can more easily maintain the major gene diversity, but only at the expense of disrupting integrated networks throughout the genome.

Empirical support for the hypothesis that coadaptation preserving inbreeding is not incompatible with maintenance of diversity at a major locus is illustrated by the mouse (*Mus musculus*) immune system. Duncan et al. (1979) report enormous variation at the H-2 self-identifier locus of the mouse major histocompatibility complex (> 100 alleles in one population and ≃ 100% individual heterozygosity). As they also note, consideration of the mouse social and mating systems and independent genetic evidence both imply that house mice are normally inbreeding in relatively small demes (e.g., Table 14, Ch. 8). They conclude, "the fact that near 100% H-2 heterozygosity occurs would mean that the effect of inbreeding is probably offset by heterozygous advantage at the H-2 loci."

When the immune response, or other complex epigenetic systems are considered, a genome might be considered a compilation of information gathered by all of its ancestors. Whether an environment is constant or fluctuating, homogeneous or heterogeneous, predictable or not in an ecological time frame, if it has been associated with a particular lineage for sufficient evolutionary time, then the information carried in each of the lineage's genomes should be current and vital to adaptation in that environment. If such lineage-environment associations are relatively stable, then parent-like genomes will usually have higher probabilities of success in offspring generations. Only radical ecological changes producing states beyond the historically normal range of variability are likely to reduce intergenerational correlations enough to favor radical genetic changes in response. Such radically changing environments are as improbable as perfectly constant ones (Maynard Smith, 1978).

The relatively slow pace of phylogenetic evolution, the stability of basic developmental processes and body plans across large taxonomic groups, and the occurrence of remarkable protein similarities betwen otherwise divergent groups are all consistent with the view that genomes may change slowly on an evolutionary time scale (for reviews, see Mayr, 1963; Simpson, 1967; Gould, 1977). Such a thesis implies that at any point in time the vast majority of living organisms are the products of relatively stable lineage-environment interactions. If true, conservative reproductive mechanisms should approach universality in nature. While this may sound novel, it may only be a restatement of the fact that the organic world is not one giant panmictic breeding unit. Instead, it is divided into more or less isolated and genetically different interbreeding groups variously designated species, subspecies, or populations. Even outbreeding, when defined as species-wide panmixis, is a relatively conservative process, when compared with the potentially more progressive, though rarely practiced, interspecific or intergeneric interbreeding.

Given that reproduction should be conservative, two questions emerge, (1) how conservative, and (2) how is the conservatism to be achieved? As stated, the argument implies that the favored level of conservatism will be controlled by the stability of a given lineage-environment association. This suggests that if either the environment or the lineage changes in a way that makes phenotypic tracking impossible, a less conservative reproductive process might be favored. I would suggest that this is exactly the case for many high fecundity organisms. First, such high fecundity ($> 10^5$ offspring/female/lifetime) organisms (e.g., marine invertebrates, some plants) are less likely to possess well-developed buffering systems (Manning, 1976b). Thus, they are more likely to respond to environmental change with genetic change. Second, by producing enormous numbers of variable progeny, high fecundity parents increase the probability that the pool of competing individuals, which includes their progeny, will differ from the pool in which they themselves proved their worth. Thus, high fecundity may be associated with lineages that fluctuate. An environment need not change radically, it need only generate conditions favoring high fecundity. The resulting association between intense selection and large numbers of variable progeny will tend to favor the more progressive outbreeding end of sexual continuum owing to the associated production of sisyphean genomes (Fig. 21, Ch. 6). I agree with Williams (1975; 1980; see also Bulmer, 1980) that the variable progeny, sib-competition models can explain the occurrence of outbreeding sex in high fecundity organisms.

If lineage-environment associations were more stable, then more conservative reproductive processes would be favored. If we assume that such stable associations were normally associated with low fecundity ($< 10^4$ OFL), then the more conservative processes (i.e., asexuality and inbreeding) would also be associated with low fecundity. In the absence of mutation and the ratchet, asexuality would be the ultimate conservator, so we can refine this prediction. If the rate of mutation per genome per generation were low enough to prevent the ratchet (Ch. 6), then low fecundity organisms should reproduce asexually. If, on the other hand, mutation rates were high enough to induce the ratchet, but low enough so that the ratchet did not operate in every generation, then low fecundity organisms could alternate bouts of asexual and sexual reproduction (i.e., a heterogonic strategy). Under such conditions, the number of asexual generations separating two sexual events should be negatively correlated with the mutation rate. Finally, if mutation rates were high enough to insure the ratchet's operation in every generation, then low fecundity organisms should inbreed in every generation (Table 10; and Bremermann, 1979a).

To examine these predictions we need only investigate the association between expected mutation rates and mating strategies. At the allelic level mutation is a physicochemical event, and absolute mutation rates may be a function of absolute time. If we assume that average mutation rates are normally minimized by natural selection (for reviews, see Williams, 1966; Maynard Smith, 1978), then decreasing generation time will decrease the number of mutations arising per generation. If we also assume that mutation occurs independently at different loci, then reducing the number of *functional* loci (i.e., decreasing genome size) will decrease the

Table 10. Predicted associations among fecundities, mutation rates, and reproductive strategies.

Mutation Rate/ Generation/ Individual[a]	Fecundity	
	Low ($< 10^4$)	High ($> 10^5$)
Low	Asexual	Asexual
Medium	Heterogonic[b]	Heterogonic
High	Inbreeding	Outbreeding

[a]The mutation rate/generation/individual (M) is equal to the mutation rate/locus/generation (10^{-9} - 10^{-4}) times the number of loci per individual (10^2 - 10^5) and so theoretically can range from about 10^{-7} to 10 mutations/generation/individual. Any M greater than 1.0 would favor obligate sexuality, since *all* asexual progeny would accumulate mutations in *every* generation regardless of selection intensities.

[b]Alternation of asexual and sexual generations, may be sporadic or cyclic.

number of mutations per genome. Thus, minimal mutation rates per genome per generation are expected in organisms with small genomes and short generation times. The latter expectation is consistent with the observed per locus mutation rates of 10^{-9} to 10^{-6} per generation characteristic of prokaryotes and many unicellular eukaryotes with short generation times (< 48 h). The higher-per-locus mutation rates (10^{-6} to 10^{-4}) observed in most higher eukaryotes with longer generation times (weeks to many years) are also in line with expectation (for reviews, see Dobzhansky et al., 1977; Wright, 1977).

In an elegant and somewhat overlooked paper (e.g., it is not cited in Maynard Smith, 1978), Manning (1967b) explored the phylogenetic distribution of asexuality and sexuality in an attempt to answer the question, "Is sex maintained to facilitate or minimize mutational advance?" He suggested that many groups had "evolved methods of making themselves independent of variations in the external environment" by employing "both behavioural and physiological buffering mechanisms." Since such organisms (primarily cephalopods, many insects, and especially the vertebrates) usually perceive the environment as fine-grained (Levins, 1968), their, in many cases, exclusive sexuality cannot be attributed to varying envrionments. He concluded that for these organisms, "the most important function of sex is to reduce the mutation load'' (by obviating the ratchet). Since such organisms also have the largest genomes and longest generation times, they further support his argument and confirm my prediction regarding the association of sex and expected mutation rates. The exclusive sexuality in these fine-grained species is not entirely consistent with the view that sex functions primarily to meet the challenges of a varying environment.

In contrast, species which perceive their environments as coarse-grained (Levins, 1968) in space or time (including bacteria, protozoa, porifera, coelenterates, platyhelminthes, bryozoa, annelids and many plant species) show a reduced capacity for homeostatic buffering, and would, therefore, be more likely to respond to fluctuating environments genetically. If sex did function to meet the demands of such varying environments, then such species should be ''predominantly sexual'' (Manning, 1976b). They are not, most being predominantly asexual or heterogonic to varying degrees. For example, Manning (1976b) noted that while the bacteria often possess parasexual processes, asexuality is their more common reproductive strategy. I would add that as predicted, it is usual in prokaryotes for many asexual events to separate independent parasexual events (i.e., the ratio of asexual to sexual generations is high). The prokaryotes also have the smallest genomes and shortest generation times of the organisms examined. Similarly, many of the short generation protozoans appear to rely almost exclusively on asexuality, while many that engage in sex do so relatively infrequently (high asexual/sexual ratio). Heterogonic life histories in the eukaryotes also appear to be associated with relatively short generation times ($\leqslant 2$ weeks), while the asexual/sexual ratio also declines as predicted (for a parallel argument developed independently, see Bremermann, 1979a).

These comparative data on the phylogenetic distribution of asexuality and the frequency of its occurrence in heterogonic species are consistent with the hypothesis that the major factor controlling the occurrence of asexuality is mutation pressure. If a species can reproduce fast enough, relative to the size of its genome, then it can beat the mutational clock. That is, if progeny can be produced with parental genomes unaltered by deleterious mutation, then asexuality will be favored over any sexuality with its reduced conservatism and increased segregational load. If, and perhaps this is more likely, mutation rates are intermediate so that deleterious mutants are assimilated, but at relatively low rates during the asexual portion of a species' life cycle, then when the assimilated load reaches some unspecified level, sex and its editor can intervene, cleansing a family of its accumulated mutations. Only when mutation rates are high enough to drive the ratchet in every generation and load *all* the progeny produced will the editor more than balance sex's segregational load and exclusive sex finally replace asexuality. In answer to Manning's question, and consistent with my predictions, it appears that sex may be maintained to minimize mutational advance, that is, to conserve parental genomes (for additional supporting evidence not pertinent to my arguments, see Manning, 1976b).

If the genomic mutation rate is high enough to induce the ratchet in every generation, then sex may be a necessity in every generation. If an organism facing this mutational challenge does not have sufficient fecundity to afford the gamble of outbreeding, then it should employ the more conservative strategy of inbreeding. Organisms characterized by large genomes, long generation times, and low fecundity (e.g., many insects and plants, almost all of the vertebrates) *should* be inbreeding. This is a testable prediction. Before attempting such a test, I feel it worthwhile to digress on the issue of whether my arguments imply anything about the intensity of inbreeding likely to be favored in particular circumstances.

Optimal Inbreeding

If we assume that inbreeding's primary function is conserving successful parental genomes, then maximum conservation (fidelity) is likely to yield maximum benefits. Maximum conservation, in turn, is likely to be achieved at maximal inbreeding intensities (i.e., selfing in hermaphrodites; parent-offspring or full-sibling incest in biparental species). Why are all low fecundity organisms not selfing or incestuous? A likely answer is the traditional answer, but from a slightly different perspective. Extreme inbreeding is associated with extreme segregational loads, or if one prefers, maximum incest depression. At times these costs may outweigh the benefits, especially when inbreeding's maximum benefits can be attained at much lower inbreeding intensities (for a detailed treatment of how random mating in small populations ($N_e < 1000$) can produce the beneficial effects of selfing or incest ($N_e \leqslant 2$), see Ch. 8). Thus, there may be an optimal level of inbreeding (also discussed as "optimal outbreeding," e.g., Wigan, 1944; Lerner, 1954;

Bateson, 1978; Price and Waser, 1979, a distinction that I believe is more than semantic, see Ch. 8).

Based solely on these genetic consequences (both genotypic and genomic, see Ch. 3), this inbreeding optimum is likely to be a compromise between two opposing forces. If natural selection can produce optimal strategies (for review, see Maynard Smith, 1978), then an inbreeding optimum may be expected to minimize the cost/benefit ratio for a particular set of circumstances (Fig. 23). Driving the optimum away from incest are the costs of segregation if dominance or heterosis are important components of fitness potential. Random mating in larger populations increases the probability that deleterious mutations carried by potential mates have arisen independently. Compared with incest, segregational loads will be lower, and recombination's editor may operate more efficiently (a greater number of parental genomes transmitted with fewer "waste" genomes, see Ch. 6). With lesser inbreeding inten-

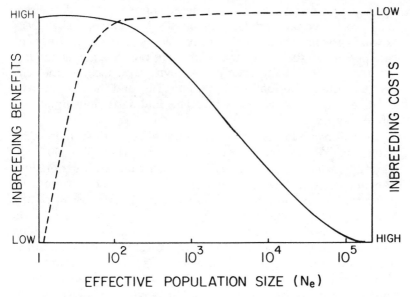

Fig. 23. A hypothetical representation of the costs and benefits associated with different inbreeding intensities. The minimum cost/benefit ratio for particular conditions will reflect an optimal inbreeding intensity for those conditions. Primary determinants of the shape and position of the curves include the relative importance of epistasis versus dominance interactions in determining fitness. As the proportional contribution of epistasis increases, inbreeding's benefits increase with increasing intensity. As the importance of dominance increases, the disadvantages of inbreeding increase with increasing intensities (see text for further discussion).

sities, deleterious mutations are more likely to be carried, at least initially, in heterozygous condition. If such mutations recur, the developmental adjustments we call dominance can evolve. This would permit production of progeny with unaltered parental phenotypes in spite of the genetic changes. Since selection tests phenotypes, this phenotypic masking of mutation further increases the conservative nature of sexual reproduction (Fisher, 1931). Finally, reduced levels of inbreeding would allow for increased segregation of favored heterozygotes in heterotic environments.

Any adaptive tendency to reduce inbreeding would ultimately be limited by the increasing probability that as mates become less related, not just novel mutations, but also the more numerous ancestral alleles of their genomes would have arisen independently. If these independent alleles had interacted epistatically in ancestral genomes, interbreeding would disrupt previously coadapted allele associations. This would generate a recombinational load and entail a genetic meiotic loss. As the degree of relatedness decreased, such costs would increase, finally driving the optimum back towards greater inbreeding intensity. Factors influencing the shape and position of such cost/benefit functions (Fig. 23), in qualitatively predictable, but quantitatively unknown ways, include: the relative importance of dominance vs. epistasis, and the absolute and relative rates of occurrence of favorable and deleterious mutations of both types.

Relative fecundity is also expected to affect optimal inbreeding intensity. Within the range of low fecundity ($2 - 10^4$ offspring/female/lifetime), increases in progeny number might reduce the impact of any segregational load. If the cost of producing young is low, either absolutely, or relative to the cost of raising them to maturity, then production of an ecological excess would allow any potential genetic deaths resulting from the mating system (e.g., the highly homozygous) to coincide with the otherwise inevitable ecological deaths associated with the excess fecundity (Ch. 4; Wallace, 1968b; 1970; 1977). In this way even intense inbreeding could be associated with relatively high levels of individual heterozygosity and population polymorphism. Should fecundity increase enough (some value between 10^4 and 10^5 OFL) to favor increased variance in fitness potential in a family of progeny, then the outbreeding end of the mating continuum would finally be favored (Table 10).

This notion of an inbreeding optimum is consistent with the occurrence of phenotypic traits which appear to function in prevention of *incest* (and not necessarily inbreeding *per se*, as is often implied) in a wide variety of organisms. These traits include such mechanisms as physiological or mechanical self-sterility in plants (for reviews, see Stebbins, 1950; Grant, 1975) and kin recognition and incest avoidance in mice (Hill, 1974), birds (Koenig and Pitelka, 1979), and especially primates (e.g., Sade, 1968; Itani, 1972; Packer, 1975; 1979), as well as less direct incest avoidance through, for example, sexual differences in dispersal (Greenwood and Harvey, 1976; Greenwood, 1980). The model also admits of the incest depression noted in many of these same organisms when the avoidance mechanisms break down (e.g., Greenwood et al., 1978; Packer, 1979; Price and Waser, 1979).

In contrast to traditional presentations, this model also admits of the positive benefits and potentially wide occurrence of relatively intense inbreeding in these same species. Such possibilities are often hidden in the "common" knowledge of inbreeding's (= incest's) detrimental effects with a resulting dismissal of inbreeding as an important evolutionary phenomenon (for review, see Carson, 1967). Unlike traditional views (Ch. 4), the model proposed here is also consistent with the frequent occurrence of extreme inbreeders. The model even implies that phenotypic traits promoting inbreeding would not necessarily be rare. If there is an optimal level of inbreeding, then on the basis of genetic consequences alone, it appears it should lie above the level of incest ($N_e > 2$), but well below what many would consider outbreeding (i.e., $N_e < 1000$ rather than $N_e > 10,000$).

The general thesis developed here suggests that long-lived (generation time > 1 yr.), low fecundity organisms should be inbreeding. If the optimality argument is correct, then most of these should be inbreeding randomly in small ($2 < N_e < 1000$), semi-isolated demes. One of the primary consequences of philopatry is that it produces just such a population structure. Philopatry may be *one* proximate mechanism that promotes inbreeding. If it is fine-tuned behaviorally, it may be the most efficient mechanism for generating optimal levels of random inbreeding. Integrating both of these arguments permits a simultaneous test of both inbreeding and philopatry hypotheses. *Philopatry, which is effective in generating relatively intense inbreeding, should occur in, and only in, low fecundity organisms. Vagrancy, effective in generating wider outbreeding, should only be associated with high fecundity organisms.*

Since control of the genetic structure of populations is not the sole function of dispersal, it is necessary to stress the actual genetic consequences of an observed dispersal strategy. For example, if a low fecundity organism were forced to disperse propagules widely owing to special ecological conditions (e.g., its normal habitat is ephemeral, patchy, or both), then the argument predicts that the organisms will use some mechanism other than philopatry to achieve adaptive levels of inbreeding. Similarly, if circumstances imposed constraints on the dispersal of a high fecundity species, it should display an alternative mechanism maintaining its optimal level of wider outbreeding.

Fecundity and Dispersal: A Positive Correlation

Marine invertebrates

With lifetime fecundities spanning seven orders of magnitude (10^2-10^9 OFL) and the presence of both philopatry and vagrancy, the marine invertebrates offer an ideal test of these predictions. Since wide vagrancy is associated with long-lived pelagic larvae (Thorson, 1950), and philopatry with nonpelagic larvae and in many cases with parental care (e.g., Thorson, 1950; Morrison, 1963; Gee and Williams, 1965; Menge, 1975; Hartnoll, 1976; Schopf and Gooch, 1977; Sanders, 1977; Hansen, 1978; Cook and Cook, 1978), an association between dispersal and fecundity immediately emerges. Thorson (1950; and Fig. 24) reviewed data from 53 benthic marine invertebrates, representing all of the major marine phyla. He demonstrated a strong association between *annual* fecundity and larval type, and therefore expected dispersal strategy, in the predicted direction (Fig. 24). The associations of low fecundity with philopatry and high fecundity with vagrancy might have been even clearer had he tabled lifetime rather than annual fecundities.

Many have attempted to explain the high fecundities observed in vagrant species as a *consequence* of the dangers of their larvae's pelagic life (e.g., Thorson, 1950; Vance, 1973; Shine, 1978). Even if true, this argument implies nothing about any association between fecundity and mating system. There is no reason intrinsic to the ecological theories explaining fecundity, why a high fecundity species should not self-fertilize. Many are hermaphroditic, yet most of these appear to be exclusive cross-fertilizers. In concert with their vagrancy, this is likely to insure relatively wide outbreeding (e.g., Gee and Williams, 1965; Menge, 1975). Like many

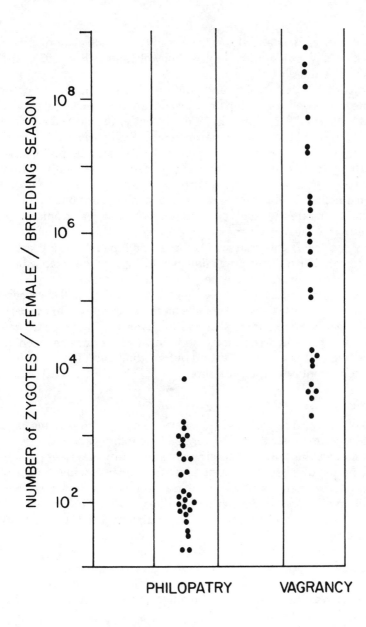

Fig. 24. The association between annual fecundity and dispersal strategies in benthic marine invertebrates. Philopatric species are either viviparous with extensive parental care or lay very large eggs and display primitive brood protection. Vagrant species produce long-lived pelagic larvae (modified from Thorson, 1950).

plant species, some of the high fecundity animals even display a rudimentary self-sterility (e.g., Longwell and Stiles, 1973, and references therein).

In contrast, self-fertility and confirmed selfing appear to occur more commonly in philopatric, low fecundity species (e.g., Gee and Williams, 1965; Hartnoll, 1976). Recently, Cronin and Forward (1979) reported on an estuarine crab, *Rhithropanoplus harrisii*, which, despite dispersing via pelagic larvae, may be philopatric. Normally pelagic larvae are expected to disperse vagrantly as they are passively carried by local currents. In this species, behavioral adjustments via vertical migration proximately controlled by tidal currents apparently result in, "retention of these planktonic larvae in estuaries near the parent populations." If this retention were truly localized, the crab would be as philopatric as any active disperser. If true, my prediction would be that the crab would possess low fecundity. In response to this prediction, Cronin (pers. comm.) presented a "best guess" of less than 10,000 progeny (range: 2500–25,000) as *R. harrisii*'s lifetime fecundity. On the basis of these broad comparisons, as well as in the specific case of *R. harrisii*, the observed associations in marine invertebrates between inbreeding and low fecundity, and outbreeding and high fecundity, are consistent with the predictions.

Plants

Not only do the higher plants (i.e., gymnosperms and angiosperms) offer as wide a range of fecundity as the marine invertebrates, but, owing to their possession of two classes of potential propagules (seeds and pollen), they offer a wider range of possible associations betwen dispersal and mating strategies. Most adult plants are sessile hermaphrodites, so that individual (vs. gene) dispersal will occur primarily via diploid seeds. The mobility of pollen will permit adjustments in mating strategy independent of requirements for individual dispersal met by seed, since pollen's primary function will be mating and gene dispersal. Thus plants offer a stronger test of the hypothesis predicting a negative correlation between fecundity and inbreeding intensity because they can falsify it in more ways.

The critical prediction remains that low fecundity will be associated with increased, and high fecundity with decreased, inbreeding. Given philopatric seed dispersal, plants can inbreed by limiting pollen dispersal. If, on the other hand, greater outbreeding is favored, a species with philopatric seed dispersal can still outbreed by dispersing its pollen vagrantly. Given vagrant seed dispersal, any pollen dispersal (either vagrant or philopatric) is expected to result in fairly wide outbreeding. This occurs because the seeds developing in proximity are likely to have been drawn from a wider area, so that near neighbors (and potential mates) are unlikely to be particularly close relatives. If a species is forced to disperse seed widely, while inbreeding is favored, then the only effective mating system would be selfing (i.e., zero pollen dispersal). Of the six potential dispersal strategies available to plants, the three promoting inbreeding should be associated with low fecundity, and the three associated with increased outbreeding should occur in high fecundity species (Table 11).

Table 11. Predicted associations between fecundity and dispersal strategies for pollen and seeds of the higher plants (gymnosperms and angiosperms).

Fecundity			
Low	Seed Philopatry + Pollen Philopatry or Selfing	or	Seed Vagrancy + Selfing
High	Seed Philopatry + Pollen Vagrancy	or	Seed Vagrancy + Pollen Philopatry or Pollen Vagrancy

Because of an absence of data collected or presented in a manner suitable for testing these predictions directly, only weaker indirect tests are possible. Over the years, plant biologists have developed a number of empirical generalizations about relationships among growth habits (annual vs. perennial), environmental stability, and mating systems (selfing vs. crossing). Perhaps the best confirmed and most widely cited of these rules is the association of selfing and the annual habit and crossing and the perennial habit (Table 12; and for reviews, Stebbins, 1950; Grant, 1958; Baker, 1959; 1963; Harper, 1977). One factor considered partially responsible for this association is the joint correlation of the annual habit and selfing with unstable habitats that place a premium on colonizing ability

(Table 13, Stebbins, 1958; Baker, 1963; Grant, 1975; but, see Jain, 1976). The rationale is that a self-fertile organism is more efficient, both ecologically (e.g., pollen always available, a single propagule enough to start a population, high intrinsic rate of increase) and genetically (owing to selfing's capacity to preserve a well-adapted genome, e.g., Grant, 1975) at colonizing suitable empty habitat. Grant (1975) explicitly suggests that the entire association may best be viewed within the theoretical frame of r- and K-selection. He concludes that unstable, i.e., ephemeral habitats, and the resulting needs of colonizing, generate r-selection favoring rapid development, "high" fecundity, and the annual habit. In contrast, stable and saturated environments select for the perennial habit and the other correlates of a more competitive K strategy.

Table 12. The relation between inbreeding intensity and growth habit in selected grass species (Gramineae, after Stebbins, 1950).[a]

Mating System	Perennials	Annuals
Self-incompatible obligate crossing	26	0
Self-compatible frequent crossing	40	3
Self-compatible cleistogamous obligate selfing	5	27

[a]Similar correlations have been demonstrated in a wide variety of angiosperm families (Grant, 1975).

Table 13. The associations between mating systems, chromosome numbers (increased number = increased recombination = greater effective outbreeding), and habitat type in plants of the composite tribe Cichoreae (after Stebbins, 1958).[a]

Mating System	Chromosome #	Habitat Types		
		Stable	Intermediate	Unstable
Crossing	9–8	47	44	7
Crossing	7–6	2	26	0
Crossing	5–3	4	13	1
Selfing	–	6	28	23

[a]Tabled values are the number of species observed.

There are difficulties with this interpretation of the factors likely to be important in controlling the occurrence of self-fertilization. For example, the interpretation is inconsistent with the associations observed in superficially similar marine invertebrates. In the animals, the colonizing, high fecundity, r-strategist species disperse passive propagules that travel great distances before settling, in much the manner of a weedy annual. Like the plants, many are hermaphrodites. Unlike the plants, almost all are exclusively cross-fertilizing and therefore outbreeders. In the marine invertebrates, selfing and other traits promoting inbreeding appear in species living in stable and saturated environments. In contrast, equivalent K-selected plant species living in stable habitats appear to cross-fertilize and outbreed.

The same plant-animal comparison illustrates some of the difficulties the fluctuating environment hypotheses have in explaining the advantage of sexual reproduction. These predict that species living in relatively unstable environments that produce progeny likely to face changed conditions should reproduce sexually. On the other hand, species living in relatively stable environments would be expected to reproduce more conservatively via increased inbreeding or even asexuality. The associations observed in the marine invertebrates appear to be consistent with this hypothesis. Yet this hypothesis is flatly contradicted by the reversed pattern observed in plants (Table 12). Must we conclude that the plant and animal kingdoms have evolved in opposite directions in response to the same selective pressures? Or is there a simpler, and perhaps more nearly universal explanation for the patterns characterizing both kingdoms?

I believe that the problem stems from concentrating on annual (clutch size) rather than lifetime fecundity (e.g., Grant's description of the higher fecundity in annuals than perennials, cf. Fig. 25). Of course it is lifetime fecundity that is important in evolutionary arguments. The association of low lifetime fecundity and the annual habit, which is correlated with selfing, supports the predicted association of low fecundity and increased inbreeding. Selfing may be adaptive in many colonizing plant species, but for different reasons than are usually offered. Given an ephemeral environment selecting for vagrant seed dispersal, the only mating system permitting inbreeding is self-fertilization (Table 10). If the annual habit and specific environmental conditions limit lifetime fecundity below the critical level necessary to favor outbreeding ($< 10^4$OFL), then an annual should inbreed (unless mutation rates are low

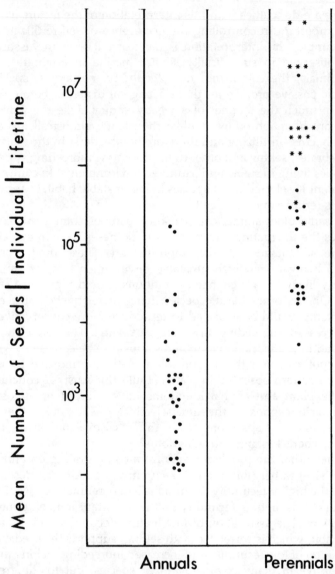

Fig. 25. The association between lifetime fecundity and an annual or perennial habit for selected plant species: herbs or shrubs (●), trees (*). Unless they were given, lifetime fecundities are the products of annual seed production (average clutch size) and minimum estimates of reproductive lifespan, i.e., 5 yrs. for herbs and shrubs, 100 yrs. for trees (taken or calculated from data in Salisbury, 1942; Harper et al., 1970; Harper and White, 1974).

enough to favor asexuality). If it is to inbreed at all, the low fecundity, colonizing annual plant must self-fertilize. Truly high fecundity plants with vagrant seeds including both annual and perennial epiphytes or parasites (e.g., orchids, reviewed in Salisbury, 1942) normally cross-fertilize and thus outbreed. Since they are also colonizers, if the more traditional arguments (e.g., Baker, 1959) were correct, they might be expected to inbreed (i.e., self). That they, like their high fecundity marine invertebrate counterparts, are actually outbreeding is more consistent with the hypothesis predicting a causal association between fecundity and mating system. From the perspective of genetic consequences, the nonoptimal selfing observed in annual plants may be the only option available if inbreeding is a necessity.

The large overlap in fecundities between annual and perennial species of plants (Fig. 25) will permit a more detailed analysis of these predictions. Since the primary determinants of seed dispersal distance by wind are seed weight, height of release, and the efficiency of auxiliary structures affecting airworthiness (Harper, 1977), increasing the number of seeds produced will usually increase vagrancy by reducing each seed's weight. If we assume that tiny "dust" seeds will disperse more vagrantly than larger seeds, then low lifetime fecundity species with large clutches of small seeds (colonizing annuals) should self-fertilize (Table 10). High fecundity species with similarly vagrant dust seeds must cross-fertilize to insure the predicted outbreeding, which they appear to do (e.g., perennial orchids like *Goodyera repens*, some trees, *Betula* spp. and *Pinus* spp., and some annuals, *Sonchus asper* and *Linaria minor*, see Salisbury, 1942; Harper and White, 1974).

When environmental pressures (e.g., the requirements of successful germination) select for larger, less motile seeds, there are three possible strategies (Table 10). In high fecundity, and therefore perennial, species, increased pollen vagrancy could increase outbreeding. Species such as Oaks (*Quercus* spp.) should, and apparently do, disperse pollen fairly widely (Grant, 1975). Finally, in noncolonizing, low and medium fecundity species, philopatric seed dispersal should be coupled with philopatric pollen dispersal or selfing, regardless of individual longevity (Table 10). The optimal inbreeding arguments (see above), however, suggest that under such conditions selfing should be rare. The expected seed and pollen philopatry within a framework of self-incompatibility resulting in random mating in small demes is extremely common in plants (e.g., Ehrlich and Raven, 1969; Levin and Kerster, 1974), and is often discussed under the apt descriptive term "vicinism" (e.g., Grant, 1971; 1975; Bradshaw, 1972; Antonovics, 1976). Although the evidence is less direct, it appears that plants, like their marine invertebrate counterparts, show the predicted association between fecundity and inbreeding intensity. That both groups show this association, while showing contradictory associations in light of common alternative explanations based on colonizing ability, or r and K selection, is perhaps the strongest evidence for a causal relation between fecundity and mating system. The actual selective pressures which help shape the associations remain unknown, but the observed correlation certainly fails to falsify the inbreeding hypotheses. Only more detailed analyses of data gathered or presented in light of the predicted associations between fecundity and mating system can lessen or increase this tentative support.

Vertebrates and insects

Since the majority of vertebrates possess relatively low fecundity, they offer fewer opportunities for comparative analysis. Yet they are also the taxa with the most extensively investigated population biology, and so offer the best chance of exploring exceptions. The fishes do offer opportunity for comparison, and their characteristics are consistent with the predicted associations between fecundity and mating system. Many of the marine fishes are very fecund (10^6-10^9 OFL). These high fecundity species normally produce pelagic eggs, free-swimming larvae, or both. These pelagic propagules are then subject to passive dispersal in water currents. Vagrancy and wide outbreeding probably result. Adults of such groups as herring, *Clupea* spp., and cod, *Gadus* spp., also tend to show less site tenacity than other vertebrates. They also show additional behaviors such as mass spawning in large groups, which would appear to increase outbreeding intensity (for review, Harden-Jones, 1968). In contrast, most fresh water, low fecundity fishes (e.g., salmon, Salmonidae, and sunfish, Centrarchidae) lay demersal eggs, pair bond, are ofen territorial, and show intense birth site philopatry, all of which would tend to promote inbreeding (Ch. 2; Harden-Jones, 1968). Thus, in all the groups with sufficient fecundity differences for comparison (i.e., plants, marine invertebrates, and fishes), fecundity and inbreeding intensity appear to be negatively correlated as predicted.

Since the remaining vertebrate classes and most of the insects are low fecundity organisms, *all* should be inbreeding. While this extreme view does not permit comparison, it does imply that philopatry, or alternative mechanisms promoting inbreeding, should be the rule. The vast majority of vertebrates and many low fecundity insects are philopatric (Ch. 2). Biparental sexuality combined with philopatry can result in optimal levels of inbreeding ($2 < N_e < 1000$) and incest with its attendant costs may be avoided. Thus, Greenwood and Harvey (Ch. 2; 1976) may have been correct in postulating that sexual differences in effective dispersal observed in many vertebrates may have evolved to prevent "too close" inbreeding. Since both sexes remain philopatric and N_e remains small, the sexual assymmetry certainly did not evolve to prevent inbreeding *per se*, an implication that they appear to have accepted (Greenwood et al., 1979b; Greenwood, 1980), though it appears to have escaped the attention of others (e.g., Packer, 1979; Koenig and Pitelka, 1979).

Broad comparisons are invariably disturbed by exceptions, and this analysis is certainly not immune. For example, many of the ducks and geese (Anatidae) mate on the wintering grounds with males following their mates to the females' natal areas (for reviews, see Mayr, 1942; 1963). The female displays birth site philopatry, while marking indicates that many males settle far from their birthplace (e.g., Cooke et al., 1975; Rockwell and Cooke, 1977). Mayr (1942; 1963) has suggested that this dispersal strategy may have evolved to insure wider outbreeding and increased gene flow. If true, it would stand at odds with my predictions, so I offer an alternative explanation. Members of this family may mate on the wintering grounds because of the short duration of benign conditions on their northern breeding grounds (Newton, 1977). If, during the evolution of winter mating, each deme within a species overwintered in their own traditional and separate area (winter philopatry), then winter mating would still permit inbreeding. If ecological conditions changed, and different demes were then forced to share wintering grounds, the likelihood of interdemic outbreeding would increase.

Outbreeding, then, would be the chance, and maladaptive, result of the destruction of these species' normal wintering areas. It could be a nonequilibrium condition, rather than an adaptive

161

strategy. This view is consistent with our knowledge of the destruction of wild coastal marshes in the last century. The tendency for members of different stocks of wildfowl to winter in different areas where habitat has not been altered is also consistent with this interpretation (e.g., Bent, 1962; Milne and Robertson, 1965). While this is an *ad hoc,* and therefore not a very satisfying, explanation of wildfowl dispersal, I do find indirect support for the inbreeding hypotheses in this exceptional group. The entire pattern offers a rather simple mechanism which could insure wide outbreeding in many migratory bird species. Why do more avian species not mate on the wintering grounds? The rarity of mechanisms which appear to promote wide outbreeding via dispersal strategies in low fecundity vertebrates is evidence that inbreeding enjoys some favor.

What of the colonizing or nomadic species of insects and vertebrates? Smaller insects with poor flying abilities disperse more passively than actively. In colonizing species, the ephemeral nature of their native habitat often makes philopatry impossible. Such organisms face the same challenge as low fecundity plants with vagrant seeds and must meet the need for inbreeding in similar fashion. In biparental species, the simplest method of insuring inbreeding is to mate prior to dispersal. This is taken to its logical extreme in the species which mate prior to birth within their mother's body (e.g., Elbadry and Tawfik, 1966; and for review, Hamilton, 1967), or more often in their singly parasitized host (e.g., *Telenomus fariai,* Dreyfus and Breuer, 1944). Either strategy results in continuous full-sib mating. Similar adaptations promoting intense or extreme inbreeding prior to dispersal have also been demonstrated in such colonizing arthropods as mites (e.g., Cooper, 1939; Mitchell, 1970), many free-living (Cowan, 1979; Greenberg, 1979) and especially parasitic hymenoptera (for review, Hamilton, 1967), and many other insects (for reviews, see Hamilton, 1967; Johnson, 1969).

Given ephemeral environments, a mobile vertebrate could also employ the passive strategy of mating prior to dispersal, with impregnated females taking the role of propagule. The only vertebrate example of this potential strategy may be the wild turkey (*Meleagris gallopavo*). It is at least possible that fertilized females may be the primary propagule in the turkey (W. Porter, pers. comm.). If the pattern does occur it will probably be rare, since it entails unnecessarily intense inbreeding for a mobile organism. Since vertebrates are usually mobile, a nomadic strategy is available that will permit colonization and optimal levels of inbreeding. Traveling in social groups, consisting of the same number of individuals with the same average relatedness as is characteristic of stationary demes, will meet both the colonizing and inbreeding needs of a species. Faithfulness to such mobile demes could be referred to as *philogamy*. Philogamy should be characteristic of such colonizing birds as crossbills (*Loxia* spp.) or Franklin's gulls (*Larus pipixcan*, Bent, 1968; Burger, 1972), as well as nomadic mammals (e.g., wildebeest or zebra, Leuthold, 1977; or even man). There is some evidence that such nomadic vertebrates normally travel in the expected groups (e.g., Mayr, 1965; and references above). There is, with one exception, little evidence regarding the relatedness of group members. In humans, such groups are clans or tribal units, usually consisting of individuals with the predicted degree of relatedness. Further study of the genetic structure of nomadic vertebrates on a wider taxonomic front would permit more sensitive tests of the philogamy hypothesis.

The robustness of the correlation between fecundity and inbreeding intensity suggests that the implied causal connection may be real (Table 9). The equally robust correlation between low fecundity and philopatry in noncolonizing organisms, supports the contention that one of the primary functions of philopatry is promoting inbreeding. Since this argument implies that philopatry is a proximate mechanism promoting the ultimate function of inbreeding, it may be worthwhile to examine how efficiently philopatry produces inbreeding.

Family Dialects: Positive Assortative Mating

If vertebrate species are usually subdivided into geographically separated and genetically different demes via philopatry (Ch. 8), then philopatry will not always insure adaptive within-deme interbreeding. For example, two growing demes (or one deme fissioning into two) will often share common spatial boundaries. Despite being philopatric, individuals born in such boundary regions will have a higher probability of dispersing into a foreign deme than individuals born near their natal deme's range center. This will increase the probability that boundary individuals will mate with foreign deme members and suffer any consequent outbreeding depression. Individuals remaining within the boundaries of their native deme, but near them, would be more likely to mate with dispersing foreigners, and would also be subject to outbreeding depression. If within-deme inbreeding were adaptive, selection would favor individuals that could distinguish between family members and foreigners. If there were a sufficient number of potential mates that choice were possible, individuals would be expected to choose deme members and shun foreigners. Such a behavioral system would permit related invaders to get together within a foreign deme's spatial range and so avoid outbreeding depression. It would also allow native individuals to recognize invaders, and so reduce their chances of engaging in less profitable interdeme matings.

Models of the evolution of premating ethological isolating mechanisms (e.g., via the Wallace Effect) may apply within as well as between good species. If philopatry is a first order isolating mechanism, then selection, ever the opportunist, may also produce additional mechanisms to prevent the postmating fitness depression permitted by philopatry acting alone. Just as species recognition and positive assortative mating makes adaptive sense, so might family recognition and positive assortative mating, and for the same reasons. The major difference would be that the cost of mistaken identity in a family system would be lower, and the expected perfection of resulting mechanisms perhaps reduced.

Likely candidates for intraspecific isolating mechanisms are those known to operate between species. Primary among these, and the only one discussed here, are communication dialects. Any stimulus, emitted by an organism, capable of being received by a conspecific via any sensory mode (e.g., auditory, olfactory, visual, tactile, electrical, for review, Smith, 1977) could be used in a dialect system. All that is necessary is that the stimulus encode information about deme membership or genetic relatedness, as opposed to phenotypic similarities uncorrelated with underlying genetic relatedness. If dialects are to be used in mate choice, of course, they must be a necessary prelude to mating. Such a system could promote genetically assortative (inbreeding) or disassortative (outbreeding) mating systems depending on the criteria for mate choice. The arguments developed here predict that dialect systems in low fecundity organisms will usually promote within-deme inbreeding. More traditional views (e.g., Jenkins, 1977; Treisman, 1978) often predict the opposite, that dialect systems will promote between-deme outbreeding.

Acoustic dialects

Although auditory species recognition has been well documented in insects (for review, Alexander, 1967), anuran amphibians (for review, Blair, 1958), and birds (e.g., Dilger, 1958), the most extensive studies of intraspecific variation in acoustic signals have been on avian vocalizations (for review, Baptista, 1975). In many bird species, male song is apparently learned early in life prior to dispersal. Males appear to pattern their songs after those of nearby males possibly including their fathers (e.g., Marler and Tamura, 1964; but see also Kroodsma, 1974; Jenkins, 1977). In these species, males with similar songs are grouped together in space, forming a dialect population. Different groups of males with different dialects are usually found in separate areas, often with little spatial overlap between them (e.g., Marler and Tamura, 1962; Thielcke, 1970; Nottebohm, 1972; Baptista, 1975; Baker and Mewaldt, 1978). In order to explain the persistence and purity of such local dialects, Nottebohm (1969), elaborating on Marler and Tamura's (1962) suggestions, implied that foreign dialects might act as proximate barriers to cross-dialect dispersal, and function to help maintain locally adapted populations (i.e., the eco-genetic hypothesis, my Ch. 2).

To promote outbreeding in such a dialect system, all that would be necessary is that one sex disperse into dialects that differ from those associated with their natal areas. This would permit the stay-at-home sex to gain the benefits of associating with relatives of the same sex, while reducing the expected risk of inbreeding (for a more detailed discussion of the hypothesis, see Greenwood and Harvey, 1976; Greenwood et al., 1979c; Treisman, 1978).

Baker and Mewaldt (1978) have demonstrated that, at least in White-crowned Sparrows (*Zonotrichia leucophrys*), song dialect boundaries act as effective barriers to both male and female dispersal. This is more consistent with an inbreeding than outbreeding function. Further support for the inbreeding hypothesis has emerged from studies which indicate that dialect groups do differ genetically, implying that they are indeed different demes (e.g, Nottebohm and Selander, 1972; Baker, 1974; 1975). Nottebohm's (1969; 1976) hypothesis that dialect-induced inbreeding helps maintain local adaptations has since been criticized as a general explanation of avian dialects (e.g., Payne, 1978; Baker and Mewaldt, 1978), because of the occurrence of dialects in homogeneous habitats. Since genetic heterogeneity is expected to arise in homogeneous habitats owing to the assimilation of different mutations by different demes in spite of similar or identical selective pressures (Ch. 5), dialects in homogeneous habitats actually do not contradict Nottebohm's hypothesis.

There is evidence that for some avian species auditory signals can and do act as intraspecific ethological isolating mechanisms promoting within-deme inbreeding (e.g., Baker and Mewaldt, 1978). Though there is little evidence on as fine a scale for insects or amphibians, I predict that investigation of the behavior associated with dialects in these taxa will yield similar results. An absence of dialects resulting in positive assortative mating in any species should not be taken as evidence falsifying the general inbreeding hypothesis (e.g., inbreeding could be achieved via other mechanisms such as philopatry). Rather, should a system of dialects be observed in nature, the inbreeding hypothesis predicts that it will be associated with promotion rather than prevention of inbreeding in low fecundity organisms, while the reverse should be true for high fecundity species.

Olfactory dialects

Pheromonal communication systems and olfactory species recognition are characteristic of many groups of insects, fishes, and mammals (for reviews, see Wilson, 1975; Smith, 1977). In many of these groups, olfactory signals indicating deme membership might be expected. If they do occur, then they too should function to promote inbreeding in low fecundity species. While I have not reviewed the literature exhaustively, I have found support for the hypotheses. Godfrey (1958), for example, demonstrated that bank voles (*Clethrionomys glareolus*) are able to discriminate between conspecifics born on the same islands and from geographically distant areas. As predicted, individuals appear to prefer mates that are born on the same island. Similarly, for mainland voles, there was a negative correlation between mating preference and the geographical distance separating the birthplaces of potential mates. Mainardi (1963) has also demonstrated that house mice (*Mus musculus*) are capable of distinguishing olfactorily between numbers of their own and different subspecies, and tend to limit mating to within subspecies, and Gilder and Slater (1978) showed that females preferred distant relatives to both siblings and nonkin. In an elegant study of laboratory mice, Yamasaki et al. (1976) showed that males prefer females that differ from them in histocompatibility alleles. They suggested that the preference was probably mediated through pheromones. As some have suggested, such a tendency may function to prevent incest (e.g., Halliday, 1978), but it is also possible that the behavior helps insure histocompatibility heterozygosity in an inbred group. Such flexibility in the immune system is expected to lead to a more efficient, and therefore more beneficial, immune response (Howard, 1977; Duncan et al., 1980).

Turning to other taxa, olfactory cues may be one proximate mechanism permitting the remarkable philopatry observed in salmonid fishes. In brown trout (*Salmo trutta*, Tilzey, 1977) and perhaps other salmonids (for review, see Nordeng, 1977), orientation to the natal area within fresh water systems appears to be a response to deme-specific odors released by juvenile forms in the natal area during the breeding adults' upstream migrations.

Visual dialects

Either external morphology or ritualized display could conceivably carry visual information about deme membership. Deme specific differences in structural elaborations (e.g., plumes or fur tufts), or in the patterns and hues of surface coloration, could easily be incorporated into a visual dialect system. Species-specific sexual imprinting on such differences is routinely explained as an interspecific isolating mechanism (e.g., Dobzhansky, 1970). In an intriguing study of the consequences of intraspecific morphological variation on sexual imprinting, Bateson (1978) tested the mate preferences of male quail that had been imprinted on specific female phenotypes in the laboratory. Such males were permitted to choose mates from females that were (1) phenotypically identical to the imprinted model (close relative), (2) similar but not identical in hue to the model (more distant relative), or (3) wholly different from the model in coloration (unrelated). Males preferred females that signaled intermediate relatedness, that is, (2). Bateson suggested that this choice would be favored because it reduced the risk of inbreeding depression, which was more likely if males had chosen (1) females, and outbreeding depression, which was more likely if they had preferred (3) females. He concluded that this pattern of sexual imprinting was favored because it promoted optimal levels of outbreeding (see also, Gilder and Slater, 1978; Slater and Clements, 1981).

Bateson's optimality argument could also apply to any of the dialect systems mediated through other senses. In any test of the hypothesis that dialects function to promote inbreeding, care must be taken to distinguish between incest avoidance and a more general inbreeding avoidance. For example, Packer (1975; 1977; 1979) suggested that male transfer behavior in olive baboons (*Papio anubis*) probably evolved as an inbreeding avoidance mechanism. He found support for this interpretation in the case of a single male which failed to transfer out of its natal troop prior to breeding. This male, and his female associates, were less successful at producing viable and vigorous offspring than were males that were transfers. Packer attributed this difference to inbreeding depression in the troop with the sedentary male. Replacing inbreeding with incest would result in a tighter and more meaningful argument. What Packer failed to emphasize was that transferring males joined nearest neighbor troops. In the framework of a single generation, such transfer behavior will reduce the probability of incestuous matings. But expanding the perspective one more generation changes the interpretation profoundly. In a second generation, males are again expected to transfer from their natal troops. Given a finite number of neighbor troops, how many of these will transfer into their fathers' natal troops? Thus the pattern of transfers may indeed avoid incest, but only much wider transfer would truly avoid inbreeding. The optimal inbreeding arguments presented here, and independently developed by Bateson (1978) and Price and Waser (1979), do admit the possibility of incest depression and hence avoidance, but in a framework which allows for more intense inbreeding than is usually considered favorable in traditional presentations.

Another primate offers an instructive contrast to Packer's baboons. Hamadryas baboons (*Papio hamadryas*) appear to possess a morphological dialect system which functions to promote intense inbreeding by limiting interbreeding to "small endogamous clans" (Abegglen, 1976). Hamadryas live in one-male social units, within which mating occurs, that consist of a single dominant male, his mates, and their younger offspring. A number of these one-male units usually sleep and forage together forming an ecological band (Kummer, 1968). Subadult "follower" males normally associate with particular one-male units. Such followers begin development of their own units by "kidnapping" a young female from their leader's unit. It turns out that kidnapping usually requires at least passive cooperation from the young female's parents before success is assured (Kummer, 1968; Abegglen, 1976).

Each of the one-male units in an area appears to be a clan of relatively close kin. The primary evidence for this is that members of each unit possess distinct and almost identical facial and pelage coloration. These color characters differ among one-male units within each band, as well as from band to band. With one exception, follower males possessed the same coloration as their leaders and his mates and offspring. When followers began their own units through kidnapping, their young females always had the same facial coloration, and presumably were fairly close kin (Abegglen, 1976).

The exceptional male, as is often the case, helped illustrate the inbreeding rule. During the early portion of Abegglen's study, this subadult consistently followed a one-male unit with disparate facial coloration. Long after similar males had kidnapped their first females, this odd male remained a failure. Despite continued attempts, behaviorally identical to those of successful males, he never gained a female. In the end, he apparently gave up, finally returning to trail a unit with his facial coloration, where he continued to be unsuccessful. Abegglen (1976) was able to observe a generational turnover in a number of Hamadryas units. In all cases, older dominant males were replaced by followers with the same facial coloration. It was only during such changes that a few females were gathered into units by males with different coloration (< 15% of the females) resulting in some gene flow between clans (Abegglen, 1976).

While the crucial choice tests were not performed, the behavior of clan females and dominant males in facilitating or frustrating follower kidnapping was consistent with a hypothesis that the clan colors were used to insure within-clan inbreeding (Abegglen, 1976). Crook (1970) has reported similar mosaics of pelage coloration in Gelada baboons (*Theropithecus gelada*). Their persistence in time and space also suggested to him that they may function to promote inbreeding in similar fashion.

I know of no evidence that ritualized visual displays vary in a manner that would permit their use in a dialect system as evisaged here. I can think of no reason why they should not. They do function in this fashion with respect to species recognition (for reviews, see Wilson, 1975; Smith, 1977), and more detailed investigation of displays in light of this hypothesis should show that they do vary geographically and can function to promote optimal levels of inbreeding in low fecundity organisms.

Sexual Selection as Isolating Mechanism

In Darwin's (1871) original discussion of "epigamic" (Huxley, 1938), or intersexual, sexual selection, female mate choice based on peculiar or extreme ornamentation, coloration, or behavior in males was considered a primary selective factor controlling the evolution of male characters. Fisher (1930) noted that such a system was likely to be self-stimulating. Once initiated, a female would benefit by choosing an "attractive" mate because she would then be more likely to produce attractive sons. These sons in turn would be more likely to be chosen when their turn came to mate (also see Weatherhead and Robertson, 1979). In his excellent review of sexual selection, Halliday (1978) echoes Fisher by emphasizing that the problem with such a system is not its maintenance but its origin. The problem is that to explain the system's initial increase in frequency, males possessing peculiar, but preferred, characters "must have some other heritable advantage, however slight, over other males," in order to explain a choosey female's expected benefit. Halliday (1978, p. 183) also suggested that, "the preferred character must be the marker of some other character that increases male fitness." The controversy surrounding the search for this predicted advantage has produced a number of intriguing hypotheses (e.g., Zahavi, 1975; Maynard Smith, 1978; Halliday, 1978). An additional alternative emerges directly from the preceding discussion of dialects and the hidden logic of sexual selection through female preference of peculiarities in their potential mates.

A novel, and therefore rare, character in a male may indicate his suitability as a mate without marking his unconditional viability or fertility. Trivers (1972) and Halliday (1978) have both suggested that one situation likely to favor epigamic sexual selection is when two closely related species occur in narrow sympatry. Under such conditions, females that choose males with the most extreme species-specific characters are less likely to hybridize and suffer reduced reproductive success. If the major difference distinguishing such species is ornamental, then their ornaments are expected to increase in intensity or form in the area of sympatry until the intrinsic self-stimulation drives the system to fixation in a much wider area. The same argument can be reduced to the level of narrowly sympatric demes, or even families within demes.

M. A. Cunningham (pers. comm.) has suggested that an implication of intense inbreeding is hidden in the logic of epigamic sexual selection. Consider a female with a heritable tendency to choose a male with a novel and peculiar character as her mate. The male character is equally heritable and is not necessarily associated with any aspect of the male's constitutional fitness. It may simply be a neutral ornament. Since her daughters are likely to inherit her tendencies to choose, and her sons their father's character stimulating such choice, intense inbreeding is likely to result. At its origin, intense inbreeding is likely to be one of the major consequences of epigamic sexual selection. Such a system will continue to promote increased levels of inbreeding until the system has diffused into many demes via the self-stimulation envisaged by Fisher (1930). Perhaps, at its inception, epigamic sexual selection increases in frequency simply because it promotes increased inbreeding with its attendant advantages. If so, it is simply another proximate mechanism, like philopatry or dialect-based assortative mating, that serves the same ultimate end of promoting inbreeding.

Finally, one class of behaviors related to mate choice appears to contradict the hypotheses about the advantages of inbreeding. The rare-male phenomenon (e.g., Petit, 1958; Ehrman, 1970; Farr, 1977) is defined as female choice of males with rare phenotypes or genotypes over males with the more common variants in a particular population. Such frequency-dependent mate selection is often characterized as disassortative mating, which could be a mechanism "to prevent inbreeding and to promote the genetic diversity of offspring" (Halliday, 1978, p. 201; and above references). The promotion of genetic diversity in offspring does not always require the prevention of inbreeding, though it may be facilitated by the avoidance of incest (Ch. 4). Perhaps the rare-male effect functions to prevent incest in much the manner of Bateson's (1978) optimal assortative mating in quail. If rare males were chosen only from potential mates that were optimally related and whose relatedness was assured through an independent mechanism (e.g., intense philopatry), then it might permit optimal inbreeding while promoting heterozygosity in inbred progeny. If significant interdeme dispersal were characteristic of a species displaying a rare-male effect in nature (where to the best of my knowledge the effect has not yet been demonstrated), then the effect would promote interdeme outbreeding and it would be expected only in high fecundity organisms. If it did occur in low fecundity species, where it appears to be most common, and was coupled with interdeme dispersal, it would flatly contradict the inbreeding hypotheses.

Williams (1975, p. 7) maintains that, "For answering questions on function in biology, comparative evidence is more reliable than mathematical reasoning." While there are problems (e.g., nonphilopatric wildfowl and perhaps the rare-male phenomenon), the bulk of the comparative evidence reviewed here is consistent with the hypothesis that inbreeding can be adaptive. The evidence also implies that inbreeding is an adaptation to relatively high mutation rates in low fecundity organisms that functions to promote more faithful transmission of successful genomes from parents to at least some of their offspring. The comparative evidence also supports the contention that one of the more frequent and widespread mechanisms producing favored levels of inbreeding is philopatry. It appears that selection may also favor other mechanisms (e.g., selfing or assortative mating based on dialect cues encoding relatedness) as reinforcements or replacements for philopatry in appropriate ecological circumstances. While the argument is far from proven, the consistency of its theoretical predictions with the empirical evidence makes further consideration appropriate.

The entire thesis strongly implies that low fecundity species, especially philopatric animals, should possess a particular population structure. In such species, megapopulations should be subdivided into relatively small and isolated groups of closely related interbreeding individuals. Such groups, of course, are what many would define as demes (e.g., Mayr, 1963; Dobzhansky, 1970).

CHAPTER **8**

Low Fecundity Species: Population Structure, Inbreeding, and Evolution

Earlier discussion of the evolution of inbreeding and philopatry (Ch. 5) emphasized the logical equivalency of the models of macrodifferentiation involved in speciation, and the model of microdifferentiation involved in subdivision of megapopulations into demes presented here. If the processes are indeed equivalent, then their end results, species and demes, should be similar. At the very least, the models do differ in referents, with speciation referring to reproductive relations among groups of organisms, while subdivision refers to reproductive relations, but among individuals within groups. With appropriate alterations in referents, species definitions may profitably be applied to demes.

Dobzhansky (1970, p. 357) argued that, "Species are, accordingly, systems of populations; the gene exchange between these systems is limited or prevented by a reproductive isolating mechanism or perhaps by a combination of several such mechanisms." I would argue that demes are, accordingly, groups of interbreeding individuals; the gene exchange between these groups being *limited* by a reproductive isolating mechanism, or perhaps several such mechanisms. As with species, isolation between conspecific demes can result from postmating factors (i.e., outbreeding depression) usually as a consequence of genetic divergence through chance or selective processes. In addition, premating mechanisms (e.g., philopatry or behavioral isolation, Ch. 7) may also occur as a result of chance divergence, or more often as an adaptive response to extant postmating factors. In this framework, a species might be considered a system of demes; the gene exchange between such

173

systems being *prevented* by one or more reproductive isolating mechanisms.

At any point in time, a widespread low fecundity species with many members would be expected to occur in more or less isolated demes. Each of these demes would be expected to consist of freely interbreeding, and therefore genetically similar, individuals. Such groups of relatively close kin (Chs. 3 and 5) would be expected, on average, to differ from one another genetically to a degree that would be negatively correlated with their degree of common ancestry. In philopatric species, the genetic difference between demes would be expected to increase with the geographical distance separating their normal ranges. Finally, the level of gene flow between demes is expected to be reduced relative to panmixia, but not eliminated as would occur if the demes were in different species. All of these predictions emerge directly from the models developed here (Chs. 2, 3 and 5), though they or similar predictions would also be consistent with a variety of alternative, complementary, or even contradictory hypotheses.

For example, such a demic population structure appears to be one of the cornerstones of Wright's (1931; 1969; 1977; 1978) shifting balance theory of evolution. When I initially recognized the similarities between the "novel" viewpoint developed here, and Wright's classic theory, I was a bit disconcerted. I felt that I might have rediscovered the wheel. Though we reached essentially identical conclusions about how many species should be structured in nature, we also appear to have traveled different routes, emphasizing different aspects of the problem along the way.

Like most population geneticists, Wright concentrated on the consequences of subdivision for the resulting populations or subdivided species (for the most recent and comprehensive review of the theory, see Wright, 1977, Ch. 13). For example, in contrasting mass selection in a panmictic species with selection in species subdivided into many semi-isolated demes, he (1931) noted,

> Finally in a large population, divided and subdivided into partially isolated local races of small size, there is a continually shifting differentiation among the latter (intensified by selection, but occurring under uniform and static conditions) which inevitably brings about an indefinitely continuing, irreversible, adaptive, and much more rapid evolution of the species.

He never explicitly offered a reason why the member individuals of a species should behave in a manner (e.g., philopatry) that insured subdivision. And while he did stress the fact that a species would evolve more quickly and efficiently if it were subdivided, then if it were panmictic, he never explicitly suggested that intraspecific reproductive isolation might be a causal factor in controlling subdivison. Neither did he comment on the correlation between lifetime fecundity and population structure implicit in this discussion of the relationship between inbreeding and the advantages of sex.

What Wright did do, and perhaps better than anyone else could have done, was to assume that various population structures could exist, and then deduce, in penetrating logical and mathematical detail, their important evolutionary consequences. His analysis convinced him and others (e.g., Miller, 1947), that neither extreme inbreeding (e.g., selfing) nor extreme outbreeding (i.e., large panmictic populations) were likely to lead easily to adaptive evolutionary advance. Too close inbreeding was inefficient because it would permit chance fixation at all segregating loci, depleting the variability a species needed to meet future environmental challenge. Too intense inbreeding, then, was expected to generate an evolutionary process governed too strictly by stochastic processes. In contrast, too wide outbreeding was considered inefficient because it resulted in mass selection which could only "trap" a species' characteristic allele frequencies at, or near, the most accessible selective peak. Too intense outbreeding, then, was expected to generate an evolutionary process governed too strictly by deterministic changes in gene frequency. Despite its facilitation of the maintenance of genetic variability, panmixis still restricted a population's capability for responding to changed or changing conditions (also, see Thompson, 1976).

In contrast to these extremes, subdivision into many partially isolated demes was expected to produce a shifting balance, with drift, owing to small population size (and resulting from inbreeding), and intrademic selection resulting in differentiated demes occupying separate selective peaks and valleys (Wright, 1956). Species-wide adaptive advance was expected to occur through interdemic selection among these demes. Interdeme selection, in turn, could occur through the excess emigration of members of more successful demes (those at adaptive peaks), the extinction of less successful demes (those in adaptive valleys), or both. Subdivided population structures were expected to generate a highly efficient evolutionary process, governed by a balance between the stochastic effects associated with small population size and the determinism of selection within and between demes. "The conclusion is that the subdivision of a species into local races provides the most effective mechanism for trial and error in the field of gene combinations" (Wright, 1932, p. 363).

Wright's primary emphasis was on the pattern of evolution in entire species. He did compare different species with different population structures and concluded that evolutionary advance was best served by the shifting balance associated with subdivision. He appears never to have applied similar reasoning to a direct comparison of alternative evolutionary processes within a single population or species. Had he done so, he might have reached conclusions similar to those reached here about the individual consequences, and therefore ultimate causes, of subdivision.

Even with his primary emphasis on species, Wright (1940, p. 235) did mention what may be the most important difference between panmixia and subdivision into demes. Although never explicitly couched in terms of individual advantage, he did suggest,

> One limitation on the effectiveness of selection in a panmictic population is that it can apply only to the *net effects* in each series of alleles. It is really the organism as a whole that is well or ill adapted. A really effective selection pressure should relate to genotypes not genes. But in a panmictic population, combinations are formed in one generation only to be broken up in the next (emphasis his).

As the level of panmixis is reduced, that is, as the level of inbreeding is increased, selection is increasingly able to discriminate between interacting systems of alleles, rather than being limited to the net effects of alternative alleles at single loci. In the extreme case of obligate selfing, "Selection would then be between genotypes" (Wright, 1940). In context, his genotype is equivalent to the genome as defined here (Ch. 4), and thus his argument did presage mine with respect to inbreeding's capacity to mold and safeguard coadapted genomes (Ch. 5).

Inbreeding, whether it results from some form of nonrandom assortative mating, or from subdivision into small semi-isolated demes, increases the size of the replicating genetic unit subject to selection until this replicator can include interacting alleles at many loci on the same or even different chromosomes. It appears to be true that the primary unit of selection in a panmictic species would be the replicating allele (e.g., Williams, 1966; Dawkins, 1976; 1978). The only thing questionable about such a view is its normal auxiliary assumption of almost universal panmixia in nature. The increased size of the selective unit associated with increased inbreeding benefits individual parents by increasing the heritability of fitness allowing parents to transmit their successful genomes with great fidelity to at least some of their offspring (Ch. 6). Such reproductive conservatism may be considered a function of the numerous morphological, physiological, and behavioral characters which result in subdivision. From this perspective, the increased evolutionary potential of the species stressed by Wright is not a function, but rather a fortuitous and unselected effect. Despite the differences, we do make similar predictions regarding the occurrence of small semi-isolated demes. This coincidence permits testing the thesis developed here within the massive theoretical and empirical framework developed by Wright and his intellectual descendants during the last 50 years. Because of the size of this base, I will necessarily abstract pertinent portions of the work rather than treat it in detail. In addition, rather than constantly citing the original work, all that follows, and more, can be found in Wright's own massive and comprehensive reviews of the subject (e.g., Wright, 1977; 1978).

Effective Population Size

Speaking of his conception of a shifting balance, Wright (1977), p. 465) noted that, ''the most serious criticisms of the theory have been that populations are in general not small enough to give a basis for appreciable sampling drift, or sufficiently isolated for enough differentiation of their genetic systems to give an adequate basis for interpopulational selection (Simpson, 1953; Mayr, 1963).'' While my thesis neither relies on nor predicts the occurrence of drift as an important evolutionary process, it does predict that low fecundity, actively dispersing organisms will normally be found in small semi-isolated demes. Since Wright's assumption about population structure is identical with my prediction, we are faced with similar crucial questions. Are the breeding units of many organisms (those of low fecundity species in my case) small enough to produce the required inbreeding (or drift)? Are demes genetically different from one another?

For our purpose, the breeding unit in question is the panmictic unit or deme (e.g., Mayr, 1963; Dobzhansky, 1970). The genetically effective size (N_e) of a deme is defined as the size of an idealized population producing the same level of inbreeding (or drift) as the population under study (Kimura and Crow, 1963). As a first approximation, the size of such a deme can be considered the number of reproductive individuals within a panmictic unit. One of the principle determinants of N_e is the species neighborhood size. A neighborhood, in turn, is defined as the geographical *area* surrounding a group of individuals, "within which the gametes which produced them may be considered to have been drawn at random" (Wright, 1978, p. 54). The *size* of such a neighborhood, as an estimator of N_e, is defined as the *number* of individuals living in a neighborhood area. Neighborhood size, then, is a joint function of both the magnitude of dispersal and the density of reproductive individuals living within range of that dispersal. For exploring questions of genetic structure and its consequences, the important parameter is effective dispersal which accounts for both dispersal and density (Ch. 2).

Wright (1938; 1943; 1951; 1978), and then others (for review, see Kimura and Ohta, 1971), developed a series of mathematical models for estimating N_e in natural populations. All were based on assumptions about the spatial distribution of individuals (e.g., continuous or clumped), and empirical estimates of local values of effective dispersal. Calculations based solely on these parameters were expected to overestimate effective population size owing to a number of common conditions which were expected to reduce N_e regardless of local patterns of dispersal and density (for reviews, see Wright, 1938; Kimura and Ohta, 1971).

For example, a skewed sex ratio of reproductive adults (e.g., owing to polygamy) will reduce N_e. In any population of cross-fertilizing organisms, N_e will be a function of the number of males (N_m) and females (N_f) which actually contribute gametes to the next generation, so that,

$$N_e = 4N_mN_f \, / \, (N_m + N_f) \qquad\qquad 8$$

As the reproductive sex ratio deviates from equality, the numbers of the rarer sex have an increasing effect on N_e, until equation 8, in the case of extreme polygyny ($N_m << N_f$), reduces to,

$$N_e = 4N_m \qquad\qquad 9$$

Cyclical fluctuations in population size with periods of a few generations will likewise result in instantaneous estimates of N_e being too high. In this case, N_e is best estimated by accounting for the temporal fluctuations such that,

$$1/N_e = t / \sum_{i=1}^{t} N_i \qquad\qquad 10$$

where N_i is the effective population size in each of t generations. Under such conditions, generations with the smaller populations, so-called genetic bottlenecks, will have disproportionate effects on the overall effective population size.

Finally, in a numerically stable population, with the average number of progeny produced per mated pair (k) equal to two, N_e will be a function of the variance in progeny production among breeding pairs (V_k), so that in a population with n reproductive members,

$$N_e = (4N - 2) / (V_k + 2) \qquad\qquad 11$$

If the actual number of progeny produced per pair were distributed randomly (i.e., following a Poisson distribution with $V_k = k = 2$), then N_e would equal N. If reproductive success were distributed nonrandomly ($V_k > 2$), then N_e would be less than N. As the disparity in individual reproductive success in a population increases, effective population size decreases. Strong selection, which by definition operates through disparate reproductive success, will usually decrease N_e, thereby increasing inbreeding intensity.

Despite the crucial importance of effective population size in determining the pattern and controlling the process of evolution, most treatments of N_e have been theoretical elaborations on this fundamental theme. Most of the studies which have actually attempted empirical estimation of N_e under natural conditions have relied solely on models based on effective dispersal. Despite the paucity of data, and in the face of inherent bias towards overestimation, many low fecundity species do appear to live in small demes (Table

14; Wright, 1978). Wright contends, and Begon (1978) demonstrates for *Drosophila subobscura* (Table 14), that as the information about factors likely to affect N_e increases, estimates of N_e tend to decrease. The intense philopatry observed in many other low fecundity species suggests that small demes are common rather than exceptional (Ch. 2). The high frequency of alternative behavioral characters which also tend to reduce deme size (e.g., polygamy, for review, Ginsberg, 1968; 1978), further reinforces this conclusion.

Although the data base is admittedly meager, I agree with Wright (1978) that for many species, and I would emphasize primarily low fecundity species, deme size is small enough to generate the inbreeding which he assumes and which I predict. I would also emphasize here that I part ways with Wright in that I would not predict that such inbreeding would necessarily result in appreciable drift.

Differentiation of Demes

Given small enough demes, Wright (e.g., 1977) assumed that they would be so isolated that they would diverge from one another solely as a result of the stochastic processes associated with small numbers. He never argued that all small demes would always, or could only, differentiate in this fashion. He only suggested that, in the absence of strong enough selection, drift would be possible. In contrast, my narrower prediction implies that any isolation between demes initially resulted, either directly or indirectly, from outbreeding depression and meiotic loss (Chs. 5 and 6). Once it originated, such isolation could permit further differentiation of other portions of the genome via drift given the proper conditions. As envisaged by Wright (1977; 1978); such drift would require "effectively neutral" alleles, which he defined as being subject to selection weak enough that the stochastic processes associated with small N_e could determine the course of differentiation. Such near neutrality is unnecessary in my model, and in fact were it commonplace, it would tend to belie my hypothesis of relatively intense inbreeding coupled with the selective maintenance of individual and deme variability. Despite these differences, both Wright and I predicted that demes would be genetically homogeneous (not homozygous) assemblages, owing to the inbreeding associated with small size. In addition, because

Table 14. Empirical estimates of genetically effective population sizes (N_e) in a variety of plant and animal species[a].

Species	N_e	Source
Plants		
Phlox pilosa	75–282	Levin & Kerster, 1974
Liatris aspera	30–191	Levin & Kerster, 1974
L. cylandracea	30–200	Levin & Kerster, 1974
Lithospermum caroliniense	2–6	Levin & Kerster, 1974
Lupinus texensis	42–94	Schaal, 1980
Animals: Invertebrates		
Cepea nemoralis	2800	Wright, 1978
C. nemoralis	190–6500	Greenwood, 1974
Drosophila pseudoobscura	25,000	Wright, 1978
D. subobscura	10,000	Begon, 1976
D. subobscura[b]	400	Begon, 1978
Apis mellifera	225–1093	Crozier, 1980
Animals: Vertebrates (Non Birds)		
Rana pipiens	112–446	Merrell, 1970
Sceloporus olivaceus	225	Kerster, 1964
Uta stansburiana	17	Tinkle, 1965
Peromyscus maniculatus	10–75	Rasmussen, 1964
P. maniculatus	80–120	Wright, 1978
P. polianotus	240–360	Wright, 1978
Mus musculus	12	Levin, et al., 1969
M. musculus	12	Defries & McClearn, 1970
Animals: Vertebrates (Birds)		
Puffinus puffinus	46,837	Barrowclough, 1980
Larus delawarensis	1250	Barrowclough, 1980
L. argentatus	1208	Barrowclough, 1980
L. novaehollandiae	174	Barrowclough, 1980
Sterna hirundo	11,447	Barrowclough, 1980
S. fuscata	64,580	Barrowclough, 1980
Riparia riparia	35	Barrowclough, 1980
Cistothorus palustris	17	Barrowclough, 1980
Troglodytes aedon	7,678	Barrowclough, 1980
Thromanes bewickii	563	Barrowclough, 1980
Phoenicurus phoenicurus	176	Barrowclough, 1980
Parus major (England)	1,806	Barrowclough, 1980
Parus major (Netherlands)	770	Barrowclough, 1980
Melospiza melodia (Ohio)	891	Barrowclough, 1980
Coereba flaveola	2,918	Barrowclough, 1980
Melospiza melodia (Ohio)	65–215	Miller, 1947
Chamaea fasciata	500	Miller, 1947

[a]Almost all estimates are conservatively high because they fail to account for all factors controlling effective population size.

[b]N_e from Begon (1976) based solely on effective dispersal from (1978) based on same populations but sex ratio, variance in reproductive success, and fluctuations in local density taken into account.

of the isolation between them, whatever its causes, we expected demes to differ genetically from one another.

Phenotypic Differentiation

In the earliest studies of differentiation, Wright (e.g., 1932; 1940) reported on the phenotypic variation observed by many naturalists in a wide variety of organisms. These included such phenomena as the occurrence of significantly different variants in Hawaiian land snails reported by Gulick (1905, cited by Wright, 1932). Snails in each valley had their own characteristic shell type, which differed among valleys in "nonutilitarian" respects. It appears that for many low fecundity organisms, such microgeographic variation in morphology is commonplace (Fig. 26; for reviews, see Dobzhansky, 1937; 1970; Mayr, 1942; 1963; Ford, 1964; Grant, 1971). Particularly striking are the cases where changes from one phenotype to another are spatially abrupt, temporally stable, and occur in the absence of obvious environmental discontinuities. These patterns suggest that "area effects" are the result of some sort of dynamic equilibrium (e.g., Dobzhansky, 1937; 1970; Epling and Dobzhansky, 1942; Epling et al., 1960; Cook, 1962; Cain, 1963; Ford, 1964; Smith et al., 1972; Oxford, 1976; Brown, 1976). The spirited discussions of whether such differences result from drift or selection (for reviews, see Ford, 1964; Wright, 1977; 1978; Cain, 1977) may have intrinsic importance, and are certainly important to Wright's thesis of a shifting balance between drift and selection, but they are less relevant to a prediction of inbreeding. If the morphological variants have a genetic basis, and are considered in the context of philopatric dispersal, their microdistribution is unequivocal, if indirect, evidence that demes are groups of related and therefore inbreeding individuals that differ from one another.

The spatial distribution of rare phenotypic "mutants" often adds weight to conclusions of inbreeding in many of these species, while offering some evidence about characteristic inbreeding intensities. In the Laysan Albatross (*Diomedea immutabilis*), an easily distinguished dwarf phenotype occurs in fewer than 1% of the nestlings born in any breeding season (Fisher, 1967). Such dwarfs are distributed nonrandomly on nesting islands, appearing in circumscribed clumps. For example, in one small (< 50 nests) patch of nesting habitat, Fisher (1967) found 6 dwarf nestlings one year, 13 the next. Since each monogamous pair produces a single nestling per year, more than 50% of the area's breeding

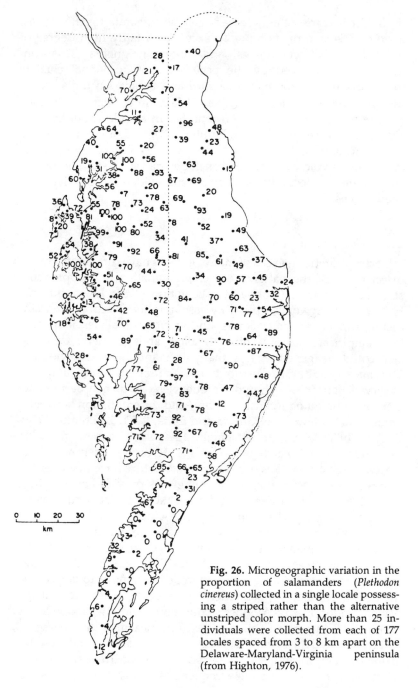

Fig. 26. Microgeographic variation in the proportion of salamanders (*Plethodon cinereus*) collected in a single locale possessing a striped rather than the alternative unstriped color morph. More than 25 individuals were collected from each of 177 locales spaced from 3 to 8 km apart on the Delaware-Maryland-Virginia peninsula (from Highton, 1976).

183

individuals carried the necessary genetic substrate for the expression of this rare phenotype. This implies a fairly high degree of relatedness between mates, and among neighbors. This conclusion is reinforced by the occurrence of additional clusters of subcolony specific morphological and behavioral traits within albatross nesting colonies (Fisher, 1976). Similar clusters of rare phenotypic variants have been reported in a wide variety of low fecundity species (e.g., snails, Hunter, 1975; rodents, Smith et al., 1972; and Barrett, 1976; lions, McBride, 1977). Thus, there is sufficient phenotypic evidence to conclude that at least some of the time, some low fecundity species are subdivided into relatively inbred demes.

Genotypic differentiation

Electrophoretic analyses of many proteins have furnished a more direct assay of the patterns of genetic variation and population structure in nature (Hubby and Lewontin, 1966; Lewontin and Hubby, 1966; Lewontin, 1974). By assuming that electrophoretically distinguishable enzymes correspond to different alleles at specific loci, empirical estimates of both allele and genotype frequencies could be generated for many loci and many individuals. The macro- and microdistribution of different alleles and the observed pattern of genotype frequencies could then be used to estimate inbreeding intensity within, and differentiation between, demes (for reviews, see Kimura and Ohta, 1971; Lewontin, 1974; Wright, 1977; 1978). Unfortunately, the ease of generating such estimates was not matched by ease in interpreting their meaning.

Most extensive studies of population structure have made use of electrophoretic techniques in the framework provided by Wright's (1943; 1965) F-statistic fixation indices, or some logically equivalent alternative (e.g., Cockerham, 1969). These indices permit the total genetic variation in any megapopulation to be partitioned into its hierarchical components (e.g., within demes, among demes, within races, among races, etc., see Ch. 3 and Wright, 1965). All of these indices use observed allele and genotype frequencies to determine the degree of heterozygote deficiency observed relative to that expected under Hardy-Weinberg conditions and megapopulation panmixia. Thus, as a fixation index, F_{IS} measures the degree of heterozygote deficiency observed within a deme, and can be estimated empirically from observed genotype frequencies and those expected based on allele frequencies in that deme. F_{ST} is the ratio of the actual variance in allele frequency among demes to the maximum expected if the demes were totally isolated and *fixed* for alternative alleles. It can be empirically estimated by

$$F_{ST} = \sigma_p^2 \, / \, \bar{p}\bar{q} \qquad\qquad 12$$

where $\bar{p}$ is the average frequency of the more common allele across demes, $\bar{q}$ the frequency of its alternative, and σ_p^2 the variance of p among demes. As a fixation index, F_{ST} measures the Wahlund (1928) effect, which occurs when different demes have assimilated different alleles at the same loci. Nei (1965) has developed an extension for estimating F_{ST} for loci carrying multiple alleles, such that

$$F_{ST} = \sigma_{jk} / \bar{p}_j \, \bar{p}_k \qquad\qquad 13$$

where σ_{jk} is the covariance of the jth and kth alleles, and $\bar{p}_j$ and $\bar{p}_k$ their mean frequencies. Finally, F_{IT} is defined as the total fixation index, and is usually estimated from F_{IS} and F_{ST} using equation 3 (Ch. 3).

Wright (1965; 1977; 1978) has repeatedly emphasized that empirically estimated fixation indices are usually *not* equivalent to inbreeding coefficients. Unless the alleles used in the estimations are effectively neutral, the indices do not measure the correlation between combining gametes as a result of coancestry. They therefore cannot be used with complete confidence to infer either presence or absence of subdivision and inbreeding. Despite his warnings, some continue to equate fixation indices and gametic correlations (e.g., Schaal, 1975), or presume little subdivision or inbreeding on the basis of low F-values (e.g., Brussard and Vawter, 1975; Yardley and Hubbs, 1976; Barrowclough, 1980).

The problem may be that Wright (e.g., 1978), and many others (e.g., Kimura, 1968; Kimura and Ohta, 1971; Ohta, 1973) do assume that much of the natural isozyme variation detected electrophoretically is effectively neutral. Such effective neutrality (i.e., selection not intense enough to obviate the genotypic consequences of small N_e, whether considered as inbreeding or drift) is a necessary condition for Wright's shifting balance theory. If the assumption of near neutrality were true, then near zero values of fixation indices would indeed imply an absence of inbreeding and subdivision. The common occurrence of such low values in a variety of low fecundity species, then, would falsify the hypothesis that they should be inbreeding. Despite this putative falsification for some species, there is an equally large and diverse group of low fecundity organisms, both plants and animals, that show substantial heterozygote deficiencies and resulting high F values (for a detailed review of empirically estimated F values, see Wright, 1978, Ch. 7). It is important that evolutionary theory be capable of explaining their obviously high levels of inbreeding functionally.

If some form of heterotic selection were operating, then fixation indices could no longer unequivocally indicate inbreeding intensity or degree of subdivision (Ch. 4; and Wright, 1978). Observable Hardy-Weinberg genotypic equilibria could result from a balance between inbreeding's reduction, and selection's increase, of heterozygote frequencies. Just such a balance has been demonstrated in nature in detailed investigations of populations of wood lice (*Porcellio scaber*, Sassaman, 1978), and *Drosophila subobscura* (Krimbas and Alevizos, 1973). In a conceptually similar fashion, Spielman et al. (1977) used electrophoretic variants to explore the levels of inbreeding and subdivision in tribal Yanomamo Indians from the Amazon. Regardless of the estimator used, observed allele and genotype frequencies implied little inbreeding or subdivision ($0.048 < F_{ST} < 0.081$). Similar studies usually stop there, but Spielman et al. (1977) performed computer simulations of mating patterns based on detailed knowledge of typical pedigrees, mate choice, and patterns of dispersal. The results of this analysis indicated that the Yanomamo were actually subdivided into small inbred demes ($0.330 < F_{ST} < 0.500$). They concluded that fixation indices "substantially underestimate the true coefficient of inbreeding in such populations," which they believed, "should be no less than 0.3 and may well be greater than 0.5." Finally, they suggested that the most likely reasons for the disparate estimates of inbreeding intensity were some form of heterotic selection or low levels of interdeme migration maintaining heterozygosity and variability in spite of the intense inbreeding (for a similar analysis and conclusion about mice, see Duncan et al., 1979). Even hindsight will not permit us to decide which, or how many, previous studies of the genetic structure of natural populations suffered similar biases against conclusions of inbreeding or subdivision. In the future, unless heterotic selection can be ruled out, perhaps fixation indices should not be used as evidence about inbreeding intensity.

Inbreeding may not equal homozygosity, but it will produce

genetic homogeneity (Ch. 4). If a locus carries more than one allele in any megapopulation, then the alleles may be distributed differentially among demes without substantial effect on within-deme heterozygosity. If a megapopulation were subdivided into semi-isolated demes, heterogeneity in the among-deme allele frequencies would be expected. Such differences could be a response to the chance effects of inbreeding, or might result from selection pressures in a heterogeneous environment. Whether such differentiation results from drift or selection may be intrinsically important, and it does bear on Wright's (1977) conception of a shifting balance. Nonetheless, like phenotypic differentiation, the occurrence of genetic microdifferentiation in and of itself would support the hypothesis that a species is inbreeding.

If low fecundity species are inbreeding owing to subdivision, and if one of the controlling factors in such a breeding system is outbreeding depression (Ch. 5), then demes should often show significant differences in allele frequencies. They might even display occasional substitution at loci with multiple alleles. Such expected differences can be investigated by simple statistics that compare allele frequencies (e.g., Snedecor and Irwin, 1933), or by calculating genetic similarities and distances (e.g., Nei, 1972). If there were considerable substitution of alternative alleles in a heterotic environment, then subdivision would produce a relatively high value for F_{ST}, but a low F_{IS}. This pattern is commonly observed in natural populations (Wright, 1978). One of the more foolproof methods for demonstrating such differences would be to map allele and genotype frequencies in space (e.g., Selander and Yang, 1969; Selander et al., 1969; Selander and Kaufman, 1975). If the sample deme represented a true deme, and if such demes were small and therefore inbred, then patterns of microgeographic variation should emerge (Fig. 27).

Empirical studies of the genetic structure of numerous organisms have been thoroughly reviewed by Wright (1978, Ch. 6). His conclusion was that many species, especially vertebrates and plants, display patterns of variability consistent with a view that they mate in small, inbred, and partially isolated demes. Rather than repeat his monumental analysis, I will just note that his conclusions are consistently reinforced by more recent studies on additional species showing the predicted patterns of variation. Such organisms include obligately cross-fertilizing, yet inbreeding, plants (e.g., Schall, 1975; 1976; 1980; Keeler, 1978; Levin, 1978),

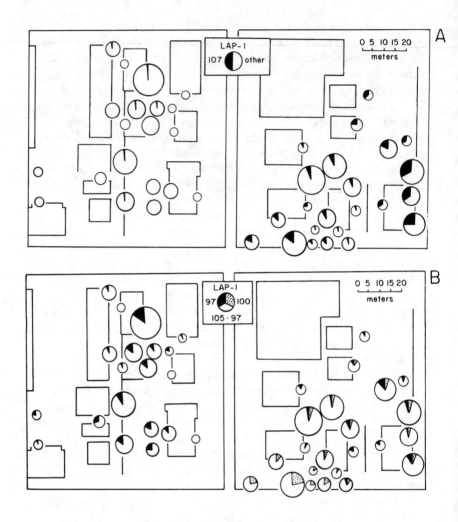

Fig. 27. Microgeographic variation in allele frequencies at the *Lap-1* locus in colonies of the snail (*Helix aspersa* on adjacent city blocks in Texas. Each circle is proportional to the number of snails in the sampled colony.   A. The distribution of the most common allele versus all others.   B. The distribution of these "other" alleles in the same set of colonies (redrawn from Selander and Kaufman, 1975).

non-Drosophilid invertebrates (e.g., Halkka et al., 1974; Coker and Kuma, 1974; Saul et al., 1978), many species of *Drosophila* (e.g., McKenzie, 1975; McKenzie and Parsons, 1974; Hoenigsberg et al., 1977; Smith et al., 1978), fish (e.g., McPhail, 1977; Child, 1977), amphibians (e.g., Bogart and Wasserman, 1972; Inger et al., 1974;

Hedgecock, 1976; Highton, 1976; Tordoff et al., 1976; Keller and Lyerla, 1977), reptiles (e.g., Gorman et al., 1975; Adest, 1977), birds (e.g., Ferrell, 1966; Baker, 1974; 1975; Barrowclough and Corbin, 1978), and mammals (e.g., Nozawa et al., 1975; Smith et al., 1975; Glover et al., 1977; Patton and Yang, 1977).

The combined evidence of phenotypic and genetic microgeographical differentiation in many low fecundity species is consistent with a view that they should be and are inbreeding. Even allowing for real exceptions, a significant number of what are usually referred to as outbreeders (e.g., Dobzhansky, 1970), are inbreeding intensely enough to significantly reduce the costs of sex below the levels assumed in current discussions of that subject (e.g., Williams, 1975; Maynard Smith, 1978).

Demes and Relatedness

It would be difficult to overestimate the importance of either the concept or the reality of genetic relatedness for evolutionary theory. Heritable, and therefore genetic, similarities among parents and progeny were cornerstones of Darwin's (1859) theory of evolution by natural selection. Individual and group relatedness is also a crucial component of the modern theories of kin selection and inclusive fitness, so important in sociobiology (e.g., Hamilton, 1964a; 1964b; Alexander, 1974; West Eberhard, 1975; Wilson, 1975; Maynard Smith, 1976b). Quantitative estimates of genetic relatedness often enter the equations of population genetics (e.g., Malecot, 1948; Jacquard, 1975), and quantitative genetics (e.g., Wright, 1977), as well as those of sociobiology. Such estimates enter these equations as controlling parameters, capable of causally determining the behavior of the systems under study. Indeed, there is even some indication that patterns of variation of relatedness among individuals may have important consequences in such systems (e.g., Barash et al., 1978; but see Dawkins, 1979).

Relatedness and inbreeding are inextricably intertwined (for review, Ch. 3). The relatedness of two individuals depends on the number of ancestors they share, which in turn is a function of the level of inbreeding that characterizes their group or species. The intensity of inbreeding, in turn, is wholly determined by the average relatedness of mates. Despite caveats that inbreeding would change the picture (e.g., Hamilton, 1972; West Eberhard, 1975), almost every intuitive and mathematical treatment of problems dependent on relatedness dismisses the possibility of inbreeding. Phrases like, "in the absence of inbreeding," are as common in treatments of social behavior as are references to kin selection (e.g., Hamilton, 1972; West Eberhard, 1975; Blick, 1977).

One of the reasons for the assumption of no inbreeding is mathematical convenience. In so-called outbred species relatedness can be calculated directly "from immediate connections shown in the pedigree" (Hamilton, 1972, p. 197). Such calculations result in the familiar average r values, e.g., r = 1/2 between parents and progeny or between full sibs, r = 1/4 between half-sibs or between aunts and nieces, and so on (Hamilton, 1972; Alexander, 1977). As Dawkins (1978) stresses, this r can be interpreted in two different ways. Following the logic of the probabilistic models of relatedness (e.g., Malecot, 1948), r can be considered the probability that two individuals carry identical copies of a particular allele at a particular locus (Davies and Krebs, 1978). Alternatively, and more frequently (e.g., Hamilton, 1954a; 1972; West Eberhard, 1975; Davies and Krebs, 1978), r has been considered equivalent to Wright's coefficient of relatedness (Ch. 3). As a correlation coefficient, r is an expectation of the proportion of two individual's genomes that are identical. While the two interpretations rely on identical mathematics, conceptually they are distinct. The probabilistic model measures relatedness from the perspective of a particular allele (Dawkins, 1978), while the correlation models measure it from the perspective of entire individuals (Hamilton, 1972). The importance of this distinction between genes and individuals depends on their importance as the primary replicating units of selection (Dawkins, 1978).

If alternative alleles are the fundamental units of selection (Williams, 1966; Maynard Smith, 1978; Dawkins, 1978), then relatedness from the perspective of alleles may be more important in determining the course of kin selection. If interacting systems of alleles at different loci are the fundamental units of selection (Wright, 1931; 1969; 1977; Mayr, 1963; De Benedictis, 1978), then individual relatedness may be more important. Without entering into a detailed discussion of the merits of either argument, I would note that the arguments of the gene selectionists heavily rely on an implicit assumption of outbreeding. It is only in an outbreeding system that recombination so tears apart genomes in every generation, that single genes, as the only reasonable unit of transmission, *must* also be the unit of selection (Dawkins, 1976; 1978).

What is this outbreeding, on which current models of relatedness and selection rely so heavily? The numbers generated offer a clear, if surprising, answer. The only way in which parents would be consistently related to their offspring by 1/2, generation after generation, is under *perfect* outbreeding. Parents must be totally unrelated, that is share zero alleles identical by descent. For outbred coefficients of relatedness to apply, there can be absolutely no inbreeding. Based on theoretical considerations perfect outbreeding is impossible (Ch. 3). Based on the genetic and ecological evidence discussed above, even species-wide panmixia is probably rare. This is especially true of the low fecundity social vertebrates, so often the objects of sociobiological speculation. Thus, the mathematically simple estimates of relatedness which assume outbreeding are unrealistic at best.

The unreliability of such coefficients is especially obvious when interpreted as measures of genomic similarity among individuals. Even with the considerable levels of genetic variability observed in nature (Lewontin, 1974), it is unlikely that an average parent in any species could share as little as 50% of its genome with its offspring. Estimates actually based on allelic identities would indicate that the vast majority of an individual's alleles would be found at least as single copies in its parents. This lack of realism has not gone unnoted, but it does appear to have been glossed over (e.g., Dawkins, 1978; Davies and Krebs, 1978).

One potential solution to this dilemma that has been advanced (Dawkins, 1978; 1979), is to restrict the concept of relatedness to probabilities of allelic identity, though this would necessarily entail acceptance of the gene selection viewpoint. Since our primary interest is likely to be in the origin and selective increase or elimination of particular traits, it may be appropriate to consider relatedness from the perspective of the alleles controlling such traits. The major, and perhaps, insurmountable difficulty with this strategy is that it can only apply to traits which are the phenotypic expression of single alleles or loci (but, see Dawkins, 1978; 1979). With this caution in mind, we can still explore the argument. Any mutation can usually be considered unique at its origin in a finite population. From such an allele's perspective, any of its carrier's potential mates would truly be unrelated, regardless of past or current inbreeding intensities. Reproduction by the original carrier would distribute such a mutant in a manner consistent with the calculus of outbred relatedness. Any of that carrier's offspring would be expected to carry the mutant with a probability of one-half. Taken as a group, 50% of these progeny would be expected to carry, and thus, their relatedness to one another with respect to the mutant would also be one-half, and so on. Outbred coefficients of relatedness can apply to a novel mutant, but *only* when it is rare. As soon as it becomes common enough to appear in both members of a mated pair, then the pair would be inbreeding with respect to that locus, and the outbred coefficients would no longer apply. The duration of a mutation's rarity is itself a function of the characteristic level of inbreeding in the species in question. Increased inbreeding (reduced N_e) would lessen the time that outbred coefficients of relatedness could apply even from the perspective of single alleles. In the end, inbreeding intensity becomes a crucial consideration in any model of selection which is based on relatedness, regardless of whether one's perspective is allelic identity or genomic similarity. Despite this importance, inbreeding in most of its guises is generally overlooked or ignored.

Treisman and Dawkins (1976) recently criticized Williams's (1975) concept of the cost of meiosis (Ch. 6). Their argument illustrates the dangers of a reduced consciousness of inbreeding. Their entire argument of there being no cost of meiosis from the perspective of a sexual allele is based entirely, if not explicitly, on inbreeding at the level of a single locus. They concluded that if sex were controlled by a single locus *homozygous* for a sexual allele, then such an allele would suffer no cost of meiosis. Even in the unlikely event that a complex character like sexual reproduction could be controlled by a single locus, the model still assumes inbreeding. The necessary homozygosity of the sexual allele produces a population with an allelic relatedness at the sexual locus equalling one. In this perfectly inbred group (at least from the sexual allele's view), there would indeed be no cost of meiosis at the sexual locus. Yet it would be the inbreeding, and not the gene selectionist view, which actually eliminated the cost. Williams's (1975) argument of a 50% cost of meiosis is valid in an outbred group, even from the perspective of single alleles. For example, if there were multiple alleles, each capable of independently producing sexuality in either single or double dose (i.e., $S_1, \ldots S_n$), then true outbreeding with mates having no sexual alleles in common would be possible. In such a group, the cost of meiosis to each sexual allele would be 50% for as long as the outbreeding remained possible. As soon as inbreeding occurred, the cost of meiosis would begin to decline until complete fixation of one allele in the population eliminated the cost just as Treisman and Dawkins argued. Inbreeding, then, can profoundly influence relatedness, which can, in turn, influence the selective value of characters like sex. Given the general importance of relatedness to evolutionary theory, and the application of such theory to inbred organisms (e.g., vertebrates), perhaps it is time to assimilate inbreeding more completely into that theory.

Inbreeding and Relatedness

Inbreeding has two theoretical effects on relatedness. One, it will tend to increase the average level of relatedness among members of an inbred group. Two, it will tend to decrease the variance in relatedness among those members (for reviews, see Wright, 1969; Jacquard, 1974; 1975). Quantitative estimates of these consequences are possible. In chapter 3, Equation (5) was presented for determining the average level of relatedness among deme members as a function of deme size, in the absence of mutation, migration, and selection,

$$\alpha_t = 1 - e^{-t/2N} \qquad\qquad 5$$

where t is the number of generations since the deme was founded, and N is its effective poupulation size. Jacquard (1974) has determined that in such a population the variance in α in any generation (V_t) will be,

$$V_t = 1/6N\,(1 - 1/2N)^{2t} \qquad\qquad 14$$

Thus, in the absence of mutation, migration, and selection, a deme's average relatedness is expected to increase continuously, ultimately approaching its limit of one. At the same time, but at a faster rate, the group's variance in average relatedness will be decreasing to zero (e.g., Table 15; Jacquard, 1974).

I do not present these formulae, nor the numbers they generate, as accurate descriptions of inbreeding's quantitative effects on relatedness. Certainly their accuracy is limited by their improbable assumptions. Selection is normally expected to act against mutations, and if outbreeding depression does discriminate against immigrants, then the accuracy of such estimates would increase. On

Table 15. The relationship between inbreeding intensity (deme size) and the mean ($\propto$) and variance (V) in relatedness among deme members as a function of number of generations since the deme was formed by "unrelated individuals," and assuming no mutation, immigration, and selection.[a]

Generation (t)	Effective Population Size (N_e)			
	25	100	400	1000
Mean ($\propto$)				
1	.020	.005	.001	.0005
10	.183	.048	.012	.005
50	.635	.221	.061	.024
100	.867	.394	.117	.048
200	.982	.633	.221	.095
500	.999	.918	.465	.221
Variance (V)				
1	6×10^{-3}	2×10^{-3}	4×10^{-4}	2×10^{-4}
10	4×10^{-3}	1×10^{-3}	4×10^{-4}	2×10^{-4}
50	9×10^{-4}	1×10^{-3}	4×10^{-4}	2×10^{-4}
100	1×10^{-4}	6×10^{-4}	3×10^{-4}	2×10^{-4}
200	2×10^{-7}	2×10^{-4}	2×10^{-4}	1×10^{-4}
500	1×10^{-11}	1×10^{-5}	1×10^{-4}	1×10^{-4}

[a]Values are estimated using equations (5) and (14), the variance is rounded to the nearest significant digit.

the other hand, heterotic selection would tend to reduce their accuracy by maintaining segregating loci in any deme, regardless of size. At the very least, such analytic coefficients of relatedness do imply something about the proportion of an individual's genome, and the proportion of a deme's gene pool, that is likely to have shared a common selective history (Ch. 3). Inbreeding undoubtedly complicates the effort to develop a realistic, accurate, and yet manageable, calculus of relatedness. I am certainly unwilling and indeed incapable of even beginning such a task (but for elegant beginnings, see Flesness, 1978; Michod and Anderson; 1979; Michod, 1979). Yet the obvious limitations on effective population size in so many organisms (e.g., Table 14), as well as the many other forms of inbreeding observed in nature (Ch. 7), together with the phenotypic and genotypic evidence that many species are indeed inbred, bankrupts the uncritical use of outbred coefficients of relatedness.

Patterns of relatedness within a group are determined by the average intensity and temporal continuity of the inbreeding characteristic of that group. Whether the group inbreeds through obligate full-sib mating (N_e = 2), or in larger but still limited demes (e.g., N_e = 100), the ultimate effects on relatedness are identical (Table 15). The average proportion of an individual's genome shared with other deme members tends to increase with increases in inbreeding intensity. In addition, the variance in relatedness among deme members decreases, and at a faster rate. Ultimately inbreeding produces a deme among whose members, "There is no more resemblance between parent and offspring than between cousins" (Haldane, 1932, p. 35). Inbreeding increases relatedness and also homogenizes it. If a deme has been small and sufficiently isolated for enough time, its members will come to share the greater portion of their genomes (the ancestral portion, see Ch. 6).

Small semi-isolated demes can be considered extended families, with all members closely resembling one another genetically. So-called unrelated individuals in such demes are actually likely to be close genetic kin regardless of their immediate pedigree relationship. That distant pedigree relatives may be extremely similar genetically may explain the random mating so characteristic of many organisms. An absence of obvious pedigree incest, or even near incest, is certainly *not* strong evidence that a species is not inbreeding, as is often asserted (e.g., Bischof, 1975; Packer, 1975; 1979; Greenwood and Harvey, 1976; Bengsston, 1978; Maynard Smith, 1978; Williams, 1980). With respect to the ancestral portion of their genomes, they may be inbreeding as intensely as any selfer. At the same time, they may avoid the potential costs associated with true incest. These, of course, are the product of the relatively minute, but nonetheless important, remainder of the genome (the mutant portion, Ch. 6). Given the deme sizes observed in many low fecundity species, especially vertebrates (Table 14), it may no longer be tenable to consider them outbreeders. Rather, the question may become, just how inbred are they (also, see Price and Waser, 1979)?

Conclusions

Some criticism may be leveled at this work for what is perceived as an overemphasis on the potential advantages, and perhaps a too facile dismissal of the potential disadvantages, of inbreeding. The bias was conscious and was offered as an antithesis to the nearly universal and more traditional thesis of inbreeding as maladaptation. The latter view has been expressed *in extremis* by Bischof (1975, p. 42), *"in the whole animal world with very few exceptions no species is known in which under natural conditions inbreeding occurs to any considerable degree"* (his emphasis).

Evidence for incest avoidance in a few natural populations of humans (e.g., Shepher, 1971; Bischof, 1975), other primates (e.g., Sade, 1968; Itani, 1972; Packer, 1979), and a variety of lesser vertebrates (e.g., mice, Hill, 1974; birds, Greenwood et al., 1978; Koenig and Pitelka, 1979) is used as primary support for this view. Such "inbreeding" avoidance is thought to be an adaptation preventing the inbreeding depression so easily demonstrated in laboratory or captive organisms (Bischof, 1975; Wright, 1977; Ralls et al., 1979) and occasionally in nature as well (e.g., Greenwood et al., 1978; Packer, 1979).

There is an alternative view of much of that evidence and additional evidence that is cited less often that flatly contradicts the view that inbreeding (or even incest) *per se* is maladaptive. For example, the human incest taboo is often considered a cultural universal (Bischof, 1975; Wilson, 1978; Alexander, 1979). Avoidance of marriage by individuals that grow up together in the same kibbutz in Israel (Shepher, 1971) is often cited as strong evidence for the naturalness of that taboo. As Livingstone (1980) pointed out, Kaffman (1977) has proposed a number of simpler cultural explanations for the absence of marriage and documented that sexual interaction between unrelated kibbutz "siblings" not only occurs but is apparently increasing in frequency. While rare, true incest between primary family members does occur, and is also apparently increasing in modern societies (Sarles, 1975). Several human societies have no incest taboo whatsoever (Schneider, 1976). There are even modern and viable societies in which intense inbreeding though not incest is preferred (e.g., uncle-niece in India, Sanghvi, 1966), and in which inbreeding depression is apparently absent (e.g., Rao and Inbaraj, 1977). Livingstone (1980) interprets this disparity as evidence against a biological view of human behavior.

The occurrence of much incest in spite of the legislated taboo is inconsistent with a view of incest avoidance as an evolved adaptation. Evolutionary theory implies that actual behavior, and not necessarily legislated mores, should be adaptive, (Alexander,

1979). Perhaps the disparity can be viewed as a misunderstanding of the adaptive nature of inbreeding, rather than a contradiction of a sociobiological theory of human behavior.

There is considerable evidence from nonhuman primates that contradicts the traditional view of detrimental inbreeding. For example, in the Cayo Santiago rhesus monkeys, Missakian (1973) reported a much higher frequency of mother-son and full-sib incest than Sade's (1968) earlier and more often cited study. Similarly, while Itani's (1972) study of "incest avoidance" in Japanese macaques did demonstrate low levels of mother-son or full-sib incest owing to juvenile male dispersal, it also suggested that owing to adult male longevity and female troop tenacity (philogamy), a high frequency of intense father-daughter incest (i.e., fathers mating with daughters born of a previous daughter, etc.) was very likely. No one, including Itani, accentuates the latter possibility.

Relatively high frequencies (10–100% of matings) of parent-offspring or full sibling incest have also been documented in natural populations of low fecundity insects (e.g., Cowan, 1979; Greenberg, 1979) and various vertebrates usually considered *a priori* outbreeders (e.g., lizards, Tinkle, 1967; albatross, Fisher, 1967; swans, Reese, 1980; great tits, Van Noordwijk and Scharloo, 1981; mice, Dice and Howard, 1951; wolves and other canids, Mech 1977; and fallow deer, Smith, 1979). Such instances are not unequivocal evidence that the adaptive theory of optimal inbreeding elaborated here is true. Nonetheless, they are unequivocal in denying the universal validity and uncritical acceptance of the alternative detrimental inbreeding hypothesis. At the very least a reappraisal of tradition appears necessary, based on *all* the evidence.

Karl Popper (1963) prefaced his classic "Conjectures and Refutations" with two quotes that apparently summarized his major thesis, and perhaps offer a prescription for science:

Experience is the name every one gives to their mistakes.
— Oscar Wilde
Our whole problem is to make mistakes as fast as possible.
— John Archibald Wheeler

I repeat them because I also believe that we learn from our mistakes. One of the easiest and quickest ways to fall into error is to follow an argument to its logical extremities. I believe that Williams's (1975) conclusion that sex was maladaptive in low fecundity organisms followed directly from his implicit assumption of an *outbreeding* biota. I believe the conclusion is an error. Yet, it was certainly an important and necessary stimulus to the thesis developed here. Whether the alternative explanation of *inbreeding* sex as an adaptation making an immediate contribution to individual inclusive fitness is judged an error is irrelevant in the long run, so long as it too can be translated heuristically into experience. I certainly do not believe that the teleonomic web I have attempted to weave, causally connecting philopatry, inbreeding, and sexual reproduction, is without blemish. I am, however, so enmeshed in it that I have probably lost much of my capacity for objectively detecting many of the blemishes. I must leave that task to the interested, or irate, reader.

As for the purpose of this book, Carson (1967, p. 283), in an earlier discussion of the role of inbreeding in evolution, suggested.

> Even now, despite the comprehensive genetic explanation of inbreeding depression and the demonstration of the apparent absence of harmful effects in "normally" inbreeding plants and animals, a tendency remains for the importance of inbreeding to be underrated. Perhaps this is partly influenced by human attitudes toward both inbreeding and outbreeding.

I applaud Carson's judgement, but suggest that even he may have underestimated the importance of inbreeding, especially misjudging the numbers and kinds of organisms to which that importance applied. I am convinced that until inbreeding, whatever its guise, or intensity, is brought into the mainstream of evolutionary theory, a comprehensive understanding of the evolutionary process will elude us. If the arguments developed and presented here help stimulate such an assimilation, then I would consider my objective achieved.

References

Abegglen, J. J. 1976. On socialization in hamadryas baboons. Ph.D. Dissertation. Univ. of Zurich, Zurich, Switzerland.

Adest, G. A. 1977. Genetic relationships in the genus *Uma* (Iguanidae). *Copeia* 1977:47–52.

Alcock, J. 1975. *Animal behavior*. Sinauer, Sunderland, Mass.

Alexander, R. D. 1967. Acoustical communication in arthropods. *Annu. Rev. Entomol.* 12:495–526.

Alexander, R. D. 1974. The evolution of social behavior. *Annu. Rev. Ecol. Syst.* 5:325–83.

Alexander, R. D. 1977. Natural selection and the analysis of human sociality. In *The changing scenes in the natural sciences, 1776–1976*. (C. E. Goulden, ed.), Academy of Natural Sciences, Philadelphia, pp. 283–337.

Alexander, R. D. and P. W. Sherman. 1977. Local mate competition and parental investment in social insects. *Science* 196:494–500.

Allard, R. W. 1975. Mating system and microevolution. *Genetics* 79: 115–26.

Allard, R. W., S. K. Jain and P. L. Workman. 1968. The genetics of inbreeding populations. *Adv. Genet.* 14:55–131.

Allard, R. W. and A. L. Kahler. 1971. Allozyme polymorphisms in plant populations. *Stadler Symp.* 3:9–24.

Allard, R. W., G. R. Babbel, M. T. Klegg and A. L. Kahler. 1972. Evidence for coadaptation in *Avena barbata*. *Proc. Nat. Acad. Sci.* (USA) 69:3043–48.

Allard, R. W. and C. Wehrhahn. 1964. A theory which predicts stable equilibrium for inversion polymorphisms in the grasshopper *Moraba scurra*. *Evolution* 18:129–30.

Allen, G. 1965. Random and non-random inbreeding. *Eug. Quart.* 12: 181–98.

Altmann, S. A. and J. Altmann. 1970. *Baboon ecology.* Univ. of Chicago Press, Chicago.

Anderson, W. W. 1968. Further evidence for coadaptation in crosses between geographic populations of *Drosophila pseudoobscura. Genet. Res.* 12:317–30.

Anderson, W. W. 1969. Genetics of natural populations XLI. The selection coefficients of heterozygotes for lethal chromosomes in *Drosophila* on different genetic backgrounds. *Genetics* 62:827–36.

Antonovics, J. 1968. Evolution in closely adjacent plant populations: V. Evolution of self-fertility. *Heredity* 23:219–38.

Antonovics, J. 1971. The effects of a heterogeneous environment on the genetics of natural populations. *Amer.Scientist* 59:593–99.

Antonovics, J. 1976. The input from population genetics: "The new ecological genetics." *Syst. Bot.* 1:233–45.

Antonovics, J., A. D. Bradshaw and R. G. Turner. 1971. Heavy metal tolerance in plants. *Adv. Ecol. Res.* 7:2–58.

Austin, O. L., Sr. 1949. Site tenacity, a behavior trait of the Common Tern. *Bird Banding* 20:1–39.

Avise, J. C. 1975. Genetics of plate morphology in an unusual population of threespine sticklebacks (*Gasterosteus aculeatus*). *Genet. Res.* 27:33–46.

Avise, J. C. 1976. Genetic differentiation during speciation. In *Molecular Evolution.* (F. J. Ayala, ed.), Sinauer, Sunderland, Mass., pp. 106–22.

Ayala, F. J. 1975. Genetic differentiation during the speciation process. *Evol. Biol.* 8:1–78.

Ayala, F. J., M. L. Tracy, L. G. Barr and J. G. Ehrenfeld. 1974. Genetic and reproductive differentiation of the subspecies *Drosophila equinoxialis caribbensis. Evolution* 28:24–41.

Ayala, F. J., M. L. Tracy, D. Hedgecock and R. C. Richmond. 1975. Genetic differentiation during the speciation process. *Evolution* 28:576–92.

Bairlein, F. 1978. Uber, die biologie einer sudwest deutschen population der Monchsgrasmuche (*Sylvia atricapilla*). *J. Ornith.* 119:14–51.

Baker, M. C. 1974. Genetic structure of two populations of white-crowned sparrows with different song dialects. *Condor* 76:351–56.

Baker, M. C. 1975. Song dialects and genetic differences in white-crowned sparrows (*Zonotrichia leucophrys*). *Evolution* 29:226–41.

Baker, M. C. and L. R. Mewaldt. 1978. Song dialects as barriers to dispersal in white-crowned sparrows, *Zonotrichia leucophrys* Nuttali. *Evolution* 32:712–22.

Baker, H. G. 1959. Reproductive methods as factors in speciation in flowering plants. *Cold Spring Harbor Symp. Quant. Biol.* 24:177–91.

Baker, H. G. 1963. Evolutionary mechanisms in pollination biology. *Science* 139:877–83.

Baker, R. R. 1978. *The evolutionary ecology of animal migration.* Hodder and Staughton, London.

Balashov, Y. S. 1975. Interpopulation genetic incompatibility in *Ornithodoros verrucosus*, in Russian, English summary in *J. Zoology* 54: 1160–68.

Balat, F. 1976. Dispersion prozesse und brutortstreue beim feldsperling *Passer montanus. Zool. Listy* 25:39–49.

Baptista, L. F. 1975. Song dialects and demes in sedentary populations of the white-crowned sparrow (*Zonotrichia leucophrys* Nuttali). *Univ. Cal. Publ. Zool.* 105:1–52.

Barash, D. P., W. G. Holmes and P. J. Greene. 1978. Exact versus probabilistic coefficients of relationship: some implications for sociobiology. *Am. Nat.* 112:355–63.

Barrett, G. W. 1976. Occurrence of a wild population of extreme dilute meadow voles. *J. Hered.* 67:109–10.

Barrowclough, G. F. 1980. Gene flow, effective population sizes, and genetic variance components in birds. *Evolution* 34:789–98.

Barrowclough, G. F. and K. W. Corbin. 1978. Genetic variation and differentiation in the Parulidae. *Auk* 95:691–702.

Bateman, A. J. 1950. Is gene dispersal normal? *Heredity* 4:353–63.

Bateson, P. P. G. 1978. Sexual imprinting and optimal outbreeding. *Nature* 273:659–60.

Begon, M. 1976. Dispersal, density and microdistribution in *Drosophila subobscura* Collin. *J. Anim. Ecol.* 45:441–56.

Begon, M. 1978. Population densities in *Drosophila obscura* Fallen and *D. subobscura* Collin. *Ecol. Ent.* 3:1–12.

Bekoff, M. 1977. Mammalian dispersal and the ontogeny of individual behavioral phenotypes. *Am. Nat:* 111:715–32.

Bengtsson, B. O. 1978. Avoiding inbreeding: at what cost? *J. theor. Biol.* 73:439–44.

Bent, A. C. 1962. *Life histories of North American wild fowl.* Parts I and II. Dover, New York.

Bent, A. C. 1968. *Life histories of North American cardinals, grosbeaks, buntings, towhees, finches, sparrows and allies.* Part I. Dover, New York.

Berger, E. 1976. Heterosis and the maintenance of enzyme polymorphism. *Am. Nat.* 110:823–39.

Berndt, R. and H. Sternberg. 1968. Terms, studies and experiments on the problems of bird dispersion. *Ibis* 110:256–69.

Bernstein, H. 1977. Germ line recombination may be primarily a manifestation of DNA repair processes. *J. theor. Biol.* 69:371–80.

Bernstein, H., G. S. Beyers and R. E. Michod. 1981. Evolution of sexual reproduction: importance of DNA repair, complementation and variation. *Am. Nat.* 117:537–49.

Bigelow, R. S. 1965. Hybrid zones and reproductive isolation. *Evolution* 19:449–58.

Bischof, N. 1975. Comparative ethology of incest avoidance. In *Biosocial anthropology*. (R. Fox, ed.), Wiley, N.Y., pp. 37–68.

Blair, W. F. 1953. Population dynamics of rodents and other small mammals. *Adv. Genet.* 5:1–41.

Blair, W. F. 1958. Mating call in the speciation of anuran amphibians. *Am. Nat.* 92:27–51.

Blair, W. F. 1960. *The rusty lizard: a population study.* Univ. of Texas Press, Austin.

Blair, W. F. 1961. *Vertebrate speciation.* Univ. of Texas Press, Austin.

Blick, J. 1977. Selection for traits which lower individual reproduction. *J. theor. Biol.* 67:597–601.

Blickenstaff, C. C. 1965. Partial intersterility of eastern and western U.S. strains of the alfalfa weevil. *Ann. Ent. Soc. Amer.* 58:523–26.

Bogart, J. P. and A. O. Wasserman. 1972. Diploid-polyploid cryptic species pairs: a possible clue to evolution by polyploidization in anuran amphibians. *Cytogenetics* 11:7–24.

Bogert, C. M. 1947. A field study of homing in the Carolina toad. *Amer. Mus. Novit.* 1355:1–24.

Bonner, J. T. 1958. The relation of spore formation to recombination. *Am. Nat.* 92:193–200.

Boorman, S. A. and P. R. Levitt. 1973. Group selection on the boundary of a stable population. *Theoret. Pop. Biol.* 4:85–128.

Bradshaw, A. D. 1972. Some of the evolutionary consequences of being a plant. *Evol. Biol.* 5:25–47.

Brannon, E. L. 1967. Genetic control of migrating behavior of newly hatched sockeye salmon fry. *Intl. Pac. Salmon Comm. Progress Repr.* No. 16. 31 pp.

Bremermann, H. J. 1979a. Theory of spontaneous cell fusion: sexuality in cell populations as an evolutionarily stable strategy. Applications to immunology and cancer. *J. theor. Biol.* 76:311–34.

Bremermann, H. J. 1979b. Fusion as a potential mechanism for generating lymphocyte diversity. *Biosystems* 11:163-65.

Bremermann, H. J. 1980. Sex and polymorphism as strategies in host-pathogen interactions. *J. theor. Biol.* 87:671-702.

Britten, R. J. and E. H. Davidson. 1969. Gene regulation for higher cells: a theory. *Science* 165:349-57.

Brown, C. K. 1976. Local variation in scale characters of *Sceloporus jarrovi* (Sauria: IGUANIDAE) inhabiting the Pinaleno Mountains of Arizona. I. Frequency of head scute polymorphisms. *Herpetol.* 32:180-97.

Brncic, D. 1954. Heterosis and the integration of the genotype in geographic populations of *Drosophila pseudoobscura. Genetics* 39:77-88.

Brncic, D. 1961. Integration of the genotype in geographic populations of *Drosophila pavani. Evolution* 15:92-97.

Brussard, P. F. and A. T. Vawter, 1975. Population structure, gene flow and natural selection in populations of *Euphydryas phaeton. Heredity* 34:407-15.

Buechner, H. K. and H. D. Roth. 1974. The lek system in Uganda Kob antelope. *Amer. Zool.* 14:145-62.

Bulmer, M. G. 1973. Inbreeding in the great tit. *Heredity* 30:313-25.

Bulmer, M. G. 1980. The sib competition model for the maintenance of sex and recombination. *J. theor. Biol.* 82:335-45.

Burger, J. 1972. Dispersal and post-fledging survival of Franklin's gulls. *Bird-Banding* 43:267-75.

Burnet, F. M. 1975. *Immunology. Readings from Scientific American.* W. H. Freeman, San Francisco, Ca.

Burt, W. H. 1940. Territorial behavior and populations of some small mammals in southern Michigan. *Misc. Publ. Mus. Zool., Univ. Mich.* 45:1-58.

Bush, G. L. 1975. Modes of animal speciation. *Annu. Rev. Ecol. Syst.* 6:339-64.

Cagle, F. R. 1944. Home range, homing behavior and migration in turtles. *Misc. Publ. Mus. Zool., Univ. Mich.*, 61:1-34.

Cain. A. J. 1963. The causes of area effects. *Heredity* 18:467-71.

Cain, A. J. 1977. The efficacy of natural selection in wild populations. *The changing scenes in the natural sciences, 1776-1976.* (C. E. Goulden, ed), Academy of Natural Sciences, Philadelphia. pp. 111-33.

Caisse, M. and J. Antonovics. 1978. Evolution in closely adjacent plant populations. IX. Evolution of reproductive isolation in clinal populations. *Heredity* 40:371-84.

Callan, H. G. and H. Spurway. 1951. A study of meiosis in inter-racial hybrids of the newt *Triturus cristatus*. *J. Genet*. 50:235–49.

Carr, A. and L. Giovanelli. 1957. The ecology and migrations of sea turtles. 2. Results of field work in Costa Rica, 1955. *Amer. Mus. Novit*. 1835:1–32.

Carr, A. and M. H. Carr. 1972. Site fixity in the Caribbean green turtle. *Ecology* 53:425–29.

Carson, H. L. 1959. Genetic conditions which promote or retard the formation of species. *Cold Spring Harbor Symp. Quant. Biol*. 24:87–105.

Carson, H. L. 1967. Inbreeding and gene fixation in natural populations. In *Heritage from Mendel*. (R. A. Brink, ed.), Univ. of Wisconsin Press, Madison., pp. 281–308.

Carson, H. L. 1975. The genetics of speciation at the diploid level. *Am. Nat*. 109:83–92.

Case, T. J. and E. A. Bender. 1981. Is recombination advantageous in fluctuating and spatially heterogeneous environments? *J. theor. Biol*. 90:181–90.

Charlesworth, B. 1976. Recombination modification in a fluctuating environment. *Genetics* 83:181–95.

Charlesworth, B. 1980a. The cost of sex in relation to mating system. *J. theor. Biol*. 84:655–71.

Charlesworth, B. 1980b. The cost of meiosis with alternation of sexual and asexual generations. *J. theor. Biol*. 87:517–28.

Charlesworth, D., B. Charlesworth and C. Strobeck. 1977. Effects of selfing on selection for recombination. *Genetics* 86:213–26.

Chetverikov, S. S. 1926. On certain aspects of the evolutionary process from the standpoint of genetics. *Zhurnal Exp. Biol*. 1:3–54 (Russian); English trans. in *Proc. Amer. Phil. Soc*. 105:167–95 (1959).

Child, A. R. 1977. Biochemical polymorphism in char (*Salvelinus alpinus* L.) from LLYNNAU Peris, Padarn, Cwellyn and Bodlyn. *Heredity* 38:359–65.

Clarke, B. C. 1979. The evolution of genetic diversity. *Proc. R. Soc. London B* 205:453–74.

Clarke, C. A. and P. M. Sheppard. 1960. The evolution of dominance under disruptive selection. *Heredity* 14:73–87.

Clarke, C. A., P. M. Sheppard and I. W. B. Thornton. 1968. The genetics of the mimetic butterfly *Papilio memnon* L. *Phil. Trans. Royal Soc. London B*. 254:37–89.

Clausen, J. 1951. *Stages in the evolution of plant species*. Hafner, New York.

Cockerham, C. C. 1969. Variance of gene frequencies. *Evolution* 23:72–84.

Cockerham, C. C. 1973. Analysis of gene frequencies. *Genetics* 74:679–700.

Cohen, D. 1967. Optimization of seasonal migratory behavior. *Am. Nat.* 101:5–17.

Coker, W. Z. and E. Kuma. 1974. A study of the genetic heterogeneity in *Bulinus globosus* populations in southern Ghana: electrophoretic patterns of esterase enzymes in snail extracts. *Ghana J. Science* 14:19–21.

Connor, J. L. and M. J. Bellucci. 1979. Natural selection resisting inbreeding depression in captive wild housemice (*Mus musculus*). *Evolution* 33:929–40.

Cook, L. M., E. W. Thomason and A. W. Young. 1976. Population structure, dynamics and dispersal of the tropical butterfly *Heliconius charitonius*. *J. Anim. Ecol.* 45:851–63.

Cook, S. B. and C. B. Cook. 1978. Tidal amplitude and activity in the pulmonate limpets *Siphonaria normalis* (Gould) and *S. alternata* (Say). *J. Exp. Mar. Biol. Ecol.* 35:119–36.

Cook, S. A. 1962. Genetic system, variation and adaptation in *Eschscholzia californica*. *Evolution* 6:278–99.

Cooke, F., C. D. Macinnes and J. P. Prevett. 1975. Gene flow between breeding populations of the lesser snow goose. *Auk* 92:493–510.

Cooper, K. W. 1939. The nuclear cytology of the grass mite, *Pediculopsis graminum* (Reut.), with special reference to karyomerokinesis. *Chromosoma* 1:51–103.

Coulson, J. C. 1971. Competition for breeding sites causing segregation and reduced young production in colonial animals. *Proc. Adv. Study Inst. Dynamics Numbers Popul.* (Oosterbeek). pp. 257–68.

Cowan, D. P. 1979. Sibling matings in a hunting wasp: adaptive inbreeding? *Science* 205:1403–5.

Cronin, T. W. and R. B. Forward, Jr. 1979. Tidal vertical migration: an endogenous rhythm in estuarine crab larvae. *Science* 205:1020–22.

Crook, J. H. 1970. *Social behavior in birds and mammals.* Academic Press, New York., pp. 103–66.

Crosby, J. L. 1970. The evolution of genetic discontinuity: computer models of the selection of barriers to interbreeding between subspecies. *Heredity* 25:253–97.

Crow, J. F. 1956. Genetics of DDT resistance in *Drosophila*. *Proc. Intern. Genet. Symp.* Tokyo (Cytologia Suppl.):408–9.

Crow, J. F. and M. Kimura. 1965. Evolution in sexual and asexual populations. *Am. Nat.* 99:439–50.

Crow, J. F. and M. Kimura. 1969. Evolution in sexual and asexual populations: a reply. *Am. Nat.* 103:89–90.

Crow, J. F. and M. Kimura. 1970. *An introduction to population genetics theory.* Harper and Row, New York.

Crozier, R. H. 1980. Genetical structure of insect populations. In *Evolution of social behavior: hypotheses and empirical tests*. (H. Markl, ed.), Verlag Chemie; Weinheim, pp. 129–46.

Cruden, R. W. 1977. Pollen-ovule ratios: a conservative indicator of breeding systems in flowering plants. *Evolution* 31:32–46.

Daly, M. 1978. The cost of mating. *Am. Nat.* 112:771–74.

Darlington, C. D. 1932. *Recent advances in cytology*. Blakiston's, Philadelphia.

Darlington, C. D. 1958. *The evolution of genetic systems*. Basic Books, New York.

Darwin, C. 1859. *On the origin of species*. John Murray, London.

Darwin, C. 1868. *The variation of animals and plants under domestication*. John Murray, London.

Darwin, C. 1871. *The descent of man and selection in relation to sex*. Appleton, New York.

Darwin, C. 1876. *The effects of cross and self-fertilization in the vegetable kingdom*. Appleton, New York.

Davidson, E. H. and R. J. Britten. 1973. Organization, transcription and regulation in the animal genome. *Quart. Rev. Biol.* 48:565–613.

Davies, N. B. and J. R. Krebs. 1978. Introduction: ecology, natural selection and social behaviour. In *Behavioural Ecology*. (J. R. Krebs and N. B. Davies, eds.), Sinauer, Sunderland, Mass., pp. 1–18.

Dawkins, R. 1976. *The selfish gene*. Oxford Univ. Press, Oxford.

Dawkins, R. 1978. Replicator selection and the extended phenotype. *Z. Tierpsychol.* 47:61–76.

Dawkins, R. 1979. Twelve misunderstandings of kin selection. *Z. Tierpsychol.* 51:184–200.

De Benedictis, P. A. 1978. Are populations characterized by their genes or by their genotypes? *Am. Nat.* 112:155–75.

Defries, J. C. and G. E. McClearn. 1970. Social dominance and Darwinian fitness in the laboratory mouse. *Am. Nat.* 104:408–11.

Defries, J. C. and G. E. McClearn. 1972. Behavior genetics and the fine structure of mouse populations: a study in microevolution. *Evol. Biol.* 5:279–91.

Dice, L. C. 1933. Fertility relationships between some of the species and subspecies of mice in the genus *Peromyscus*. *J. Mammal.* 14:208–305.

Dice, L. R. and W. E. Howard. 1951. Distance of dispersal by prairie deermice from birthplace to breeding sites. *Contr. Lab Vert. Biol. Univ. Mich.* 50:1–15.

Dilger, W. C. 1956. Hostile behavior and reproductive isolating mechanisms in the avian genera *Catharus* and *Hylocichla*. *Auk* 73:313–53.

Dobzhansky, T. 1937. *Genetics and the origin of species*. 1st ed. Columbia Univ. Press, New York.

Dobzhansky, T. 1948. Genetics of natural populations XVIII. Experiments on chromosomes of *Drosophila pseudoobscura* from different geographic regions. *Genetics* 33:588–602.

Dobzhansky, T. 1950. Genetics of natural populations XIX. Origin of heterosis through natural selection in populations of *Drosophila pseudoobscura*. *Genetics* 35:288–302.

Dobzhansky, T. 1951. *Genetics and the origin of species*. 3rd ed. Columbia Univ. Press, New York.

Dobzhansky, T. 1970. *Genetics of the evolutionary process*. Columbia Univ. Press, New York.

Dobzhansky, T. 1972. Species of *Drosophila*. *Science* 177:664–69.

Dobzhansky, T. 1974. Genetic analysis of hybrid sterility within the species *Drosophila pseudoobscura*. *Hereditas* 77:81–88.

Dobzhansky, T., F. J. Ayala, G. L. Stebbins and J. W. Valentine. 1977. *Evolution*. W. H. Freeman, San Francisco.

Dobzhansky, T. and B. Spassky. 1968. Genetics of natural populations. XL. Heterotic and deleterious effect of recessive lethals in populations of *Drosophila pseudoobscura*. *Genetics* 59:411–25.

Dobzhansky, T. and S. Wright. 1943. Genetics of natural populations X. Dispersion rates in *Drosophila pseudoobscura*. *Genetics* 28:304–40.

Dodson, E. O. 1953. Comments on the origin of sex and of meiosis. *Evolution* 7:387–88.

Dougherty, E. C. 1955. Comparative evolution and the origin of sexuality. *Syst. Zool.* 4:145–69, 190.

Dreyfus, A. and M. E. Breuer. 1944. Chromosomes and sex determination in the parasitic hymenopteran *Telenomus fariai* (Lima). *Genetics* 29:75–82.

Duncan, W. R., E. K. Wakeland and J. Klein. 1979. Heterozygosity of H-2 loci in wild mice. *Nature* 281:603–5.

East, E. M. and D. F. Jones. 1919. *Inbreeding and Outbreeding*. J. B. Lippincott Co., Philadelphia.

Ehrlich, P. R. and P. H. Raven. 1969. Differentiation of populations. *Science* 165:1228–32.

Ehrlich, P. R., R. R. White, M. C. Singer, S. W. McKechnie and L. E. Gilbert. 1975. Checkerspot butterflies: a historical perspective. *Science* 188:221–28.

Ehrman, L. 1960. The genetics of hybrid sterility in *Drosophila paulistorum*. *Evolution* 14:212–23.

Ehrman, L. 1970. The mating advantage of rare males in *Drosophila*. *Proceed. Nat. Acad. Sci.* (USA) 65:345–48.

Elbadry, E. A. and M. S. F. Tawfik. 1966. Life cycle of the mite *Adaetylidium* sp. (Acarina: Pyemotidae), a predator of thrips eggs in the United Arab Republic. *Ann. Entomol. Soc.* 59:458–61.

Elliot, L. 1978. Social behavior and foraging ecology of the eastern chipmunk (*Tamias striatus*) in the Adirondack Mountains. *Smithsonian Contr. Zool.* 265:1–107.

Emlen, J. M. 1973. *Ecology: an evolutionary approach.* Addison-Wesley. Reading, Mass.

Emlen, J. T. 1978. Density anomalies and regulatory mechanisms in land bird populations on the Florida peninsula. *Am. Nat.* 112:265–86.

Emlen, S. T. and L. W. Oring. 1977. Ecology, sexual selection, and the evolution of mating systems. *Science* 197:215–23.

Endler, J. A. 1973. Gene flow and population differentiation. *Science* 179:243–50.

Endler, J. A. 1977. *Geographic variation, speciation and clines.* Princeton Univ. Press, N. J.

Endler, J. A. 1979. Gene flow and life history patterns. *Genetics* 93:263–84.

Enfield, F. D. 1977. Selection experiments in *Tribolium* designed to look at gene action issues. *Proc. Int. Conf. Quant. Genetics* 1:177–90.

Epling, C. and T. Dobzhansky. 1942. Microgeographic races in *Linanthus parryae. Genetics* 27:317–32.

Epling, C., H. Lewis and F. M. Ball. 1960. The breeding group and seed storage: a study in population dynamics. *Evolution* 14:238–55.

Erlinge, S. 1977. Spacing strategy in stoat *Mustela ermina. Oikos* 28:32–42.

Faegri, K. and L. Van Der Pijl. 1971. *Principles of pollination ecology.* Pergamon Press, Oxford.

Falconer, D. S. 1960. *Introduction to quantitative genetics.* Ronald Press, New York.

Farr, J. A. 1977. Male rarity or novelty, female choice behavior, and sexual selection in the guppy. *Poecilia reticulata* Peters (Pisces: Poeciliidae). *Evolution* 31:162–68.

Felsenstein, J. 1974. The evolutionary advantage of recombination. *Genetics* 78:737–56.

Felsenstein, J. 1975. A pain in the torus: some difficulties with models of isolation by distance. *Am. Nat.* 109:359–68.

Felsenstein, J. and S. Yokoyama. 1976. The evolutionary advantage of recombination II. Individual selection for recombination. *Genetics* 83:845–59.

Ferrell, G. T. 1966. Variation in blood frequencies in populations of song sparrows of the San Francisco Bay region. *Evolution* 20:369–82.

Festing, M. and S. Atwood. 1970. The maintenance of inbred strains of laboratory animals. *J. Inst. Animal Tech.* 21:50–57.

Fischer, E. A. 1980. The relationship between mating system and simultaneous hermaphroditism in the coral reef fish, *Hypoplectrus nigricans* (Serranidae). *Anim. Behav.* 28:620–33.

Fisher, H. I. 1966. Aerial census of Laysan Albatrosses breeding on Midway atoll in December, 1962. *Auk* 83:670–73.

Fisher, H. I. 1967. Body weights of Laysan Albatrosses *Diomedea immutabilis*. Ibis 109:373–82.

Fisher, H. I. 1971a. Experiments on homing in Laysan Albatrosses *Diomedea immutabilis*. *Condor* 73:389–400.

Fisher, H. I. 1971b. The Laysan Albatross: its incubation, hatching and associated behaviors. *Living Bird* 10:19–78.

Fisher, H. I. 1975. Mortality and survival in the Laysan Albatross *Diomedea immutabilis*. *Pacific Science* 29:279–300.

Fisher, H. I. 1976. Some dynamics of a breeding colony of Laysan Albatrosses. *Wilson Bull.* 88:121–42.

Fisher, H. I. and M. L. Fisher. 1969. The visits of Laysan Albatrosses to the breeding colony. *Micronesica* 5:173–221.

Fisher, R. A. 1930. *The genetical theory of natural selection.* 1958 ed., rev. Dover, New York.

Fisher, R. A. 1931. The evolution of dominance. *Biol. Rev.* 6:345–68.

Fisher, R. A. 1949. *The theory of inbreeding.* 2nd ed., 1965. Oliver and Boyd, London.

Flesness, N. R. 1978. Kinship asymmetry in diploids. *Nature* 276:495–96.

Ford, E. B. 1949. Early stages in allopatric speciation. In *Genetics, paleontology and evolution.* (Jepsen, G., E. Mayr, and G. G. Simpson, eds.), Princeton Univ. Press, N.J.

Ford, E. B. 1964. *Ecological genetics.* Methuen, London.

Forester, D. C. 1977. Comments on the female reproductive cycle and philopatry by *Desmognathus ochrophaeus* (Amphibia, Urodela, Plethodontidae). *J. Herpetol.* 11:311–16.

Franklin, I. R. 1977. The distribution of the proportion of the genome which is homozygous by descent in inbred individuals. *Theor. Popul. Biol.* 11:60–80.

Gadgil, M. 1971. Dispersal: population consequences and evolution. *Ecology* 52:253-61.

Gauthreaux, S. A., Jr. 1978. The ecological significance of behavioral dominance. In *Perspectives in ethology*. Vol. 3. (P.P.G. Bateson and P. H. Klopfer, ed.), Plenum, London, pp. 17-54.

Geddes, P. and J. A. Thompson. 1914. *Sex*. Henry Holt, New York.

Gee, J. M. and G. B. Williams. 1965. Self and cross-fertilization in *Spirorbis borealis* and *S. pagenstecheri*. *J. Mar. Bio. Assoc.* 45:275-85.

Gerking, S. D. 1959. The restricted movements of fish populations. *Biol. Rev.* 34:221-42.

Ghiselin, M. T. 1969. The evolution of hermaphroditism among animals. *Quart. Rev. Biol.* 44:189-208.

Ghiselin, M. T. 1974. *The economy of nature and the evolution of sex.* Univ. Cal. Press, Berkeley, Cal.

Gilder, P. M. and P. J. B. Slater, 1978. Interest of mice in conspecific male odours is influenced by degree of kinship. *Nature* 274:364-65.

Ginsberg, B. E. 1968. Breeding structure and social behavior of mammals: a servomechanism for the avoidance of panmixia. In *Genetics, biology and behavior series*. (B. C. Glass, ed.), Rockefeller Univ. Press, N.Y.

Ginsberg, B. E. 1978. The genetics of social behavior. In *Perspectives in ethology*. (P. P. G. Bateson and P. H. Klopfer, eds.), Plenum, New York, pp. 1-15.

Glesener, R. R. and D. Tilman. 1978. Sexuality and the components of environmental uncertainty: clues from geographic parthenogenesis. *Am. Nat.* 112:659-73.

Glover, D. G., M. H. Smith, L. Ames, J. Joule and J. M. Dubach. 1977. Genetic variation in pika populations. *Can. J. Zool.* 55:1841-45.

Godfrey, J. 1958. The origin of sexual isolation between bank boles. *Proc. R. Phys. Soc. Edinb.* 27:47-55.

Goldschmidt, R. 1934. Lymantria. *Bibliogr. Genetica* 11:1-186.

Gordon, H. and M. Gordon. 1957. Maintenance of polymorphism by potentially injurious genes in eight natural populations of the platy fish *Xiphophorus maculatus*. *J. Genet.* 55:1-44.

Gorman, G. C., M. Soule, S. Y. Yang and E. Nevo. 1975. Evolutionary genetics of insular adriatic lizards. *Evolution* 29:52-71.

Gottlieb, L. D. 1971. Evolutionary relationships in outcrossing diploid annual species of *Stephanomeria* (Compositae). *Evolution* 25:312-29.

Gould, S. J. 1977. *Ontogeny and phylogeny*. Belknap Press, Harvard Univ. Press, Cambridge, Mass.

Gowen, J. W. 1952. *Heterosis*. Iowa State College Press, Ames, Iowa.

Grant, V. 1958. The regulation of recombination in plants. *Cold Spring Harbor Symp. Quant. Biol.* 23:337–63.

Grant, V. 1963. *The origin of adaptations.* Columbia Univ. Press, New York.

Grant, V. 1971. *Plant speciation.* Columbia Univ. Press, New York.

Grant, V. 1975. *Genetics of flowering plants.* Columbia Univ. Press, New York.

Grant, V. and A. Grant. 1960. Genetic and taxonomic studies in *Gilia* XI. Fertility relationships of the diploid cobwebby *Gilias. Aliso* 4:435–81.

Greenberg, L. 1979. Genetic component of bee odor in kin recognition. *Science* 206:1095–97.

Greenwood, J. J. D. 1974. Effective population numbers in the snail *Cepaea nemoralis. Evolution* 28:513–26.

Greenwood, P. J. 1980. Mating systems, philopatry, and dispersal in birds and mammals. *Anim. Behav.* 28:1140–62.

Greenwood, P. J. and P. H. Harvey. 1976. The adaptive significance of variation in breeding area fidelity of the blackbird (*Turdus merula* L.). *J. Anim. Ecol.* 45:887–98.

Greenwood, P. J., P. H. Harvey and C. M. Perrins. 1978. Inbreeding and dispersal in the great tit. *Nature* 271:52–54.

Greenwood, P. J., P. H. Harvey and C. M. Perrins. 1979a. The role of dispersal in the great tit (*Parus major*): the causes, consequences and heritability of natal dispersal. *J. Anim. Ecol.* 48:123–42.

Greenwood, P. J., P. H. Harvey and C. M. Perrins. 1979b. Mate selection in the great tit, *Parus major*, in relation to age, status and natal dispersal. *Ornis. Fenn.* 56:75–86.

Greenwood, P. J., P. H. Harvey and C. M. Perrins. 1979c. Kin selection and territoriality in birds? A test. *Anim. Behav.* 27:645–51.

Hadfield, M. G. 1972. Flexibility in larval life patterns. *Amer. Zool.* 13:721–33.

Haldane, J. B. S. 1932. *The causes of evolution.* Longmans, Green, London.

Haldane, J. B. S. 1936. The amount of heterozygosis to be expected in an approximately pure line. *J. Genet.* 32:375–91.

Haldane, J. B. S. 1937. Some theoretical results of continued brother-sister mating. *J. Genet.* 34:265–74.

Haldane, J. B. S. 1964. A defense of beanbag genetics. *Persp. Biol. Med.* 7:343–59.

Halkka, D., M. Raatikainen and L. Halkka. 1974. The founder principle, founder selection and evolutionary divergence and convergence in natural populations of *Philaenus. Hereditas* 78:73–84.

Hall, W. P. and R. K. Selander. 1973. Hybridization of karyotypically differentiated populations in the *Sceloporus grammicus* complex (Iguanidae). *Evolution* 27:226–42.

Halliburton, R. and L. R. Mewaldt. 1976. Survival and mobility in a population of Pacific coast song sparrows (*Melospiza melodia gouldii*). *Condor* 78:499–504.

Halliday, T. R. 1978. Sexual selection and mate choice. In *Behavioural Ecology*. (J. R. Krebs and N. B. Davies, eds.), Sinauer, Sunderland, Mass., pp. 180–213.

Hamilton, W. D. 1964a. The genetical evolution of social behavior I. *J. theor. Biol.* 7:1–16.

Hamilton, W. D. 1964b. The genetical evolution of social behavior II. *J. theor. Biol.* 7:17–52.

Hamilton, W. D. 1967. Extraordinary sex ratios. *Science* 156:477–88.

Hamilton, W. D. 1972. Altruism and related phenomena, mainly in social insects. *Annu. Rev. Ecol. Syst.* 3:193–232.

Hamilton, W. D. and. R. M. May. 1977. Dispersal in stable habitats. *Nature* 269:578–81.

Hamilton, W. D., P. A. Henderson and N. A. Moran. 1981. Fluctuation of environment and coevolved antagonist polymorphism as factors in the maintenance of sex. In *Natural Selection and Social Behavior*. (R. D. Alexander and D. W. Tinkle, eds.), Chiron Press, N.Y., pp. 363–381.

Hamrick, J. L. and R. W. Allard. 1972. Correlations between quantitative characters and enzyme genotypes in *Avena barbata*. *Evolution* 29:438–42.

Hansen, T. A. 1978. Larval dispersal and species longevity in lower tertiary gastropods. *Science* 199:885–87.

Harden-Jones, F. R. 1968. *Fish migration*. Edward Arnold Ltd., London.

Harland, S. C. 1936. The genetical conception of the species. *Biol. Rev.* 11:83–112.

Harper, J. L. 1977. *Population biology of plants*. Academic Press, London.

Harper, J. L., P. H. Lovell and K. G. Moore. 1970. The shapes and sizes of seeds. *Annu. Rev. Ecol. Syst.* 1:327–56.

Harper, J. L. and J. White. 1974. The demography of plants. *Annu. Rev. Ecol. Syst.* 5:419–63.

Hartnoll, R. G. 1976. Reproductive strategy in two British species of Alcyonium. In *Biology of benthis organisms*. (B. F. Keegan, P. O. Cedigh and P. J. S. Boaden, eds.), Pergamon Press, Oxford, pp. 321–28.

Hartung, J. 1981. Transfer RNA, genome parliaments and sex with the red queen. In *Natural selection and social behavior*. (R. D. Alexander and D. W. Tinkle, eds.). Chiron Press, N. Y., pp. 382–402.

Hasler, A. D., A. T. Scholz and R. M. Horrall. 1978. Olfactory imprinting and homing in salmon. *Amer. Scientist* 66:347–55.

Hayman, B. I. and K. Mather. 1953. The progress of inbreeding when homozygotes are at a disadvantage. *Heredity* 7:165–83.

Hedgecock, D. 1976. Genetic variation in two widespread species of salamanders, *Taricha granulosa* and *Taricha torosa*. *Biochem. Genet.* 14:561–76.

Hedgecock, D. 1978. Population subdivision and genetic divergence in the red-bellied newt, *Taricha rivularis*. *Evolution* 32:271–86.

Hedrick, P., S. Jain and L. Holden. 1978. Multilocus systems in evolution. *Evol. Biol.* 11:101–83.

Heller, R. and J. Maynard Smith. 1979. Does Muller's ratchet work with selfing? *Genet. Res.* 32:289–93.

Hempel, C. G. 1966. *Philosophy of natural science*. Prentice-Hall, Englewood Cliffs, N. J.

Heusser, H. 1969. Die Lebensweise der Erdhrote, *Bufo bufo* (L.): Das Orientierungs-problem. *Rev. Suisse Zool.* 76:443–518.

Highton, R. 1975. Geographic variation in genetic dominance of the color morphs of the red-backed salamander, *Plethodon cinereus*. *Genetics* 80:363–74.

Highton, R. 1977. Comparison of microgeographic variation in morphological and electrophoretic traits. *Evol. Biol.* 10:397–436.

Hilden, O. 1965. Habitat selection in birds. *Ann. Zool. Fenn.* 2:53–75.

Hill, J. L. 1974. Peromyscus: effect of early pairing on reproduction. *Science* 186:1042–44.

Hill, W. G. and A. Robertson. 1966. The effects of linkage on limits to artificial selection. *Genet. Res.* 8:269–94.

Hill, W. G. and A. Robertson. 1968. The effects of inbreeding at loci with heterozygote advantage. *Genetics* 60:615–28.

Hinde, R. A. 1956. The biological significance of the territories of birds. *Ibis* 98:340–69.

Hoenigsberg, H. F., J. J. Palomino, M. J. Hayes, I. Z. Zandstra and G. C. Rojas. 1977. Population genetics in the American tropics. X. Genetic load differences in *Drosophila willistoni* from Columbia. *Evolution* 31:805–11.

Howard, J. C. 1977. H_2 and mating preferences. *Nature* 266:406–8.

Howard, W. E. 1960. Innate and environmental dispersal of vertebrates. *Amer. Midl. Natur.* 63:152–61.

Hubby, J. L. and R. C. Lewontin. 1966. A molecular approach to the study of genetic heterozygosity in natural populations. I. The number of alleles at different loci in *Drosophila pseudoobscura*. *Genetics* 54:577–94.

Hughes, K. W. and R. K. Vickery, Jr. 1974. Patterns of heterosis and crossing barriers resulting from increasing genetic distance between populations of the *Mimulus luteus* complex. *J. Genet.* 61:235–45.

Hunter, R. D. 1975. Variation in populations of *Lymnaea palustris* in upstate New York. *Amer. Midl. Natur.* 94:401–20.

Huxley, J. S. 1938. The present standing of the theory of sexual selection. In *Essays on aspects of evolutionary biology presented to E. S. Goodrich* (G. R. de Beer, ed.), Clarendon Press, Oxford.

Huxley, J. S. 1942. *Evolution, the modern synthesis.* G. Allen and Unwin, London.

Immelmann, K. 1975. Ecological significance of imprinting and early learning. *Ann. Rev. Ecol. Syst.* 6:15–37.

Inger, R. F., H. K. Voris and H. H. Voris. 1974. Genetic variation and population ecology of some southeast Asian frogs of the genera *Bufo* and *Rana. Biochem. Genet.* 12:121–45.

Itani, J. 1972. A preliminary essay on the relationship between social organization and incest avoidance in non-human primates. In *Primate socialization.* (F. E. Poirer, ed.), Random House, N. Y., pp. 165–71.

Jacquard, T. L. A. 1974. Homogeneisation de l'apparentement dans une population limitee. *Ann. Genet.* 17:99–103.

Jacquard, A. 1975. Inbreeding: one word, several meanings. *Theor. Pop. Biol.* 7:338–63.

Jaenike, J. 1978. An hypothesis to account for the maintenance of sex within populations. *Evol. Theory* 3:191–94.

Jain, S. K. 1976. The evolution of inbreeding in plants. *Annu. Rev. Ecol. Syst.* 7:469–95.

Jain, S. K. and R. W. Allard. 1966. The effects of linkage, epistasis and inbreeding on population changes under selection. *Genetics* 53: 633–59.

Jain, S. K. and A. D. Bradshaw. 1966. Evolutionary divergence among adjacent plant populations I. The evidence and its theoretical analysis. *Heredity* 21:407–41.

James, S. H. 1970. A demonstration of a possible mechanism of sympatric divergence using stimulation techniques. *Heredity* 25:241–52.

Jameson, D. L. 1957. Population structure and homing responses in the Pacific treefrog. *Copeia* 1957:221–28.

Jenkins, P. F. 1977. Cultural transmission of song patterns and dialect development in a free-living bird population. *Anim. Behav.* 25:50–78.

Jerne, N. K. 1974. Towards a network theory of the immune system. *Ann. Immunol.* (Inst. Pasteur) 125C:373–89.

Jewell, P. A. and P. J. Fullagar. 1965. Fertility among races of the field mouse (*Apodemus sylvaticus*) and their failure to form hybrids with the yellow-necked mouse (*A. flavicallis*). *Evolution* 19:175–81.

Jinks, J. L. 1955. A survey of the genetical basis of heterosis in a variety of diallele crosses. *Heredity* 9:223–38.

Jinks, J. L. and K. Mather. 1955. Stability in development of hetero-zygotes and homozygotes. *Proc. R. Soc. London B.* 143:561–78.

Johnson, C. G. 1966. A functional system of adaptive dispersal by flight. *Annu. Rev. Ent.* 11:233–60.

Johnson, C. G. 1969. *Migration and dispersal of insects by flight*. Methuen, London.

Johnson, W. W. 1974. Coadaptation and recessive lethal content in DDT resistant populations of *Drosophila melanogaster*. *Evolution* 28:251–58.

Johnston, J. S. and W. B. Heed. 1976. Dispersal of desert-adapted *Drosophila*: the saguaro-breeding *D. nigrospiracula*. *Am. Nat.* 110:629–51.

Johnston, R. F. 1961. Population movements of birds. *Condor* 63:386–89.

Kaffman, M. 1977. Sexual standards and behavior of the kibbutz adolescent. *Amer. J. Orthopsychiatry.* 47:207–17.

Kalmus, H. and C. A. B. Smith. 1960. Evolutionary origin of sexual differentiation and the sex-ratio. *Nature* 186:1004–5.

Karlin, S. and J. MacGregor. 1974. Towards a theory of the evolution of modifier genes. *Theor. Popul. Biol.* 5:59–103.

Keeler, K. H. 1978. Intra-population differentiation in annual plants. II. Electrophoretic variation in *Veronica peregrina*. *Evolution* 32:638–45.

Keller, A. J. and T. A. Lyerla. 1977. Lactate dehydrogenase poly-morphism in the spring peeper, *Hyla crucifer*. *Copeia* 1977:691–94.

Kempton, R. A. 1974. A model of selective migration. *Heredity* 33:79–86.

Kenyon, K. W. 1960. Territorial behavior and homing in the Alaska fur seal. *Mammalia* 24:431–44.

Kerster, H. W. 1964. Neighborhood size in the rusty lizard, *Sceloporus olivaceus*. *Evolution* 18:445–57.

Kimura, M. 1968. Evolutionary rate at the molecular level. *Nature* 217:624–26.

Kimura, M. and J. F. Crow. 1963. The measurement of effective popu-lation number. *Evolution* 17:279–88.

Kimura, M. and T. Ohta. 1971. *Theoretical aspects of population genetics*. Princeton Univ. Press, Princeton, N.J.

Kimura, M. and G. Weiss. 1964. The stepping stone model of popula-tion structure and the decrease of genetic correlation with distance. *Genetics* 49:561–76.

King, H. D. 1918a. Studies on inbreeding: I. The effects of inbreeding on the growth and variability in body weight of the albino rat. *J. Exp. Zool.* 26:1-54.

King, H. D. 1918b. Studies in inbreeding: II. The effects of inbreeding on the fertility and on the constitutional vigor of the albino rat. *J. Exp. Zool.* 26:55-98.

King, H. D. 1918c. Studies on inbreeding: III. The effets on inbreeding with selection on the sex ratio of the albino rat. *J. Exp. Zool.* 27:1-35.

King. H. D. 1919. Studies on inbreeding: IV. A further study of the effects of inbreeding on the growth and variability in body weights of the albino rat. *J. Exp. Zool.* 29:134-75.

King. J. C. 1955. Evidence for the integration of the genepool from studies of DDT resistance in *Drosophila. Cold Spring Harbor Symp. Quant. Biol.* 20:311-17.

King. J. L. 1967. Continuously distributed factors affecting fitness. *Genetics* 55:483-92.

Koehn, R. K. 1975. Migration and population structure in the pelagically dispersing marine invertebrate, *Mytilus edulis.* In *Isozymes* Vol. 4. (C. L. Markert, ed.), Academic Press, N. Y., pp. 945-59.

Koehn, R. K., F. J. Turano and J. B. Mitton. 1973. Population genetics of marine pelecypods. II. Genetic differences in microhabitats of *Modiolus demissus. Evolution* 27:100-105.

Koehn, R. K. and G. C. Williams. 1978. Genetic differentiation without isolation in the American eel, *Anguilla rostrata* II. Temporal stability of geographic patterns. *Evolution* 32:624-37.

Koenig, W. D. and F. A. Pitelka. 1979. Relatedness and inbreeding avoidance: counter plays in a communally nesting acorn woodpecker. *Science* 206:1103-05.

Krimbas, C. B. and V. Alevizos. 1973. The genetics of *Drosophila subobscura* populations IV. Further data on inversion polymorphism in Greece—evidence of microdifferentiation. *Egypt. J. Genet. Cytol.* 2:121-32.

Kroodsma, D. E. 1974. Song learning, dialects and dispersal in Bewick's wren. *Z. Tierpsychol.* 35:352-80.

Kruckeberg, A. R. 1957. Variation in fertility of hybrids between isolated populations of the serpentine species, *Streptanthus glandulosus* Hook. *Evolution* 11:185-211.

Kummer, H. 1968. *Social organization of* Hamadryas *baboons.* Univ. Chicago Press, Chicago.

Lack, D. 1954. *The natural regulation of animal numbers.* Clarendon Press, Oxford.

Lack, D. 1958. The evolution of reproductive rates. In *Evolution as a process*. (J. Huxley, A. C. Hardy and E. B. Ford, eds.), George Allen and Unwin, London, pp. 143–56.

Lack, D. 1966. *Population studies of birds*. Clarendon Press, Oxford.

Lande, R. 1977. The influence of the mating system on the maintenance of genetic variability in polygenic characters. *Genetics* 86:485–98.

Leggett, W. C. 1977. The ecology of fish migrations. *Annu. Rev. Ecol. Syst.* 8:285–308.

Lerner, I. M. 1954. *Genetic homeostasis*. Oliver and Boyd, Edinburgh.

Leslie, J. F. and R. C. Vrijenhoek, 1978. Genetic dissection of clonally inherited genomes of *Poeciliopsis*, I. Linkage analysis and preliminary assessment of deleterious gene loads. *Genetics* 90:801–11.

Leslie, J. F. and R. C. Vrijenhoek. 1980. Consideration of Muller's ratchet mechanism through studies of genetic linkage and genomic compatibilities in clonally reproducing *Poeciliopsis*. *Evolution* 34:1105–15.

Leuthold, W. 1975. *African ungulates*. Springer-Verlag, Berlin.

Levin, B. R., M. L. Petras and D. I. Rasmussen. 1969. The effect of migration on the maintenance of a lethal polymorphism in the house mouse. *Am. Nat.* 103:647–61.

Levin, D. A. 1975. Pest pressure and recombination systems in plants. *Am. Nat.* 109:437–51.

Levin, D. A. 1978. Genetic variation in annual phlox: self-compatible versus self-incompatible species. *Evolution* 32:245–63.

Levin, D. A. and H. W. Kerster. 1974. Gene flow in seed plants. *Evol. Biol.* 7:139–220.

Levins, R. 1968. *Evolution in changing environments*. Princeton Univ. Press, Princeton, N. J.

Lewis, D. 1942. The evolution of sex in flowering plants. *Biol. Rev.* 17:46–67.

Lewis, H. 1973. The origin of diploid neospecies in *Clarkia*. *Am. Nat.* 107:161–70.

Lewontin, R. C. 1974. *The genetic basis of evolutionary change*. Columbia Univ. Press, New York.

Lewontin, R. C. and K. Kojima. 1960. The evolutionary dynamics of complex polymorphisms. *Evolution* 14:458–72.

Lewontin, R. C. and J. L. Hubby. 1966. A molecular approach to the study of genic heterozygosity in natural populations. II. Amount of variation and degree of heterozygosity in natural populations of *Drosophila pseudoobscura*. *Genetics* 54:595–609.

Li, C. C. 1955. *Population genetics.* Univ. of Chicago Press, Chicago.

Li, W. H. and M. Nei. 1974. Stable linkage disequilibrium without epistasis in subdivided populations. *Theor. Pop. Biol.* 6:173–83.

Lidicker, W. Z., Jr. 1962. Emigration as a possible mechanism permitting the regulation of population density below carrying capacity. *Am. Nat.* 96:29–33.

Livingstone, F. B. 1969. Genetics, ecology, and the origins of incest and exogamy. *Curr. Anthro.* 10:45–62.

Livingstone, F. B. 1980. Cultural causes of genetic change. In *Sociobiology: beyond nature/nurture.* (G. W. Barlow and J. Silverberg, eds.), Westview Press, Boulder, Colorodo, pp. 307–29.

Lloyd, D. G. 1980. Benefits and handicaps of sexual reproduction. *Evol. Biol.* 13:69–111.

Loeb, L. and H. D. King. 1927. Transplantation and individuality differentials in strains of inbred rats. *Am. J. Pathol.* 3:143–67.

Loeb, L., H. D. King and H. T. Blumenthal. 1943. Transplantation and individuality differentials in inbred strains of rats. *Biol. Bull.* 84:1–12.

Loncke, D. J. and M. E. Obbard. 1977. Tag success, dimensions, clutch size and nesting site fidelity for the snapping turtle, *Chelydra serpentina* (Reptilia, Testudines, Chelydridae) in Algonquin Park, Ontario, Canada. *J. Herpetol.* 11:243–44.

Longwell, A. C. and S. S. Stiles. 1973. Gamete cross incompatibility and inbreeding in the commercial American oyster, *Crassostrea virginica* Gmelin. *Cytologia* 38:521–33.

Lynch, C. B. 1977. Inbreeding effects upon animals derived from a wild population of *Mus musculus. Evolution* 31:526–37.

Mainardi, D., M. Marsan and A. Pasquali. 1965. Causation of sexual preferences of the house mice. *Atti Societa Italiana Scienze Naturale Museo Civico Storia Naturale, Milano.* 54:325–38.

Malecot, G. 1948. *The mathematics of heredity.* (1969 trans. by D. M. Yermanas). W. H. Freeman, San Francisco.

Malmberg, R. L. 1977. The evolution of epistasis and the advantage of recombination in populations of *Bacteriophage* T4. *Genetics* 68:607–21.

Manning, J. T. 1976a. Gamete dimorphism and the cost of sexual reproduction: are they separate phenomena? *J. theor. Biol.* 55:393–95.

Manning, J. T. 1976b. Is sex maintained to facilitate or minimize mutational advance? *Heredity* 36:351–57.

Marler, P. and M. Tamura. 1962. Song dialects in three populations of white-crowned sparrows. *Condor* 64:368–77.

Marler, P. and M. Tamura. 1964. Culturally transmitted patterns of vocal behavior in sparrows. *Science* 146:1483–86.

Maruyama, T. 1969. Genetic correlation in the stepping stone model with non-symmetric migration rates. *J. Appl. Prob.* 6:463–77.

Maruyama, T. 1970. On the rate of decrease of heterozygosity in circular stepping stone models of populations. *Theor. Popul. Biol.* 1:101–19.

Mason, W. 1979. Ontogeny of social behavior. In *Handbook of Behavioral Neurobiology V. II. Social behavior and communication.* (P. Marler and J. G. Vandenbergh, eds.), Plenum Press, N.Y., pp. 1–28.

Mather, K. 1943. Polygenic inheritance and natural selection. *Biol. Rev.* 18:32–64.

Mather, K. 1953. The genetical structure of populations. *Symp. Soc. Exper. Biol.* 7:66–95.

Mather, K. 1973. *Genetical structure of populations.* Chapman and Hall, London.

Mather, K. and P. D. S. Caligari. 1976. Genotype X environment interactions. IV. The effect of the background genotype. *Heredity* 36:41–48.

Mather, K. and B. I. Hayman. 1952. The progress of inbreeding where heterozygotes are at an advantage. *Biometrics* 8:176.

May, R. M., J. A. Endler and R. E. McMurtie. 1975. Gene frequency clines in the presence of selecton opposed by gene flow. *Am. Nat.* 109:659–76.

Maynard Smith, J. 1966. Sympatric speciation. *Am. Nat.* 100:637–50.

Maynard Smith, J. 1968. Evolution in sexual and asexual populations. *Am. Nat.* 102:469–73.

Maynard Smith, J. 1971a. What use is sex? *J. theor. Biol.* 39:319–35.

Maynard Smith, J. 1971b. The origin and maintenance of sex. In *Group selection,* (G. C. Williams, ed.). Aldine-Atherton, Chicago. pp. 163–75.

Maynard Smith, J. 1974. Recombination and the rate of evolution. *Genetics* 78:299–304.

Maynard Smith, J. 1976a. Group selecton. *Quart. Rev. Biol.* 51:277–83.

Maynard Smith, J. 1976b. A short-term advantage for sex and recombination through sib-competition. *J. theor. Biol.* 63:245–58.

Maynard Smith, J. 1977. Why the genome does not congeal. *Nature* 268:693–96.

Maynard Smith, J. 1978. *The evolution of sex.* Cambridge Univ. Press, Cambridge.

Maynard Smith, J. 1979. The effects of normalizing and disruptive selection on genes for recombination. *Genet. Res.* 33:121–28.

Maynard Smith, J. and J. Haigh. 1974. The hitchhiking effect of a favourable gene. *Genet. Res.* 23:23–35.

Maynard Smith, J. and G. R. Price. 1973. The logic of animal conflicts. *Nature* 246:15–18.

Mayr, E. 1942. *Systematics and the origin of species.* Columbia Univ. Press, New York.

Mayr, E. 1947. Ecological factors in speciation. *Evolution* 1:263–88.

Mayr, E. 1954. Change of genetic environment and evolution. In *Evolution as a process.* (J. Huxley, A. C. Hardy and E. B. Ford, eds.), Allen and Unwin, London, pp. 157–80.

Mayr, E. 1955. Integration of genotypes: synthesis. *Cold Spring Harbor Symp. Quant. Biol.* 20:327–33.

Mayr, E. 1963. *Animal species and evolution.* Belknap Press, Harvard Univ. Press, Cambridge, Mass.

Mayr, E. 1969a. Species, speciation and chromosomes. In *Comparative mammalian cytogenetics.* (K. Benirschke, ed.), Springer-Verlag, New York. pp. 1–7.

Mayr, E. 1969b. *Principles of systematic zoology.* McGraw-Hill, New York.

Mayr, E. 1974. Teleological and teleonomic: a new analysis. *Boston Studies Phil. Sci.* 14:91–117.

Mayr, E. 1975. The unity of genotype. *Biol. Zbl.* 94:377–88.

McBride, C. 1977. *The white lions of Timbavati.* Paddington Press, New York.

McFarquhar, A. M. and F. W. Robertson. 1963. The lack of evidence for co-adaptation in crosses between geographical races of *Drosophila subobscura. Coll. Genet. Res.* 4:104–31.

McKenzie, J. A. 1975. Gene flow and selection in a natural population of *Drosophila melanogaster. Genetics* 80:349–61.

McKenzie, J. A. and P. A. Parsons. 1974. Microdifferentiation in a natural population of *Drosophila melanogaster* to alcohol in the environment. *Genetics* 77:385–94.

McPhail, J. D. 1977. Inherited interpopulation differences in size at first reproduction in threespine stickleback *Gasterosteus aculeatus* L. *Heredity* 38:53–60.

Mech, L. D. 1970. *The wolf: the ecology and behavior of an endangered species.* Natural History Press, Garden City, New York.

Mech, L. D. 1977. Wolf-pack buffer zones as prey reservoirs. *Science* 198:320–21.

Menge, B. A. 1975. Brood or broadcast? The adaptive significance of different reproductive strategies in the two intertidal sea stars, *Leptasterias hexactis* and *Pisaster ochraceus. Mar. Biol.* 31:87–100.

Merrell, D. J. 1970. Migration and gene dispersal in *Rana pipiens*. *Amer. Zool.* 10:47–52.

Merritt, R. B., J. F. Rogers and B. J. Kurz. 1978. Genic variability in the longnose dace, *Rhinichthys cataractae*. *Evolution* 32:116–24.

Mettler, L. E. and T. G. Gregg. 1969. *Population genetics and evolution.* Prentice-Hall, Englewood Cliffs, N. J.

Metz, C. W. 1938. Chromosome behavior, inheritance and sex determination in *Sciara*. *Am. Nat.* 72:485–520.

Michener, G. R. and D. R. Michener. 1977. Population structure and dispersal in Richardson's ground squirrels. *Ecology* 58:359–68.

Michod, R. E. 1979. Genetical aspects of kin selection: effects of inbreeding. *J. theor. Biol.* 81:223–34.

Michod, R. E. and W. W. Anderson. 1979. Measures of genetic relationship and the concept of inclusive fitness. *Am. Nat.* 114:637–47.

Mileikovsky, S. A. 1971. Types of larval development in marine bottom invertebrates, their distribution and ecological significance: a reevalution. *Mar. Biol.* 10:193–213.

Milkman, R. D. 1967. Heterosis as a major cause of heterozygosity in nature. *Genetics* 55:493–95.

Miller, A. H. 1947. Panmixia and population size with reference to birds. *Evolution* 1:186–90.

Miller, B. A. and R. A. Croker. 1972. Distribution and abundance of *Terebra gouldi* (Gastropoda: Terebridae) on a Hawaiian subtidal sand flat. *Ecology* 53:1120–26.

Milne, H. and F. W. Robertson. 1965. Polymorphism in egg albumen protein and behaviour in the eider duck. *Nature* 205:367–69.

Missakian, E. A. 1973. Genealogical mating activity in free-ranging groups of rhesus monkeys (*Macaca mulatta*) on Cayo Santiago. *Behaviour* 45:225–41.

Mitchell, R. 1970. An analysis of dispersal in mites. *Am. Nat.* 104:425–31.

Moore, J. A. 1950. Further studies on *Rana pipiens* Schreber. *Evolution* 3:1–24.

Moore, J. A. 1975. *Rana pipiens* - the changing paradigm. *Amer. Zool.* 15:837–49.

Moore, W. S. and W. G. S. Hines. 1981. Sex in random environments. *J. theor. Biol.* 92:301–16.

Morrison, J. P. E. 1963. Notes on American *Siphonaria*. *Bull. Am. Malac. Union* 1963:7–9.

Morvan, R. and R. Campan. 1976. Les displacements du grillon des bois: conditions d'aquisition et de maintien d'une orientation dominante. *Terre Vie* 30:276–94.

Muller, H. J. 1932. Some genetic aspects of sex. *Am. Nat.* 66:118–38.

Muller, H. J. 1958. Evolution by mutation. *Bull. Amer. Math. Soc.* 64:137–60.

Muller, H. J. 1964. The relation of recombination to mutational advance. *Mutation Res.* 1:2–9.

Murray, B. G., Jr. 1967. Dispersal in vertebrates. *Ecology* 48:975–78.

Murray, J. J. 1972. *Genetic diversity and natural selection.* Oliver and Boyd, Edinburgh.

Nagylaki, T. 1976. The relation between distant individuals in geographically structured populations. *Math. Biostat.* 28:73–80.

Nei, M. 1965. Variation and covariation of gene frequencies in subdivided populations. *Evolution* 19:256–58.

Nei, M. 1972. Genetic distance between populations. *Am. Nat.* 106: 283–92.

Nei, M. and M. W. Feldman. 1972. Identity of genes by descent within and between populations under mutation and migration pressures. *Theor. Popul. Biol.* 3:460–65.

Nei, M. and W. H. Li. 1973. Linkage disequilibrium in subdivided populations. *Genetics* 75:213–19.

Nevo, E. 1978. Genetic variation in natural populations: patterns and theory. *Theor. Popul. Biol.* 13:121–77.

Newton, I. 1977. Timing and success of breeding in tundra-nesting geese. In *Evolutionary ecology.* (B. Stonehouse and C. Perrins, eds.). MacMillan Press, London.

Nice, M. M. 1964a. *Studies in the life history of the song sparrow.* Vol I. *A population study of the song sparrow and other passerines.* Dover, New York.

Nice, M. M. 1964b. *Studies in the life history of the song sparrow.* Vol II. *The behavior of the song sparrow and other passerines.* Dover, New York.

Nordeng, H. 1977. A pheromone hypothesis for homeward migration in anadromous salmonids. *Oikos* 28:155–59.

Nottebohm, F. 1969. The song of the chingolo, *Zonotrichia capensis,* in Argentina: description and evaluation of a system of dialects. *Condor* 71:299–315.

Nottebohm, F. 1972. The origins of vocal learning. *Am. Nat.* 106:116–40.

Nottebohm, F. 1976. Continental patterns of song variability in *Zonotrichia capensis*: some possible ecological correlates. *Proc. Intl. Ornithol. Cong.* 16:337–54.

Nottebohm, F. and R. K. Selander. 1972. Vocal dialects and gene frequencies in the chingolo sparrow (*Zonotrichia capensis*). *Condor* 74:137–43.

Nozawa, K., T. Shotake and Y. Okura. 1975. Blood protenin polymorphisms and population structure of the Japanese macaque, *Macaca fuscata fuscata*. In, *Isozymes*. Vol. 4. (C. L. Market, ed.), Academic Press, N. Y., pp. 225–42.

Nyberg, D. 1975. Evolution of sex. I. Primitive sex. *J. theor. Biol.* 50:429–36.

Ohta, T. 1973. Slightly deleterious mutant substitutions in evolution. *Nature* 246:96–98.

Oliver, C. G. 1972. Genetic and phenotypic differentiation and geographic distance in four species of Lepidoptera. *Evolution* 26:227–41.

Oliver, C. G. 1977. Genetic incompatibility between populations of the nymphalid butterfly *Boloria selene* from England and the United States. *Heredity* 39:249–85.

Oliver, C. G. 1979. Genetic differentiation and hybrid viability within and between some Lepidoptera species. *Am. Nat.* 114:681–94.

Orr, R. T. 1970. *Animals in migration*. MacMillan, London.

Oxford, G. S. 1976. The colour polymorphism in *Enoplognatha ovatum* (Clerck) (Araneae: Theridiidae). Temporal stability and spatial variability. *Heredity* 36:369–81.

Packer, C. 1975. Male transfer in olive baboons. *Nature* 255:219–20.

Packer, C. 1979. Inter-troop transfer and inbreeding avoidance in *Papio anubis*. *Anim. Behav.* 27:1–36.

Palenzona, D. L., M. Mochi and E. Boschieri. 1974. Investigation of the founder effect. *Genetica* 45:1–10.

Palenzona, D. L., R. Alicchio and G. Rocchetta. 1975. Interaction between artificial and natural selection. *Theor. and Appl. Genet.* 46:223–38.

Palmer, R. S. 1962. *Handbook of North American birds*. Vol. I. *Loons through flamingos*. Yale Univ. Press, New Haven, Conn.

Paraense, W. L. 1959. One-sided reproductive isolation between geographically remote populations of a planorbid snail. *Am. Nat.* 93:93–101.

Patton, J. L. 1972. Patterns of geographic variation in karyotype in the pocket gopher, *Thomomys bottae* (Eydoux and Gervois). *Evolution* 26:574–86.

Patton, J. L. and S. Y. Yang. 1977. Genetic variation in *Thomomys bottae* pocket gophers: macrogeographic patterns. *Evolution* 31:697–720.

Payne, R. B. 1973. Wingflap dialects in the flappet lark, *Mirafra rufocinnamomea*. *Ibis* 115:270–74.

Payne, R. B. 1978. Local dialects in the wingflaps of flappet larks, *Mirafra rufocinnamomea*. *Ibis* 120:204–7.

Pearl, R. 1914. Studies on inbreeding V. Inbreeding and relationship coefficients. *Am. Nat.* 48:513–19.

Perrins, C. M. 1956. Territory in the blue tit. *Ibis* 98:378–87.

Petit, C. 1958. Le determinisme genetique et psychophysiologique de la competition sexuelle chez *Drosophila melanogaster. Bull. Biol. France et Belgique* 92:248–329.

Pimental, D., G. J. C. Smith and J. S. Soans. 1967. A population model of sympatric speciation. *Am. Nat.* 101:493–504.

Pittendrigh, C. S. 1958. Adaptation, natural selection and behavior. In *Behavior and evolution.* (A. Roe and G. G. Simpson, eds.), Yale Univ. Press, New Haven, Conn., pp. 390–416.

Popper, K. R. 1963. *Conjectures and refutations.* Harper and Row, New York.

Popper, K. R. 1968. *The logic of scientific discovery.* Harper and Row, New York.

Powell, J. R. 1975. Protein variation in natural populations of animals. *Evol. Biol.* 8:79–119.

Powers, L. 1944. An expansion of Jones' theory for the explanation of heterosis. *Am. Nat.* 78:275–80.

Price, M. V. and N. M. Waser. 1979. Pollen dispersal and optimal outcrossing in *Delphinium nelsoni. Nature* 277:294–97.

Pulliam, H. R. and C. Dunford. 1980. *Programmed to learn.* Columbia Univ. Press, New York.

Ralls, K., K. Brugger and J. Ballou. 1979. Inbreeding and juvenile mortality in small populations of ungulates. *Science* 206:1101–3.

Rao, P. S. S. and S. G. Inbaraj. 1977. Inbreeding effects on human reproduction in Taniil Nadu of south India. *Ann. Hum. Genet.* 41:87–97.

Rasmussen, D. I. 1964. Blood group polymorphism and inbreeding in natural populations of the deer mouse, *Peromyscus maniculatus. Evolution* 18:219–29.

Reese, J. G. 1980. Demography of European Mute Swans in Chesapeake Bay. *Auk* 97:449–64.

Reeve, E. C. R. 1955. Inbreeding with the homozygotes at a disadvantage. *Ann. Human Genet.* 19:332–46.

Reeve, E. C. R. 1957. Inbreeding with selection and linkage. I. Selfing. *Ann. Human Genet.* 21:277–88.

Reeve, E. C. R. and J. C. Gower. 1958. Inbreeding with selection and linkage. II. Sib-mating. *Ann. Human Genet.* 23:36–49.

Rheinwald, G. 1975. The pattern of settling distances in a population of house martins *Delichon urbica. Ardea* 63:136–45.

Richdale, L. E. 1957. *A population study of penguins.* Oxford Univ. Press, London.

Robertson, A. 1952. The effect of inbreeding on the variation due to recessive genes. *Genetics* 37:189–207.

Robertson, A. 1962. Selection for heterozygotes in small populations. *Genetics* 47:1291–1300.

Rockwell, R. F. and F. Cooke. 1977. Gene flow and local adaptation in a colonially nesting dimorphic bird: the lesser snow goose (*Anser caerulescens caerulescens*). *Am. Nat.* 111:91–97.

Rogers, J. S. 1972. Measures of genetic similarity and genetic distance. *Univ. Texas Publ.* 7213:145–53.

Rothman, E. D., C. F. Sing and A. R. Templeton. 1974. A model for analysis of population structure. *Genetics* 76:943–60.

Ryman, N., F. W. Allendorf and G. Stahl. 1979. Reproductive isolation with little genetic divergence in sympatric populations of brown trout (*Salmo trutta*). *Genetics* 92:247–62.

Sade, D. S. 1968. Inhibition of son-mother mating among free-ranging rhesus monkeys. *Scient. Psychoanalyst* 12:18–27.

Salisbury, E. J. 1942. *The reproductive capacity of plants.* G. Bell, London.

Sanghvi, L. D. 1966. Inbreeding in India. *Eugen. Quart.* 13:291–301.

Sarles, R. M. 1975. Incest. *Pediat. Clin. N.A.* 22:633–41.

Sassaman, C. 1978. Dynamics of a lactate dehydrogenase polymorphism in the wood louse *Porcellio xaber* Latr.: evidence for partial assortative mating and heterosis in natural populations. *Genetics* 88:591–609.

Saul, S. H., M. J. Sinsko, P. R. Grimstad and G. B. Craig, Jr. 1978. Population genetics of the mosquito *Aedes triseriatus*: genetic-ecological correlation at an esterase locus. *Am. Nat.* 112:333–39.

Schaal, B. A. 1975. Population structure and local differentiation in *Liatris cylindracea. Am. Nat.* 109:511–28.

Schaal, B. A. 1976. Genetic diversity in *Liatris cylindracea. Syst. Bot.* 1:163–68.

Schaal, B. A. 1980. Measurement of gene flow in *Lupinus texensis. Nature* 284:450–51.

Scheltema, R. S. 1971. The dispersal of the larvae of shoal-water benthic invertebrate species over long distances by ocean currents. *European Mar. Biol. Symp.* 4:7–28.

Schneider, D. M. 1976. The meaning of incest. *J. Polynes. Soc.* 85:149–69.

Schopf, T. J. M. and J. L. Gooch. 1977. Gene frequencies in a marine ectoproct: a cline in natural populations related to sea temperature. *Evolution* 25:286–89.

Schull, W. J. and J. V. Neel. 1965. *The effects of inbreeding on Japanese children.* Harper and Row, New York.

Schull, W. J. and J. V. Neel. 1966. Some further observations on the effect of inbreeding on mortality in Kure, Japan. *Amer. J. Human Genet.* 18:144–52.

Scudder, G. G. E. 1974. Species concepts and speciation. *Can. J. Zool.* 52:1121–34.

Selander, R. K. 1970. Behavior and genetic variation in natural populations. *Amer. Zool.* 10:53–66.

Selander, R. K. and R. O. Hudson. 1976. Animal population structure under close inbreeding: the land snail *Rumina* in southern France. *Am. Nat.* 110:695–718.

Selander, R. K., W. G. Hunt and S. Y. Yang. 1969. Protein polymorphism and genic heterozygosity in two European subspecies of the house mouse. *Evolution* 23:279–90.

Selander, R. K. and W. E. Johnson. 1973. Genetic variation among vertebrate species. *Annu. Rev. Evol. Syst.* 4:75–91.

Selander, R. K. and D. W. Kaufman. 1973. Genic variability and strategies of adaptation in animals. *Proc. Natl. Acad. Sci.* (USA) 70:1875–77.

Selander, R. K. and D. W. Kaufman. 1975. Genetic population structure and breeding systems. In *Isozymes*. Vol. 4. (C. L. Markert, ed.), Academic Press, New York.

Selander, R. K. and S. Y. Yang. 1969. Protein polymorphism and genic heterozygosity in a wild population of the house mouse (*Mus musculus*). *Genetics* 63:653–67.

Shepher, J. 1971. Mate selection among second generation kibbutz adolescents and adults: incest avoidance and negative imprinting. *Arch. Sex. Behav.* 1:293–307.

Sherman, P. W. 1977. Nepotism and the evolution of alarm calls. *Science* 197:1246–53.

Shields, W. M. 1979. Philopatry, inbreeding, and the adaptive advantages of sex. Ph.D. Dissertation. Ohio State University, Columbus.

Shields, W. M. 1982a. Optimal inbreeding and the evolution of philopatry. In *The ecology of animal movement*. (I. R. Swingland and P. J. Greenwood, eds.). Oxford Univ. Press, Oxford.

Shields, W. M. 1982b. Inbreeding and the paradox of sex: a resolution? *Evol. Theory* 5:245–79.

Shine, R. 1978. Propagule size and parental care: The "safe harbor" hypothesis. *J. theor. Biol.* 75:417–24.

Simpson, G. G. 1953. *The major features of evolution*. Columbia Univ. Press, New York.

Simpson, G. G. 1967. *The meaning of evoluton.* 2nd ed., rev. Yale Univ. Press, New Haven, Conn.

Slater, P. J. B. and F. A. Clements. 1981. Incestuous mating in zebra finches. *Z. Tierpsychol.* 57:201–08.

Slatkin, M. 1973. Gene flow and selection in a cline. *Genetics* 75:733–56.

Slatkin, M. 1975. Gene flow and selection in a two locus system. *Genetics* 81:787–802.

Smith, A. T. 1974. The distribution and dispersal of pikas: consequences of insular population structure. *Ecology* 55:1112–19.

Smith, D. B., C.H. Langley and F. M. Johnson. 1978. Variance component analysis of allozyme frequency data from eastern populations of *Drosophila melanogaster. Genetics* 88:121–37.

Smith, M. H., J. L. Carmon and J. B. Gentry. 1972. Pelage color polymorphism in *Peromyscus polionotus. J. Mammal.* 53:824–33.

Smith, M. H., C. T. Garten, Jr. and P. R. Ramsey. 1975. Genic heterozygosity and population dynamics in small mammals. In *Isozymes.* Vol. 4. (C. L. Markert, ed.), Academic Press, N. Y., pp. 85–102.

Smith, R. H. 1979. On selection for inbreeding in polygynous animals. *Heredity* 43:205–11.

Smith, W. J. 1977. *The behavior of communicating.* Harvard Univ. Press, Cambridge, Mass.

Snedecor, G. and M. R. Irwin. 1933. On the chi-square test for homogeneity. *Iowa State Coll. J. Sci.* 8:75–81.

Soule, M. 1973. The epistasis cycle: a theory of marginal populations. *Annu. Rev. Ecol. Syst.* 4:165–87.

Soule, M. 1980. Thresholds for survival: maintaining fitness and evolutionary potential. In *Conservation Biology.* (M. E. Soule and B. A. Wilcox, eds.), Sinauer Assoc., Sunderland, Mass., pp. 151–69.

Spielman, R. S., J. V. Neel and F. H. F. Li. 1977. Inbreeding estimation from population data: models, procedures and implications. *Genetics* 85:355–71.

Spieth, P. T. 1974. Gene flow and genetic differentiation. *Genetics* 78:961–65.

Spurway, H. 1953. Genetics of specific and subspecific differences in European newts. *Symp. Soc. Exp. Biol.* 7:200–37.

Stanley, S. M. 1975. Clades vs. clones in evolution: why we have sex. *Science* 190:382–83.

Stebbins, G. L. 1950. *Variation and evolution in plants.* Columbia Univ. Press, New York.

Stebbins, G. L. 1957. Self-fertilization and population variability in the higher plants. *Am. Nat.* 91:337–54.

Stebbins, G. L. 1958. Longevity, habitat and release of genetic variability in higher plants. *Cold Spring Harbor Symp. Quant. Biol.* 23:365–78.

Stebbins, G. L. 1971. *Processes of organic evolution* 2nd ed. Prentice-Hall, Englewood Cliffs, N. J.

Stevenson, A. C., H. A. Johnston, M. I. P. Stewart and D. R. Golding. 1966. *Congenital Malformations.* World Health Organizatoin, Geneva.

Stirling, I. 1975. Factors affecting the evolution of social behaviour in the pinnipedia. *Rapp. P. v. Reun. Cons. Int. Explor. Mer.* 169:205–12.

Strobeck, C., J. Maynard Smith and B. Charlesworth. 1976. The effects of hitchhiking on a gene for recombination. *Genetics* 82:547–58.

Sved, J. A., T. E. Reed and W. F. Bodmer. 1967. The number of balanced polymorphisms that can be maintained in a natural population. *Genetics* 55:469–81.

Taylor, P. D. 1979. An analytical model for a short-term advantage for sex. *J. theor. Biol.* 81:407–12.

Taylor, P. D. 1981. Intra-sex and inter-sex sib interactions as sex ratio determinants. *Nature* 291:64–66.

Taylor, P. D. and M. G. Bulmer. 1980. Local mate competition and the sex ratio. *J. theor. Biol.* 86:409–19.

Teague, R. 1977. A model of migration modification. *Theor. Popul. Biol.* 12:86–94.

Tenaza, R. R. and R. L. Tilson. 1977. Evolution of long-distance alarm calls in Kloss's gibbon. *Nature* 268:233–35.

Thaeler, C. S., Jr. 1974. Four contacts between ranges of different chromosome forms of the *Thomomys talpoides* complex (Rodentia: Geomyidae). *Syst. Zool.* 23:343–54.

Thoday, J. M. 1958. Effects of disruptive select: the experimental production of a polymorphic population. *Nature* 181:1124–25.

Thoday, J. M. 1972. Disruptive selection. *Proc. R. Soc. London B.* 182:109–43.

Thoday, J. M. and J. B. Gibson. 1962. Isolation by disruptive selection. *Nature* 193:1164–66.

Thoday, J. M. and J. B. Gibson. 1970. The probability of isolation by disruptive selection. *Am. Nat.* 104:219–30.

Thompson, V. 1976. Does sex accelerate evolution? *Evol. Theory* 1:131–56.

Thompson, V. 1977 Recombination and response to selection in *Drosophila melanogaster. Genetics* 85:125–40.

Thorson, G. 1950. Reproductive and larval ecology of marine bottom invertebrates. *Biol. Rev.* 25:1–45.

Till, J. E. 1981. Cellular diversity in the blood forming system. *Amer. Scientist* 69:522–27.

Tilzey, R. D. J. 1977. Repeat homing of brown trout (*Salmo trutta*) in Lake Eucumbene, New South Wales, Australia. *J. Fish. Res. Bd. Canada* 34:1085–94.

Tinkle, D. W. 1965. Population structure and effective size of a lizard population. *Evolution* 19:569–73.

Tinkle, D. W. 1967. Home range, density, dynamics and structure of a Texas population of the lizard, *Uta stansburiana*. In *Lizard ecology: a symposium*. (W. M. Milstead, ed.), Univ. of Missouri Press, Columbia, Missouri.

Tordoff, W. III, D. Pettus and T. C. Matthews. 1976. Microgeographic variation in gene frequencies in *Pseudacris triseriata* (Amphibia, Anura, Hylidae). *J. Herpetol.* 10:35–40.

Treisman, M. 1976. The evolution of sexual reproduction: a model which assumes individual selection. *J. theor. Biol.* 60:421–31.

Treisman, M. 1978. Bird song dialects, repertoire size and kin association. *Anim. Behav.* 26:814–17.

Treisman, M. and R. Dawkins. 1976. The "cost of meiosis": is there any? *J. theor. Biol.* 63:479–84.

Trivers, R. L. 1972. Parental investment and sexual selection. In *Sexual selection and the descent of man*. (B. Campbell, ed.), Aldine, Chicago, pp. 136–79.

Turner, J. R. G. 1967a. Why does the genotype not congeal? *Evolution* 21:645–56.

Turner, J. R. G. 1967b. On supergenes. I. The evolution of super-genes. *Am. Nat.* 101:195–222.

Twitty, V. C. 1961. Experiments on homing behavior and speciation in *Taricha*. In *Vertebrate speciation*. (W. F. Blair, ed.), Univ. of Texas Press, Austin, pp. 415–59.

Udvardy, M. D. F. 1969. *Dynamic zoogeography, with special reference to land animals*. Van Nostrand Reinhold, New York.

Van Noordwijk, A. J. and W. Scharloo. 1981. Inbreeding in an island population of the great tit. *Evolution* 35:674–88.

Van Ryzin, M. T. and H. I. Fisher. 1976. The age of Laysan albatrosses, *Diomedea immutabilis*, at first breeding. *Condor* 78:1–9.

Vance, R. R. 1973. On reproductive strategies in marine benthic invertebrates. *Am. Nat.* 107:339–52.

Van Valen, L. 1971. Group selection and the evolution of dispersal. *Evolution* 25:591-98.

Van Valen, L. 1975. Group selection, sex and fossils. *Evolution* 29:87-94.

Vetukhiv, M. 1954. Integration of the genotype in local populations of three species of *Drosophila*. *Evolution* 8:241-51.

Vetukhiv, M. 1956. Fecundity of hybrids between geographic populations of *Drosophila pseudoobscura*. *Evolution* 10:139-46.

Vetukhiv, M. 1957. Longevity of hybrids between geographic populations of *Drosophila pseudoobscura*. *Evolution* 11:348-60.

Vickery, R. K., Jr. 1959. Barriers to gene exchange within *Mimulus guttatus* (Scrophularicaceae). *Evolution* 13:300-310.

Waddington, C. H. 1957. *The strategy of the genes*. Allen and Unwin, London.

Wahlund. S. 1928. Zusammensetzung von Population und Korrelationserscheinung vom Standpunkt der Verebungslehre aus Betrachtet. *Hereditas* 11:65-105.

Wallace, B. 1955. Interpopulation hybrids in *Drosophila melanogaster*. *Evolution* 9:302-16.

Wallace, B. 1968a. On the dispersal of *Drosophila*. *Am. Nat.* 100:86-87.

Wallace, B. 1968b. *Topics in population genetics*. W. W. Norton, New York.

Wallace, B. 1970. *Genetic load*. Prentice-Hall, Englewood Cliffs, N.J.

Wallace, B. 1977. Automatic culling and population fitness. *Evol. Biol.* 10:265-76.

Wallace, B. and M. Vetukhiv. 1955. Adaptive organization of the gene-pools of *Drosophila* populations. *Cold Spring Harbor Symp. Quant. Biol.* 20:303-10.

Warham, J. 1964. Breeding behavior in Procellariiformes. In *Biologie Antarctique*. Proc, 1st. Symp. on Anarct. Biol. (R. M. Carrick, M. W. Holdgate and J. Prevost, eds.), Paris, pp. 389-94.

Watanabe, T. K. 1969. Frequency of deleterious chromosomes and allelism between lethal genes in Japanese natural populations of *Drosophila melanogaster*. *Jap. J. Gen.* 44:171-87.

Weatherhead, P. J. and R. J. Robertson. 1979. Offspring quality and the polygny threshold: "the sexy son hypothesis." *Am. Nat.* 113:201-8.

Weir, B. S., R. W. Allard and A. L. Kahler. 1972. Analysis of complex allozyme polymorphisms in a barley population. *Genetics* 72:505-23.

Weismann, A. 1891. The significance of sexual reproduction in the theory of natural selection, 1886. In *Essays upon heredity and kindred biological problems*. (E. B. Poulton, S. Schonland and A. E. Shipley, eds.), Vol. I. 2nd. ed. Clarendon Press, Oxford, pp. 257-342.

Weiss, G. H. and M. Kimura. 1965. A mathematical analysis of the stepping stone model of genetic correlation. *J. Appl. Prob.* 2:129-49.

Wells, K. D. and R. A. Wells. 1976. Patterns of movement in a population of the slimy salamander, *Plethodon glutinosus*, with observations on aggregations. *Herpetologica* 32:156-62.

West Eberhard, M. J. 1975. The evolution of social behavior by kin selection. *Quart. Rev. Biol.* 50:1-33.

White, M. J. D. 1957. Cytogenetics of the grasshopper, *Moraba scurra* II. Heterotic systems and their interaction. *Aust. J. Zool.* 5:305-37.

White, M. J. D. 1968. Models of speciation. *Science* 159:1065-70.

White, M. J. D. 1973. *Animal cytology and evolution*. 3rd ed. Cambridge Univ. Press, Cambridge.

White, M. J. D. 1974. Speciation in the Australian morabine grasshoppers: the cytogenetic evidence. In *Genetic mechanisms of speciation in insects.* (M. J. D. white, ed.), Australia and New Zealand Book Co., Sydney, pp. 57-68.

White, M. J. D. 1978a. *Modes of speciation.* Freeman, San Francisco.

White, M. J. D. 1978b. Chian processes in chromosomal speciation. *Syst. Zool.* 27:285-98.

Wigan, L. G. 1944. Balance and potence in natural populations. *J. Genet.* 46:150-60.

Williams, G. C. 1966. *Adaptation and natural selection*. Princeton Univ. Press, Princeton, N. J.

Williams, G. C. 1971. *Group selection*. Aldne-Atherton, Chicago.

Williams, G. C. 1975. *Sex and evolution*. Princeton Univ. Press, Princeton, N. J.

Williams, G. C. 1980. Kin selection and the paradox of sexuality. In *Sociobioloby: beyond nature/nurture.* (G. W. Barlow and J. Silverberg, eds.), Westview Press, Boulder, Colorado, pp. 371-84.

Williams, G. C., R. K. Koehn and J. B. Mitton. 1973. Genetic differentiation in the American eel, *Anguilla rostrata*. *Evolution* 27:192-204.

Williams, G. C. and J. B. Mitton. 1973. Why reproduce sexually? *J. theor. Biol.* 39:545-54.

Wilson, A. C. 1976. Gene regulation in evolution. In *Molecular evolution.* (F. J. Ayala, Ed.), Sinauer, Sunderland, Mass., pp. 225-36.

Wilson, D. S. 1980. *The natural selection of populations and communities.* Benjamin/Cummings, Menlo Park, Cal.

Wilson, E. O. 1963. Social modifications related to rareness in ant species. *Evolution* 17:249-53.

Wilson, E. O. 1975. *Sociobiology*. Belknap Press, Harvard Univ. Press, Cambridge, Mass.

Wilson, E. O. 1978. *On human nature.* Harvard Univ. Press, Cambridge, Mass.

Wolfenbarger, D. O. 1946. Dispersion of small organisms. *Amer. Midl. Natur.* 35:1-152.

Wool, D. and E. Sverdlov. 1976. Sib-mating populations in an unpredictable environment: effects on components of fitness. *Evolution* 30:119-29.

Wright, S. 1921. Systems of mating. *Genetics* 6:111-78.

Wright, S. 1922. Coefficients of inbreeding and relationship. *Am. Nat.* 56:330-38.

Wright, S. 1931. Evolution in mendelian populations. *Genetics* 16:97-159.

Wright, S. 1932. The roles of mutation, inbreeding, cross-breeding and selection in evolution. *Proc. 6th. Intl. Cong. Genetics* pp. 356-66.

Wright, S. 1938. Size of population and breeding structure in relation to evolution. *Science* 87:430-31.

Wright, S. 1940. Breeding structure of populations in relation to speciation. *Am. Nat.* 74:232-48.

Wright, S. 1943. Isolation by distance. *Genetics* 28:114-38.

Wright, S. 1951. The genetical structure of populations. *Ann. Eugenics* 15:323-54.

Wright, S. 1956. Modes of selection. *Am. Nat.* 90:7-24.

Wright, S. 1965. The interpretation of population structure by f-statistics with special regard to systems of mating. *Evolution* 19:395-420.

Wright, S. 1968. *Evolution and the genetics of populations.* Vol. 1. *Genetic and biometric foundations.* Univ. of Chicago Press, Chicago.

Wright, S. 1969. *Evolution and the genetics of populatoins.* Vol. 2. *Theory of gene frequencies.* Univ. of Chicago Press, Chicago.

Wright, S. 1977. *Evolution and the genetics of populations.* Vol. 3. *Experimental results and evolutionary deductions.* Univ. of Chicago Press, Chicago.

Wright, S. 1978. *Evolution and the genetics of populations.* Vol. 4. *Variability within and among natural populations.* Univ. of Chicago Press, Chicago.

Wynne-Edwards, V. C. 1962. *Animal dispersion in relation to social behavior.* Hafner Publ., New York.

Yamasaki, K., E. A. Boyse, V. Mike, H. T. Thaler, B. J. Mathieson, J. Abbott, J. Boyse, Z. A. Zayas and L. Thomas. 1976. Control of mating preferences in mice by genes in the major histocompatibility complex. *J. Exp. Med.* 144:-1324-35.

Yardley, D. and C. Hubbs. 1976. An electrophoretic study of two species of mosquitofish with notes on genetic subdivision. *Copeia* 1976:117–20.

Zahavi, A. 1975. Mate selection - a selection for a handicap. *J. theor. Biol.* 53:205–14.

Zirkle, C. 1952. Early ideas of inbreeding and cross-breeding. In *Heterosis*, (J. W. Gowen, ed.). Iowa State Coll. Press, Ames, Iowa.

Zornoza, P. and C. Lopez-Fanjul. 1975. The effect of inbreeding on egg laying of *T. castaneum*. In *Tribolium Inform. Bull.* No. 18, (A. Sokoloff, ed.). pp. 152–65.

Zouros, E. 1973. Genic differentiation associated with the early stages of speciation in the *mulleri* subgroup of *Drosophila. Evolution* 27:601–21.

Author Index

Abegglen, J. J., 168–69
Adest, G. A., 189
Alcock, J., 22
Alevizos, V., 186
Alexander, R. D., 29, 53–54, 126, 165, 189–90, 196
Allard, R. W., 46–47, 63, 129–30
Allen, G., 38
Altmann, J., 17
Altmann, S. A., 17
Anderson, W. W., 88, 194
Antonovics, J., 24, 91, 94–95, 160
Atwood, S., 62
Austin, O. L., Sr., 20, 26
Avise, J. C., 84–85, 88
Ayala, F. J., 76, 84, 88

Bairlein, F., 15
Baker, H. G., 54, 155–56, 159
Baker, M. C., 15, 99, 165–66, 189
Baker, R. R., 7, 12, 17, 21
Balashov, Y. S., 89
Balat, F., 13, 15
Baptista, L. F., 165
Barash, D. P., 189
Barrett, G. W., 184
Barrowclough, G. F., 181, 185, 189
Bateman, A. J., 12
Bateson, P. P. G., 89, 149, 167–68, 171
Begon, M., 12, 180–81
Bekoff, M., 17
Bellucci, M. J., 63
Bender, E. A., 101, 111
Bengtsson, B. O., 21, 53, 55, 125, 195
Bent, A. C., 162–63
Berger, E., 44, 86

Berndt, R., 12, 14–18
Bernstein, H., 133–35, 137
Bigelow, R. S., 72
Bischof, N., 195–96
Blair, W. F., 8, 12, 15, 17, 21–22, 165
Blick, J., 190
Blickenstaff, C. C., 89
Bogart, J. P., 188
Bogert, C. M., 12
Bonner, J. T., 104
Bradshaw, A. D., 91, 94, 160
Brannon, E. L., 24
Bremermann, H. J., 104, 110, 133–34, 137, 140–42, 145, 147
Breuer, M. E., 162
Britten, R. J., 66
Brncic, D., 88–89
Brown, C. K., 182
Brussard, P. F., 185
Buechner, H. K., 17
Bulmer, M. G., 15–16, 52, 64, 116, 128–29, 145
Burger, J., 163
Burnet, F. M., 140–42
Burt, W. H., 21
Bush, G. L., 68, 78, 84

Cagle, F. R., 14
Cain, A. J., 96–97, 182
Caisse, M., 91, 94–95
Caligari, P. D. S., 67
Callan, H. G., 89
Campan, R., 17
Carr, A., 14–15, 20, 26
Carr, M. H., 14–15, 20, 26
Carson, H. L., 2, 38, 40, 46, 52, 55, 73, 151, 198

235

Index

Case, T. J., 104, 111
Charlesworth, B., 104, 106–7, 124, 129
Charlesworth, D., 129, 135
Chetverikov, S. S., 66
Child, A. R., 188
Clarke, B. A., 60
Clarke, C. A., 88
Clausen, J., 89
Clements, F. A., 167
Cockerham, C. C., 39, 129, 184
Cohen, D., 6, 21
Coker, W. Z., 188
Conner, J. L., 63
Cook, C. B., 152
Cook, L. M., 17
Cook, S. A., 182
Cook, S. B., 152
Cooke, F., 161
Cooper, K. W., 162
Corbin, K. W., 189
Coulson, J. C., 14, 26
Cowan, D. P., 162, 197
Cronin, T. W., 154
Crook, J. H., 169
Crosby, J. L., 91
Crow, J. F., 2, 23, 27, 31–32, 34–35,
    38–41, 48, 50–52, 61, 82, 86, 94,
    102–3, 131, 137, 178
Crozier, R. H., 181
Cruden, R. W., 106, 126

Daly, M., 109
Darlington, C. D., 2, 31, 103, 109, 135
Darwin, C., 50, 170, 189
Davidson, E. H., 66
Davies, N. B., 190–91
Dawkins, R., 104, 118, 125, 177, 189–92
De Benedictis, P. A., 190
Defries, J. C., 181
Dice, L. C., 90–91
Dice, S. D., 8, 12, 15, 197
Dilger, W. C., 165
Dobzhansky, T., 10, 12, 22, 24, 27,
    32–34, 52, 66–68, 71–74, 76–78, 84,
    86, 88, 94, 103, 109, 123, 131, 146,
    167, 172–73, 178, 182, 189
Dodson, E. O., 104
Dougherty, E. C., 137
Dreyfus, A., 162
Duncan, W. R., 143, 167, 186
Dunford, C., 140

East, E. M., 31, 56–57
Ehrlich, P. R., 17, 26, 94–95, 160

Ehrman, L., 52, 88, 171
Elbadry, E. A., 128, 162
Elliot, L., 15
Emlen, J. M., 113, 130
Emlen, J. T., 87, 94
Emlen, S. T., 127
Endler, J. A., 7, 12, 17, 66, 68,
    84–85, 88, 90–91, 94–95
Enfield, F. D., 61
Epling, C., 182
Erlinge, S., 12

Faegri, K., 33
Falconer, D. S., 2, 27, 31–32, 34–35,
    38, 40, 48, 52–53, 56–57
Farr, J. A., 52, 171
Feldman, M. W., 42
Felsenstein, J., 93, 104, 109, 117–19,
    122, 133, 137
Ferrell, G. T., 189
Festing, M., 62
Fischer, E. A., 107
Fisher, H. I., 15, 20, 25–26, 182,
    184, 197
Fisher, M. L., 25
Fisher, R. A., 2, 4, 22–24, 38, 40, 51,
    66–67, 78, 94, 103–4, 108–9, 119,
    137, 150, 170–71
Flesness, N. R., 194
Ford, E. B., 22, 25, 33, 87–90, 97,
    109, 182
Forester, D. C., 12, 22
Forward, R. B., Jr., 154
Franklin, I. R., 38, 60, 63
Fullagar, P. J., 90

Gadgil, M., 19, 21
Gauthreaux, S. A., Jr., 18–19
Geddes, P., 123, 137
Gee, J. M., 152, 154
Gerking, S. D., 12
Ghiselin, M. T., 22, 104–5
Gibson, J. B., 91
Gilder, P. M., 166–67
Ginsberg, B. E., 180
Giovanelli, L., 14
Glesener, R. R., 104, 110
Glover, D. G., 189
Godfrey, J., 166
Goldschmidt, R., 89
Gooch, J. L., 152
Gordon, H., 88
Gordon, M., 88
Gorman, G. C., 189

Gottlieb, L. D., 89
Gould, S. J., 144
Gowen, J. W., 86
Gower, J. C., 46
Grant, A., 89
Grant, V., 12, 32, 38, 65, 68, 71,
 73, 79, 89, 135, 137, 151, 155–56,
 159–60, 182
Greenberg, L., 162, 197
Greenwood, J. J. D., 181
Greenwood, P. J., 10, 12–13, 15–16, 21,
 52–54, 64, 151, 161, 165, 195–96
Gregg, T. G., 38

Haigh, J., 118
Haldane, J. B. S., 2, 38, 40, 43, 55,
 67, 78, 195
Halkka, D., 188
Hall, W. P., 79, 90
Halliburton, R., 15–17, 19
Halliday, T. R., 167, 170–71
Hamilton, W. D., 6, 21, 54, 59, 107,
 110–11, 126, 128, 162, 189–90
Hamrick, J. L., 63, 129
Hansen, T. A., 152
Harden-Jones, F. R., 12, 17, 22, 160
Harland, S. C., 82
Harper, J. L., 12, 58, 155, 158–59
Hartnoll, R. G., 152, 154
Hartung, J., 91, 104, 116
Harvey, P. H., 21, 54, 151, 161, 165,
 195
Hasler, A. D., 17, 20, 22–23
Hayman, B. I., 44
Hedgecock, D., 85, 99, 189
Hedrick, P., 66, 82, 90–91, 93
Heed, W. B., 8, 12
Heller, R., 133–34
Hempel, C. G., 5
Heusser, H., 14
Highton, R., 85, 88, 183, 189
Hilden, O., 17
Hill, J. L., 53, 151, 196
Hill, W. G., 46, 117
Hinde, R. A., 21
Hines, W. G. S., 104, 110–11, 134
Hoenigsberg, H. F., 188
Howard, J. C., 167
Howard, W. E., 1, 8, 12, 15, 17, 19,
 53, 197
Hubbs, C., 185
Hubby, J. L., 184
Hudson, R. O., 16, 26
Hughes, K. W., 89

Hunter, R. D., 184
Huxley, J. S., 94, 170

Immelmann, K., 23
Inbaraj, S. G., 196
Inger, R. F., 188
Irwin, M. R., 187
Itani, J., 53, 151, 196–97

Jacquard, A., 2, 29, 35, 37, 39–40,
 42, 189, 193
Jaenike, J., 110
Jain, S. K., 33, 46–47, 54–55, 91, 94,
 129, 156
James, S. H., 79
Jameson, D. L., 14
Jenkins, P. F., 164–65
Jerne, N. K., 140–41
Jewell, P. A., 90
Jinks, J. L., 55, 82
Johnson, C. G., 17, 162
Johnson, W. E., 84
Johnson, W. W., 91, 98
Johnston, J. S., 8, 12
Johnston, R. F., 12, 17–19
Jones, D. F., 31, 56–57

Kaffman, M., 196
Kalmus, H., 53
Karlin, S., 96–97
Kaufman, D. W., 98, 187–88
Keeler, K. H., 187
Keller, A. J., 189
Kempton, R. A., 96
Kenyon, K. W., 14, 20
Kerster, H. W., 12, 17, 160, 181
Kimura, M., 2, 23, 27, 31–32, 34–35,
 38–42, 46, 48, 50–52, 61, 70, 82,
 86, 93–94, 103, 131, 178, 184–85
King, H. D., 62, 65
King, J. C., 91, 98
King, J. L., 60
Koenig, W. D., 53, 151, 161, 196
Kojima, K., 116
Krebs, J. R., 190–91
Krimbas, C. B., 186
Kroodsma, D. E., 165
Kruckeberg, A. R., 89, 99–100
Kuma, E., 188
Kummer, H., 168

Lack, D., 21, 32, 64
Lande, R., 38, 63
Leggett, W. C., 21

Lerner, I. M., 2, 32, 38, 49–51, 55, 57, 61–62, 66, 72, 86, 140, 148
Leslie, J. F., 123
Leuthold, W., 1, 17, 163
Levin, B. R., 181
Levin, D. A., 12, 17, 104, 110, 160, 181, 187
Levins, R., 6, 25–27, 146–47
Lewis, D., 103
Lewis, H., 79
Lewontin, R. C., 46, 73, 84, 86, 116–17, 184, 191
Li, C. C., 40
Li, W. H., 129
Lidicker, W. Z., Jr., 19, 21
Livingstone, F. B., 55, 196
Lloyd, D. G., 110, 141–42
Loeb, L., 62
Loncke, D. J., 14
Longwell, A. C., 154
Lopez-Fanjul, C., 61
Lyerla, T. A., 189
Lynch, C. B., 57

MacGregor, J., 96–97
Mainardi, D., 166
Malecot, G., 35, 37, 40, 93, 189–90
Malmberg, R. L., 102
Manning, J. T., 106, 109, 137, 144, 146–48
Marler, P., 165
Maruyama, T., 42, 93
Mason, W., 140
Mather, K., 2, 34, 38, 44–46, 55, 66–67, 82, 89, 103, 131
May, R. M., 6, 21, 91
Maynard Smith, J., 3, 6, 50, 70, 104–13, 115–16, 118–19, 122–24, 126–28, 131–35, 144–46, 149, 170, 189–90, 195
Mayr, E., vii, 10, 12, 19, 22, 24, 27, 32, 34, 50, 52–53, 61, 66, 68, 71–73, 77–79, 82, 84–85, 87, 91, 94–95, 97, 104, 144, 161, 163, 172, 177–78, 182, 190
McBride, C., 184
McClearn, G. E., 181
McFarquhar, A. M., 88
McKenzie, J. A., 188
McPhail, J. D., 188
Mech, L. D., 17, 197
Menge, B. A., 152
Merrell, D. J., 181
Merritt, R. B., 99

Mettler, L. E., 38
Metz, C. W., 52
Mewaldt, L. R., 15–17, 19, 165–66
Michener, D. R., 15
Michener, G. R., 15
Michod, R. E., 194
Milkman, R. D., 60
Miller, A. H., 12, 17, 175, 181
Milne, H., 162
Missakian, E. A., 197
Mitchell, R., 162
Mitton, J. B., 104, 113
Moore, J. A., 89
Moore, W. S., 104, 110–11, 134
Morrison, J. P. E., 152
Morvan, R., 17
Muller, H. J., 4, 102–3, 119–20
Murray, B. G., Jr., 19–20, 22
Murray, J. J., 84

Nagylaki, T., 93
Neel, J. V., 63–65
Nei, M., 42, 70, 76, 85, 129, 185, 187
Nevo, E., 84
Newton, I., 161
Nice, M. M., 15–16
Nordeng, H., 167
Nottebohm, F., 165
Nozawa, K., 189
Nyberg, D., 104

Obbard, M. E., 14
Ohta, T., 40, 42, 46, 70, 93, 103, 178, 184–85
Oliver, C. G., 68, 89–99
Oring, L. W., 127
Orr, R. T., 20
Oxford, G. S., 182

Packer, C., 53, 64, 151, 161, 168, 195–96
Palenzona, D. L., 91, 98
Palmer, R. S., 26
Paraense, W. L., 89, 99
Parsons, P. A., 188
Patton, J. L., 79, 99, 189
Payne, R. B., 165
Pearl, R., 31, 36
Perrins, C. M., 15
Petit, C., 171
Pimental, D., 91
Pitelka, F. A., 53, 151, 161, 196
Pittendrigh, C. S., vii
Popper, K. R., 197

Powell, J. R., 84
Powers, L., 82
Price, G. R., 6, 106
Price, M. V., 25, 65, 89, 99–102, 149,
    151, 168, 195
Pulliam, H. R., 140

Ralls, K., 65, 196
Rao, P. S. S., 196
Rasmussen, D. I., 181
Raven, P. H., 17, 94–95, 160
Reese, J. G., 197
Reeve, E. C. R., 46
Rheinwald, G., 8
Richdale, L. E., 26
Robertson, A., 46, 117
Robertson, F. W., 88, 162
Robertson, R. J., 170
Rockwell, R. F., 161
Rogers, J. S., 85
Roth, H. D., 17
Rothman, E. D., 39
Ryman, N., 27

Sade, D. S., 151, 196–97
Salisbury, E. J., 158–59
Sanghvi, L. D., 196
Sarles, R. M., 196
Sassaman, C., 186
Saul, S. H., 16, 188
Schaal, B. A., 8, 102, 129, 181, 185, 187
Scharloo, W., 64–65, 90, 197
Schneider, D. M., 196
Schopf, T. J. M., 152
Schull, W. J., 63–65
Scudder, G. G. E., 84
Selander, R. K., 16, 26, 79, 84, 90,
    98–99, 165, 187–88
Shepher, J., 196
Sheppard, P. M., 88
Sherman, P. W., 10, 14–15, 126
Shields, W. M., 10, 41, 100, 102,
    104, 124, 127–29, 133–34, 137,
    141, 143
Shine, R., 152
Simpson, G. G., 144, 177
Slater, P. J. B., 166–67
Slatkin, M., 91, 94, 111–12
Smith, A. T., 17
Smith, C. A. B., 53
Smith, D. B., 188
Smith, M. H., 182, 184, 189
Smith, R. H., 197
Smith, W. J., 164, 166, 169

Snedecor, G., 187
Soule, M., 65, 82, 91
Spassky, B., 86
Spielman, R. S., 186
Spieth, P. T., 93
Spurway, H., 89
Stanley, S. M., 104, 123
Stebbins, G. L., 32, 52, 71, 84, 90,
    103, 123, 132, 135, 151, 155–56
Sternberg, H., 12, 14–18
Stevenson, A. C., 63
Stiles, S. S., 154
Stirling, I., 26
Strobeck, C., 118–19
Sved, J. A., 60
Sverdlov, E., 61–62

Tamura, M., 165
Tawfik, M. S. F., 128, 162
Taylor, P. D., 116, 128–29
Teague, R., 96–97
Tenaza, R. R., 17
Thaeler, C. S., Jr., 79
Thoday, J. M., 91, 94
Thompson, J. A., 123, 137
Thompson, V., 3, 103–5, 175
Thorson, G., 12, 152–53
Till, J. E., 140–41
Tilman, D., 104, 110
Tilson, R. L., 17
Tilzey, R. D. J., 167
Tinkle, D. W., 12, 15, 181, 197
Tordoff, W., III, 189
Treisman, M., 104, 116, 164–65, 192
Trivers, R. L., 170
Turner, J. R. G., 105, 109
Twitty, V. C., 12, 14

Udvardy, M. D. F., 19

Vance, R. R., 152
Van der Pijl, L., 33
Van Noordwijk, A. J., 64–65, 90, 197
Van Ryzin, M. T., 25
Van Valen, L., 17–19, 21, 104
Vawter, A. T., 185
Vetukhiv, M., 88
Vickery, R. K., Jr., 89
Vrijenhoek, R. C., 123

Waddington, C. H., 66, 140
Wahlund, S., 185
Wallace, B., 4, 12, 17, 38, 44, 46,
    52, 60, 86, 88–89, 94, 131, 150

Warham, J., 26
Waser, N. M., 25, 65, 89, 99–102, 149, 151, 168, 195
Wasserman, A. O., 188
Watanabe, T. K., 87
Weatherhead, P. J., 170
Wehrhahn, C., 129
Weir, B. S., 129
Weismann, A., 104
Weiss, G. H., 41–42, 93
Wells, K. D., 15
Wells, R. A., 15
West-Eberhard, M. J., 107, 189–90
White, J., 158–59
White, M. J. D., 16, 68, 71–72, 75, 79, 84–85, 94–95, 97, 135
Wigan, L. G., 82, 89, 148
Williams, G. B., 152, 154
Williams, G. C., vii, 2–3, 103–9, 113, 115–16, 123–24, 126–28, 130–32, 138–39, 145, 172, 177, 189–90, 192, 195, 197

Wilson, A. C., 66
Wilson, D. S., 19
Wilson, E. O., 19, 23, 27, 32, 38, 51, 54, 166, 169, 189, 196
Wool, D., 61–62
Wright, S., 2–4, 10, 12, 17, 23, 30, 32, 35–36, 38–41, 44–47, 50–53, 56–57, 61–63, 66, 71, 91, 93–94, 109, 123, 137, 140, 146, 174–78, 180–82, 184–87, 189–90, 193, 196
Wynne-Edwards, V. C., 17–19

Yamasaki, K., 166
Yang, S. Y., 26, 99, 187, 189
Yardley, D., 185
Yokoyama, S., 104, 110, 117–18, 133

Zahavi, A., 170
Zirkle, C., 50, 53
Zornoza, P., 61
Zouros, E., 88

Subject Index

Adactylidium, 128
Adaptability, 51, 104–5, 132
Alteration of generations. *See*
    Heterogony
Amphibians, 12, 14, 89, 99, 165, 188
Anatidae, 161–62
Animal breeding, 58, 63
Annuals, 12, 156–60
Anolis, 85
Apis mellifera, 181
Area effects, 182
Arthropods, 89, 123, 126
Asexual reproduction, 103. *See also*
    Parthenogenesis
    advantages, 107–8
    disadvantages, 121–23, 132–33
    extinction, 123–24
Assortative mating, 163–69
Automixis, 134–35
Avena barbata, 63

Bacteria, 147
Betula, 159
Birds, 12–14, 53, 90, 97, 99, 151,
    165–66, 189
Butterflies, 12, 17, 26, 87

Canalization, 139
Canis lupus, 17, 197
Centrarchidae, 160
Cepea nemoralis, 181
Chamaea fasciata, 181
Chelonia mydas, 15
Chromosomes, 68, 75, 78–84, 109
Cichoreae, 156
Cistothorus palustris, 181
Clarkia, 79

Clethrionomys glareolus, 166
Clupea, 160
Coadaptation, 2–3, 66–68, 80–84,
    87–93, 96–97, 108–9, 136–38, 143
Coereba flaveola, 181
Consanguinity. *See* Relatedness
Composer. *See* Sexual reproduction,
    composer effect
Cost of males, 106–8, 126–29, 138
Cost of meiosis, 3, 106–8, 124–26, 138,
    150
Cyprinidae, 85

D D T resistance, 98
Delichon urbica, 8
Delphinium nelsoni, 100–102
Deme. *See* Population
Developmental homeostasis, 49, 139
Dialects, 164
    acoustic, 165–66
    olfactory, 166–67
    visual, 167–69
Differentiation
    chromosomal, 78–80
    clinal, 84
    definition, 69–70
    drift, 70–71
    gene flow, 70–71
    genetic, 80–83, 184–89
    geographic, 71–73
    macro-, 173
    micro-, 74–75, 173, 182–83, 187–89
    mosaic, 85, 182–83
    mutational, 69–71, 74–75
    phenotypic, 182–84
Diomedea immutabilis, 15, 25–27, 182–83,
    197

Index

Dipodomys, 85
Disassortative mating. *See* Assortative mating
Dispersal
  absolute, 6–7, 14–17
  active, 1
  age bias, 12–15
  breeding, 12
  defined, 1
  effective, 10–11, 14–17, 178, 181
  environmental, 17–19
  function, 6
  group benefit, 17–19
  individual benefit, 6, 21
  innate, 17–19
  insects, 160–63
  marine invertebrates, 28, 152–54
  natal, 12
  nomadic, 1, 162–63
  philopatric. *See* Philopatry
  plants, 9, 12, 28, 154–60
  population structure, 17, 19, 23, 93–102, 154–60
  quanta, 7
  sex bias, 12–15, 53, 151, 161
  vagrant. *See* Vagrancy
  variable environments, 22–27
  vertebrates, 8–9, 160–63
Drift. *See* Genetic drift
Drosophila, 12, 109, 124, 188
  bipectinata, 85
  melanogaster, 87, 98
  nigrospiracula, 8
  obscura, 85
  pseudoobscura, 86, 89, 181
  repleta, 85
  subobscura, 180–81, 186
  willistoni, 85, 89

Ecological cost of sex. *See* Cost of males
Editor. *See* Sexual reproduction, editor effect
Environmental variation, 22–27, 109–12, 139–40
Epistasis, 66, 80–83, 143, 149–50

F-statistics, 36–37, 47, 184–89
Family, 48
Fecundity, lifetime, 113–16, 144–46, 151–63
Fish, 17, 52, 188
Fitness, 58–59, 107
Fitness potential. *See* Fitness

Fixation
  indices. *See* F-statistics
  rates, 40–42

Gadus, 160
Gene flow, 25, 41, 70–73, 77, 94–96, 174
Gene migration. *See* Gene flow
Gene pool, 34, 70–71, 80
Genetic cost of sex. *See* Cost of meiosis
Genetic distance, 76
Genetic drift, 40, 70–71, 93, 173–80
Genetic environment, 67, 97–98
Genetic homeostasis, 72, 139
Genetic homogeneity, 180, 186
Genetic identity, 76, 85, 99
Genetic load
  migrational, 23
  mutational, 120–24, 133–35, 138, 146–48
  recombinational, 3, 88–93, 108–9, 129–31, 136–38, 150. *See also* Outbreeding, depression
  segregational, 4, 56, 60, 131, 138, 148–51
Genetic similarity. *See* Genetic identity
Genome, 46, 66–67
Geographic isolation, 71–72
Good mixer genes, 94
Goodyera repens, 159
Gramineae, 156
Guinea pig, 63

Heavy metal tolerance, 24
Helix aspersa, 99, 188
Heterogony, 122–23, 145–48
Heterosis, 44, 81–82, 86–89, 90–93, 143, 149–50, 186–87, 194
Hill-Robertson effect, 109, 116–18
Histocompatability, 62, 140–44
Hitch-hiking effect, 118–19
Home range, 6–7, 14–16
Host-pathogen interactions, 140–43
Humans, 17, 29–30, 53, 63–64, 163, 186, 196
Hybrid breakdown, 90–93
Hybrid dysgenesis, 89, 97. *See also* Hybrid breakdown
Hybrid vigor, 88–90, 92
Hybridization, 67–69, 88–93
Hymenoptera, 54, 126, 128, 162

Identical-by-descent, 37

Immune system, 140–44
Imprinting, 167–68
Inbreeding. *See also* Incest
  advantages, 2, 54, 68–69, 81–83,
    135–38, 172
  animal breeding, 51, 56, 58
  avoidance, 52–53, 168
  coadaptation, 80–81, 95–98, 132–38
  coefficients, 35–39, 47, 61, 185–87
  definitions, 2, 29–35, 38–39
  deleterious recessives, 43, 51–52,
    55–56
  depression, 2, 44–47, 50–52, 57–63,
    81–83, 92, 167, 175, 196
    economic, 58–59
    laboratory, 51, 53, 61–63
    natural, 52, 63–64, 100
  dominance, 43
  enhancement, 61–64
  finite populations, 35, 37, 125
  genomic consequences, 46–47, 139,
    172, 151–60, 181, 197
  genotype frequencies, 29, 38–46
  heterosis, 44–46, 56–60
  nonrandom, 35
  occurrence, 54, 151–60
  phenotypic consequences, 48–49
  philopatry, 5, 23, 96–97, 102
  plant breeding, 51, 56, 58
  random, 35
  ratchet, 133–35
  recombination, 129–30, 132–35
  selection, 60–63
  sex ratios, 127–29
  sexual reproduction, 124–26, 129–31,
    138
  sexual selection, 170–71
  underdominance, 43–44
  variability, 2, 38
Incest, 54, 125–26, 148, 162, 195–97.
  See also Inbreeding
  definitions, 34–35, 168
  avoidance, 151, 168, 196–97
  depression, 65, 90, 100, 134–35,
    150–51, 167–68
Insects, 52, 162, 165, 197
Isolation-by-distance, 93

K-selection, 156
Kin selection. *See* Selection, kin
Kinship, 29, 36–37. *See also* Relatedness

Larus, 21, 163, 181

Laysan albatross. *See Diomedea
  immutabilis*
Lepomis, 85
Liatris, 181
Linaria minor, 159
Linkage disequilibrium, 109, 116–23
Lithospermum caroliniense, 181
Local adaptation, 22–25, 165–66. *See
  also* Philopatry, ecogenetic model
Local mate competition, 126
Loxia, 163
Lupinus texensis, 9, 181
Luxuriance. *See* Hybrid vigor

Macaca, 197
Mammals, 12, 99, 189
Maniola jurtina, 97
Marine invertebrates, 144, 152–54
Mate choice. *See* Assortative mating
Meiotic loss. *See* Cost of meiosis
Meleagris gallopavo, 162
Melospiza melodia, 15–16, 181
Migration, 23, 41–42, 46, 111–13
Migrational load. *See* Genetic load,
  migrational
Modifier alleles, 66, 82, 87–88, 97
Morabine grasshoppers, 79
Muller's ratchet, 4, 119–23, 132–35,
  145–48
Mus musculus, 26, 53, 85, 166–67, 181
Musicapa hypoleuca, 15
Mutation
  allelic, 67, 74
  breeding systems, 117–23, 145–48
  chromosomal, 75, 78–81
  differentiation, 69–71, 73–75, 97–98
  fixation, 40–41, 46
  inbreeding, 35
  rates, 74, 145–46
  somatic, 142
Mutational load. *See* Genetic load,
  mutational

N_e. *See* Population, effective size
Neighborhood, genetic, 178

Oncorhynchus nerka, 24
Optimal inbreeding, 54, 81–83, 89–90,
  137, 148–52, 167–69, 171–72. *See
  also* Inbreeding
Optimal outbreeding. *See* Optimal
  inbreeding
Ortstreue, 17. *See also* Philopatry

Outbreeding, 27, 55, 72–73, 152, 157, 160–61
  definitions, 3, 31–35, 144
  depression, 66–69, 75, 77–82, 86–91, 96–102, 167, 173–75, 187
  occurrence, 53, 151–60
Outcrossing, 33
Overdominance. *See* Heterosis

Panmixia. *See* Random mating
Papilio, 88
Papio anubis, 64, 168
Papio hamadryas, 168–69
parthenogenesis, 106–8, 123. *See also* Asexual reproduction
Parus major, 13, 15–16, 52, 64, 181, 197
Passer montanus, 13, 15
Pathogen evolution, 140–43
Pedigree, 30–33
Perennials, 12, 156–60
Peromyscus, 9, 15, 85, 91, 181, 197
Phenotypic variance, 48–49, 113–14, 144–45
Phenotypic differentiation. *See* Differentiation, phenotypic
Phenotypic tracking, 139–44
Pheromones, 166–67
Philogamy, 162, 197
Philopatry
  adaptive value, 5, 17–19, 21–25, 27, 96–97, 102, 163
  definition, 10–11
  ecogenetic model, 22–24, 165
  genetic consequences, 5, 23
  genetic model, 26–28, 96–102, 151
  nonadaptive model, 19–20
  occurrence, 8–17, 25–26, 151–60, 181
  phenotypic model, 22
  somatic benefits, 21–22
Phlox pilosa, 181
Phoenicurus phoenicurus, 181
Pinus, 159
Plant breeding, 58, 63
Plants, 89, 129,154–60, 187
Pleiotropy, 66
Plethodon, 15, 183
Poeciliopsis monacha-lucida, 123
Population
  definitions, 10, 34, 163, 172–78, 195
  effective size, 10, 35, 151, 177–80
  subdivision, 36–38, 70–71, 173–77, 184–89
  structure, 38, 41, 93–97, 151, 178–79
Porcellio scaber, 186

Primates, nonhuman, 17, 53, 64, 151, 168–69, 197
Protozoa, 123
Puffinus puffinus, 181

Quercus, 159

R-selection, 156
Rana pipiens, 181
Random mating, 27, 34, 49, 71, 85, 173–77, 195
Rare-male effect, 52, 171–72
Ratchet. *See* Muller's ratchet
Rattus norvegicus, 62
Recombination, 103, 105, 108–9, 117–23, 129–31, 135
Recombinational load. *See* Genetic load, recombinational
Regulatory genes, 66, 68
Relatedness, 29–35, 68, 76–77, 98–99, 106–7, 124–26, 163–64, 189–92, 193–95
  coefficients, 36–39, 193–94
Replicator, 176–77, 190–91
Reproduction, 132–33
Reproductive isolation, 70–73, 76–77, 173–75. *See also* Outbreeding, depression
  postmating, 72
  premating, 73, 95, 164
Reptiles, 12, 90, 189
Rhithropanoplus harrisii, 154
Riparia riparia, 181
Rodents, 17, 184

Salmonidae, 160
Salmo trutta, 27, 167
Sceloporus, 8, 15, 79, 85, 181
Sciara, 52
Seals, 14, 22
Segregational load. *See* Genetic load, segregational
Selection
  artificial, 58, 62
  disruptive, 84, 94, 97–98
  frequency dependent, 44, 143
  gene, 118, 125–26
  group, 78, 103–4
  heterotic. *See* Heterosis
  individual, 58
  interdemic, 175–76
  kin, 107, 125–26, 189
  sexual, 170–71
  species, 104

Index

Self-discrimination, 140
Self-fertilization, 4, 33, 54, 63, 152–54, 156–60
Self-sterility, 52, 151, 154
Selfing. *See* Self-fertilization
Sex ratios, 53, 107, 126–29, 178–79
Sexual reproduction
  abiotic variation, 110
  advantages, 104, 109, 141–42
  biotic adaptation, 103–5
  biotic variation, 110–12, 141–42
  composer effect, 117–24
  definitions, 2–4, 103
  disadvantages, 105–9
  ecological models, 109
  editor effect, 4, 117–24
  function, 103–5, 109, 123
  genetic models, 109
  inbreeding, 124–26, 129–31
  individual adaptation, 104–5, 141
  lottery, 113, 115, 139
  outbreeding, 124–26, 130
  rates of evolution, 103–5
  sib competition, 113–15, 145
Sexual selection. *See* Selection, sexual
Shifting balance, 174–78, 180
Sigmodon, 85
Sisyphean, 113, 115, 145
Site tenacity, 1, 12–13
Sitta europaea, 15
Snails, 12, 16, 26, 87–89, 182, 184
Sonchus asper, 159

Species, definitions, 72, 173–74
Speciation, 68, 70–84
Spermophilus, 15
Sterna, 181
Streptanthus glandulosus, 100
Supergenes, 87–88, 109, 129
Sylvia atricapilla, 15
Syngamy, 103, 106–8. *See also* Sexual reproduction

Tamias striatus, 15
Taricha, 85
Telenomus fariai, 162
Theropithecus gelada, 169
Thomomys, 79, 85
Thromanes bewickii, 181
Tribolium, 61–62
Triphaena comes, 87
Troglodytes aedon, 181

Underdominance, 43–44
Uta stansburiana, 15, 181, 197

Vagrancy, 10–12, 20–21, 23, 53, 159–60
Vicinism, 12, 160

Wallace effect, 73, 76, 95, 164

Yanomamo indians, 186

Zonotrichia leucophrys, 15, 165–66